Math Work Stations
Independent Learning You Can Count On, K–2

Debbie Diller

Stenhouse Publishers
Portland, Maine

Pembroke Publishers
Markham Ontario

Stenhouse Publishers
www.stenhouse.com

Pembroke Publishers
www.pembrokepublishers.com

Library of Congress Cataloging-in-Publication Data
Diller, Debbie, 1954–
    Math work stations : independent learning you can count on, K–2 / Debbie Diller.
    p. cm.
    Includes bibliographical references.
    ISBN 978-1-57110-793-0 (alk. paper)
    1. Mathematics—Study and teaching (Early childhood) 2. Early childhood education. I. Title.
    QA135.6.D55 2010
    372.7—dc22
    2010032048

Cover design, interior design, and typesetting by Martha Drury

Manufactured in the United States of America

PRINTED ON 30% PCW
RECYCLED PAPER

16 15 14 13   9 8 7 6

To Dad, a math guy—

You'd have loved this one!

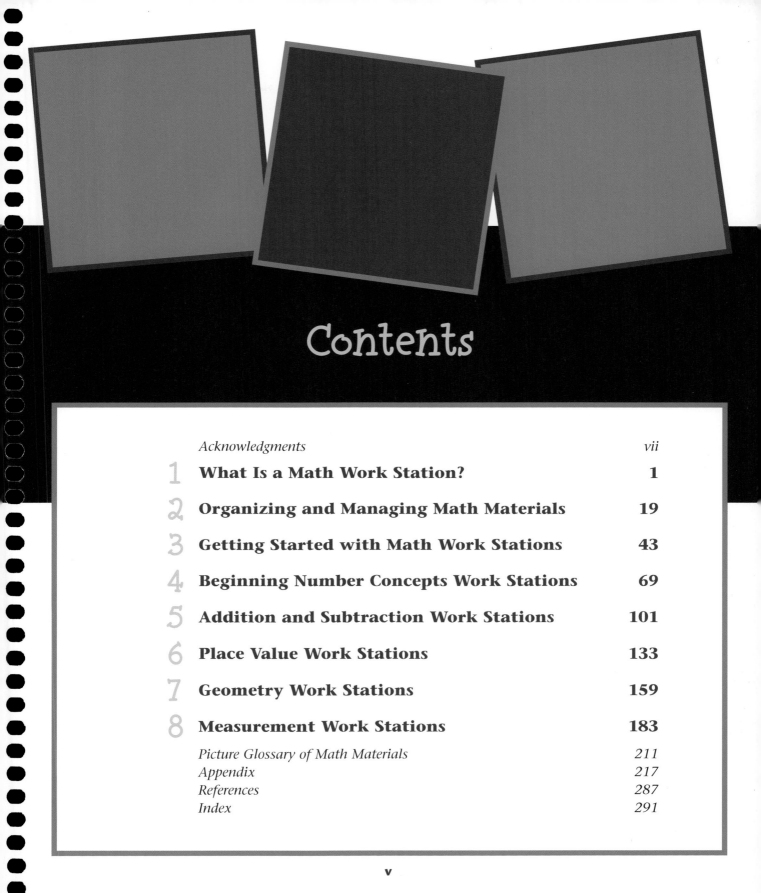

Contents

Acknowledgments

After I had been speaking and writing about literacy work stations for years, teachers began raising the question, "Could we do this in math, too?" Absolutely! So, to you, the teachers wondering how to create math work stations, I thank you for encouraging me to study this topic. I knew the management would be similar, but what about the math content?

In order to make math stations work, strong math instruction had to be the starting point. Although I presented math workshops in the 1990s, I'd devoted most of my time since then developing expertise in the field of literacy. I'm indebted to my friend and colleague Christe Cantu, a trained Math Recovery teacher and math coach, who read and responded to early drafts of this book with much on-the-spot assistance.

In the 1970s, I studied the work of Dr. Lola May under the tutelage of Professor Joseph Rousseau at Millersville State College in Pennsylvania, and I am grateful for the foundation they provided about the importance of "hands-on" math instruction, a new idea at the time. Mary

Baratta-Lorton's *Workjobs* (1972), followed by her classic *Mathematics Their Way* (1975) and Marilyn Burns's *The I Hate Mathematics! Book* (1975) were also new on the scene. I am so thankful for the work of these mathematics pioneers.

More recently, I had the privilege of working with the following teacher pioneers as we explored how to teach with math work stations:

- Maria Diaz-Albertini, first-grade teacher at Lawhon Elementary, Pearland ISD: Muchas gracias! Getting organized made all the difference. Thanks for being my stations partner.
- Mary Brown, first-grade teacher at Martin Elementary, Alief ISD: I love you and your sweet kids! I'm so pleased that you're becoming a Math Recovery teacher. You are an amazing small-group math teacher. Thank you for being open to my "new ideas."
- Heather Gaines, literacy/math coach at Lovett Elementary, Houston ISD: You rock! Thank you for setting up math stations and doing so much work behind the scenes. You devoted

countless hours to this project, and I am indebted to you. Thanks, too, to your son, Austin, who had to wait on us many days after school.

■ Katherine Kraitman, kindergarten teacher at Lovett Elementary, Houston ISD: I am grateful for the chance to work with you and your fabulous students. Thanks for opening your classroom to the possibility of math work stations.

■ Jamila Steen, second-grade teacher at Walnut Bend Elementary, Houston ISD: What fun we had making over your classroom and your math stations! You gave me so much insight into how to meet the needs of diverse learners in math.

■ Patty Terry, retired first-grade teacher in Alief ISD (and now an interventionist in Katy ISD): It all started with you, girl! You showed me it could be done in our earliest attempts at Hearne Elementary in Alief. We'll never stop teaching and learning.

■ Heather Thrash, former kindergarten teacher at Creech Elementary, Katy ISD, and third-grade interventionist at Briargrove Elementary in Houston ISD: You are one of the most thoughtful, intentional teachers I've ever met. Your questions and thinking always take me deeper. Thank you for your help with the Literature Links sections, too.

I couldn't have gone into schools to study without the support of the principals who opened their doors to me. A big thank-you to Susan Monaghan of Lovett Elementary, Julie Fernandez of Walnut Bend Elementary, and Mechiel Rozas of Gabriel Mistral Center for Early Childhood (all in Houston ISD). Thanks also to Sandy Taylor at Martin Elementary in Alief ISD and to Raymond Stubblefield and Kristin Fox Craft, both principals in Aldine ISD.

I am very blessed to work with my friends at Stenhouse Publishers. Your support means so much to me. Philippa, thank you for once more trusting me to tackle a new topic and become a "crossover artist." You believed in my vision for a math work stations book and made it happen (in color, no less). To Toby, my new math editor, it's been an amazing journey! Thank you for your encouragement along the way; you kept nudging me forward and turned me into a math writer.

A special thanks to Jay, Chris, Erin, and Martha, whose production work, design, and cover art made this book come alive, and to Dan and Nate, for your guidance and support (and for going with me to visit an old friend in Philly!). To Chuck, your help with my spring and summer institutes has been invaluable. And to Zsofi—I am loving the blog and Facebook.

Also, I appreciate the work of all the behind-the-scenes folks who answer the phones, process the orders, ship the books, and so on. You are the best! Thanks, too, to the Stenhouse and Pembroke reps for being at conferences and conventions on my behalf and making sure teachers get those books in their hands.

This book would not have been written without a group of friends who gave me special encouragement during a difficult time in my life. Laura Robb, your picture hangs in my office, reminding me to keep on writing. Thank you for your wisdom and loving care. Tangye Stephney, your stories about high school kids and teachers you work with keeps me pursuing that foundational understanding of mathematics in primary grades. And to my Friday Night Out group and prayer partners—you help to ground me.

Math Work Stations was written in many places— in airports, on Southwest flights, in hotel rooms while traveling to schools across the country—and over countless hours in hospital waiting rooms. Special thanks to all the pilots, chefs, hotel workers, doctors, and nurses who kept me moving along.

As I write these final pages, I sit at MD Anderson Cancer Center in Houston alongside my dear husband, Tom, as he continues to receive treatment during a stem cell transplant. Thank you, Tom, for all you do to help me. You are my partner for life—for richer, for poorer, in sickness, and in health. I need you on the road with me.

Finally, heartfelt appreciation to all my friends at Debbie Diller & Associates. Kelly Simmons, you are an angel sent from Chevy Chase. Gretchen Childs, Pam Pierce, and Christe Cantu, I couldn't do any of this without you. You have supported me through the best and worst of times. And you were right—I did finish the book!

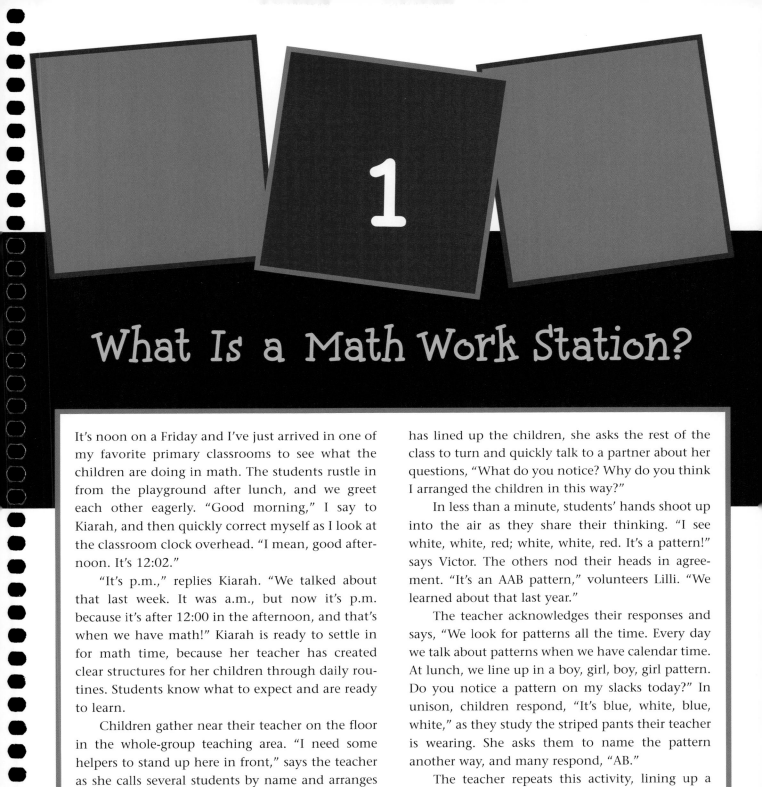

What Is a Math Work Station?

It's noon on a Friday and I've just arrived in one of my favorite primary classrooms to see what the children are doing in math. The students rustle in from the playground after lunch, and we greet each other eagerly. "Good morning," I say to Kiarah, and then quickly correct myself as I look at the classroom clock overhead. "I mean, good afternoon. It's 12:02."

"It's p.m.," replies Kiarah. "We talked about that last week. It was a.m., but now it's p.m. because it's after 12:00 in the afternoon, and that's when we have math!" Kiarah is ready to settle in for math time, because her teacher has created clear structures for her children through daily routines. Students know what to expect and are ready to learn.

Children gather near their teacher on the floor in the whole-group teaching area. "I need some helpers to stand up here in front," says the teacher as she calls several students by name and arranges them in a line. By doing this, she gets the children's attention and prepares them to think about the math concept being studied—patterns. After she has lined up the children, she asks the rest of the class to turn and quickly talk to a partner about her questions, "What do you notice? Why do you think I arranged the children in this way?"

In less than a minute, students' hands shoot up into the air as they share their thinking. "I see white, white, red; white, white, red. It's a pattern!" says Victor. The others nod their heads in agreement. "It's an AAB pattern," volunteers Lilli. "We learned about that last year."

The teacher acknowledges their responses and says, "We look for patterns all the time. Every day we talk about patterns when we have calendar time. At lunch, we line up in a boy, girl, boy, girl pattern. Do you notice a pattern on my slacks today?" In unison, children respond, "It's blue, white, blue, white," as they study the striped pants their teacher is wearing. She asks them to name the pattern another way, and many respond, "AB."

The teacher repeats this activity, lining up a new set of students. I listen in to snippets of students' paired conversations: "It's not blue, blue, blue, white." "Is it short, tall, short, tall?" "No, that

The teacher arranges students in front of the room and asks the class to tell what they notice.

doesn't work." "Is it skirt, shorts, skirt, shorts?" Finally, they get it. "It's boy, girl, boy, girl." To check their thinking, the teacher walks behind each child in the line as the class says the pattern together: "Boy, girl, boy, girl . . ." When she gets to the last student, the teacher asks, "Who would come next if we continued the pattern?"

"A boy," the students say enthusiastically.

"Why?" asks the teacher.

"Because the last person was a girl, so next would be a boy. It's boy, girl, boy, girl," says William. "Just like we were lining up for lunch." The teacher also has students say the pattern: A, B, A, B . . ." as she walks behind each child in line again. She's teaching them to think in flexible ways about patterns.

Following this brief warm-up, the teacher tells the children, "Here's a new book from one of our favorite math authors, Stuart J. Murphy [2000]— *Beep Beep, Vroom Vroom!* Do you hear a pattern already? I think you'll enjoy this story about a little sister named Molly who plays with her big brother's cars while he is out of the room. As you listen, pay attention to the patterns in this book."

As the teacher reads aloud this book, the children quickly catch on to the patterns and participate in naming how Molly arranges the cars. They mention the colors of the cars, and some notice the cars' shapes. A few even catch on to the pattern of sounds in the book: *beep, beep, vroom, vroom, crash, crash*. However, we notice that some students are reading the pattern from right to left. So we are explicit in telling students to read the patterns from left to right, just like when reading a book.

At the end of the story, the teacher lines up colored cubes to match the cars in the book (yellow, red, blue, purple, and orange). She places them in the chalk tray behind her and has students take turns showing some of the patterns Molly could make with the cars. Students volunteer their ideas:

The class names the pattern as the teacher moves from one child to the next: ABAB, or girl, boy, girl, boy.

The teacher reads aloud *Beep Beep, Vroom Vroom!* to the class to introduce the concept of repeating patterns.

"Molly could make a purple, green, purple, green pattern. That's an AB pattern." "Or she could do green, green, purple, green, green, purple—an AAB pattern." "If she shared with Kevin, they could put them together and do red, yellow, green, purple, blue . . . or all kinds of patterns!"

The teacher has planted a seed with this book and will return to it on another day to reinforce the idea of repeating patterns. Over time, she will extend the children's thinking to growing patterns and ultimately to number patterns.

The children have been sitting for a while, so she moves them to their desks and distributes pattern blocks to each table. Using a projection device, she models how to make an AB pattern with her blocks and demonstrates that she wants students to "make it, say it, write it." She makes her pattern, reads it in several ways ("ABAB"; "triangle, square, triangle, square"; "green, orange, green, orange"), and then she show students how to represent their work on paper by drawing a picture and labeling the pattern.

As children work independently building three different patterns (AB, then ABC, then AAB), the teacher walks around the room to confer with individuals. She helps one child build the pattern from left to right instead of right to left. She asks another to name his pattern. He says AB, so she extends his thinking by asking, "Can you say it another way?" and helps him to name the pattern with colors and then with shapes.

At the end of this hands-on lesson, the teacher asks students what they have learned and then

After the read-aloud, children make AB patterns with pattern blocks. The teacher circulates among them, conferring with individuals about their work. She has them "make it, say it, and write it."

summarizes with them: "Today we worked with patterns. We made AB, ABC, and AAB patterns that repeat. Let's pay attention to patterns all day long. I'll bet we'll notice many!" The materials she has used in her lesson will be added to a math station for practice with patterns over the next few days.

One Week Later

When I return to this classroom a week later, I visit during math stations time. They have just finished whole-group math instruction, and the teacher announces that it's time to go to stations. The children cheer, and the teacher reminds them to find their name and photo on the stations management board. She calls a few students at a time to move smoothly to their places by saying, "If you are wearing a red shirt, you and your partner may go to your first station." All children work with a partner using familiar materials from previous whole-group (and sometimes, small-group) lessons.

The materials are stored in plastic, lidded containers on a wooden shelf. Each container is labeled with a number from 1 to 10. Students take turns getting their math bin and taking it to a numbered spot in the room that corresponds with their numbered container. In pairs, they walk quickly and quietly to gather materials and set to work immediately. After all students are situated, the teacher goes to the small-group table to join the four students whose names on the management board show that they'll meet with her. She begins a lesson matched to their needs.

The class works productively for about thirty minutes—at the first station for fifteen minutes and at a second station for fifteen minutes—while the teacher works with two different small groups, focusing on the particular needs of students in those groups. Some days she may walk around the stations observing and noting the children at work; other days, like today, she meets with one or two groups. Children switch to their second station,

Two children work at a math station using connecting cubes and task cards to make an ABC pattern.

which is also noted on the management board, when the teacher rings a bell.

Students in the math stations are engaged in a variety of tasks. At some of the stations they are using materials the teacher included in the previous

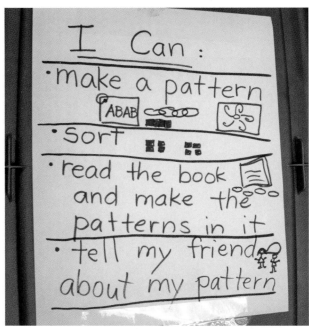

An "I Can" list made with the class helps students remember what to do at this station on working with patterns.

week's lessons on patterns. For example, I see a pair of children seated at desks, using connecting cubes to make patterns much like they did in whole group a week ago. They use task cards on a ring to help them decide which pattern to make. "Look, Mrs. Diller, we made an ABC pattern," they tell me proudly. "We are doing make it, say it, write it!" They use an "I Can" list to keep them focused so they don't finish early and start building towers. (See page 52 for more information on "I Can" lists.)

At another station, I spot children using the *Beep Beep, Vroom Vroom!* book from the previous week. They are working with cubes that match the colors of the cars in the illustrations. They sit beside each other on the floor and use the book to act out the story as they re-create patterns found there. When they get to the last page, they make new patterns using these familiar materials. They use paper provided and draw the pattern they think Molly and Kevin will create next. Behind them, two more children sit on the carpet playing a counting game that was introduced several days earlier.

In another work station, two children are collecting data. They are armed with clipboards and are taking a survey of other students in the classroom. "Which do you like better, reading alone, buddy reading, or when an adult reads to you?" they inquire of a classmate. They walk quietly around the room, stopping off to question a few of their peers

A pair of students uses the book *Beep Beep, Vroom Vroom!* to create patterns using colored connecting cubes that match the colors of the cars in the book.

Familiar materials and an "I Can" list are included at this station, where children work with patterns.

who are playing another counting game. They will share what they learned at the end of math time.

The rest of the children are working at other math stations with partners or are meeting with the teacher in small group. At the end of stations time, the teacher rings a bell as a signal to clean up and meet on the carpet in the whole-group teaching area. The children promptly put away all their materials and gather on the floor. The teacher leads a short discussion during which students take turns showing and telling about what they did and learned this day in small group and/or at math work stations. The teacher asks, "What did you do? What did you explore? Were there any problems at

<table>
<tr><td colspan="3">Name _____

SURVEY

Which do you like better?</td></tr>
<tr><td>reading alone</td><td>buddy reading</td><td>adult reads</td></tr>
</table>

Two students take a survey as part of math stations work for data collection and analysis. They ask their classmates about how they prefer to read, and then record the results. Over time, they will create graphs too.

stations today, and how did you solve them?" These questions and others are written on sharing time cards (found on page 224 in the appendix) to help the teacher lead the discussion. The teacher chooses one or two questions a day to keep the children engaged during this five-minute sharing time.

A child who worked with the *Beep Beep, Vroom Vroom!* book tells how much fun he and his partner had making patterns with cubes and shows a drawing of some of the patterns they made. Some of the other kids comment that they can't wait to go there. Students from the survey station show the data they

At the close of math stations time, a student shares his ideas on how to solve a problem with the rest of the class.

collected. "We counted 5 kids that like to read alone," says Austin.

"And 3 said they like buddy reading the best," adds his partner.

"How many students liked having an adult read to them?" prompts the teacher.

"Oh, 6," the surveyors say. "It was the one that got the most votes."

Andrea raises her hand and shares, "We had a problem today. Sam and I liked the counting game at our station, but somebody didn't put the dice back where they belong." The class decides to place a small container on top of the math stations shelf with extra dice, so students won't waste time looking for these materials if needed. If someone finds an extra die, he or she can simply put that material in this container, labeled *dice*.

Student Engagement

As you can tell from this classroom scenario, providing quality instruction with connected independent practice through math work stations is a structure that highly engages students. Instead of sitting at their desks filling out worksheets while the teacher monitors their work, the children in the classroom described are motivated to practice and learn. This frees up the teacher either to meet with differentiated small groups or to observe and take anecdotal notes about children working at stations.

I began using the term *work stations* rather than *centers* to remind the children that what they are doing during this time is their work. It is not like indoor recess or a free play time. The term *work stations* also helps signal to teachers that these are not an extra. They are not something students turn to when their work is finished. Work stations are for all children. The tasks that students do at their work stations take the place of worksheets. The emphasis is on hands-on learning and problem solving that engages students.

While visiting numerous classrooms across the United States and Canada, I have never met a child who told me he or she didn't like work stations. In fact, students often hug me and tell me how much they love going to stations. They are eager to participate in this format.

Eric Jensen writes about getting the brain's attention in his book *Teaching with the Brain in Mind* (1998). He suggests that to increase students' intrinsic motivation and keep their attention, teachers should provide choices, make learning relevant and personal, and make it engaging (emotional, energetic, and physical). These are exactly the factors that make math work stations successful in classrooms.

Jensen writes that a change in location is one of the easiest ways to get the brain's attention. At math work stations, students move to various places in the classroom to participate in learning with partners. Jensen also suggests that teachers provide a rich balance of novelty and ritual. In contrast to seatwork, math work stations provide novelty as children partake in a variety of tasks around the classroom. In each chapter that follows I show how to maintain novelty in work stations and thus engage students (and reduce behavior problems). See the sections titled "Ways to Keep Stations Going Throughout the Year" in Chapters 4 to 8 for ideas.

Teachers can do much to set up success for students by considering what students pay attention to and what engages them. To increase students' attention to tasks, have them do these things:

- Play a game.
- Make something.
- Talk with a partner.
- Act something out.
- Tell a story.
- Solve a problem.
- Record ideas by writing or drawing.
- Move.
- Do something new.

Math work stations provide all of the preceding and more.

Defining Math Work Stations

Math work stations are areas within the classroom where students work with a partner and use instructional materials to explore and expand their mathematical thinking. During math stations, a variety of activities reinforces and/or extends prior instruction, allowing children the opportunity to develop their mathematical understanding. Math work stations are a time for children to practice problem solving while reasoning, representing, communicating, and making connections among mathematical topics as the teacher observes and interacts with individuals at work or meets with a small group for differentiated math instruction.

Areas Within the Classroom

The physical setup of math stations is somewhat different from literacy work stations. For many literacy stations, teachers use existing classroom furniture, such as an easel for a big book station, a tape recorder for a listening station, and a pocket chart for a pocket chart station. With math work stations, because there are so many manipulatives, you may want to use portable containers stored in one area. I like clear plastic tubs with lids (and handles, if possible). Label the front of each container with a number (these are *math* stations!). Number the stations from 1 to 10 if you have twenty to twenty-four students. If you're fortunate enough to have a smaller class size, adjust accordingly. If you have more than twenty-four students, add a math station for every additional pair of children. Before you panic, know that you may duplicate stations to make this more manageable. Also, don't worry about setting up all of these immediately. You will want to introduce them one at a time over several weeks early in the school year. A system for doing this will be described in Chapter 3.

Each station will house materials for students to share with a partner at various places around the room. Choose a central location to keep these numbered math stations. You might use a shelf or countertop that is easily accessible to your students.

It is possible to use some of your literacy work station areas for math station areas if you'd like. For example, if you have a pocket chart literacy station, you might want to use math activities involving a pocket chart in that same location during math time. Simply post a numeral there to correspond with the appropriate numbered container of math pocket chart materials. Likewise, the computer can be used for both literacy and math stations. (See the sections titled "Technology Connections" in Chapters 4 through 8 for ideas for a math computer station.) A computer is a "computer station" for literacy work stations and may be "station 3" during math stations time. The "writing station," which is a place to write stories, letters, and responses during reading time, can also be a place to make math-related books or write problems during math time, when it would be called "station 6."

Students take their numbered containers to places around the classroom that are labeled with corresponding numerals. Use every inch of your

Math stations are organized in numbered clear plastic tubs with lids and handles in one kindergarten classroom. This system makes it easy for students to find and return their station materials. The tubs are stored on a shelf that's easy for children to access. A basket on top holds oversize materials that don't fit in the tubs.

classroom to spread kids all around the room. Use student desks, the floor (or carpet squares on the floor if needed), carpet space (if you have it), even pocket charts that may hang on a bulletin board or stand. You might also have some students work at computers or with your interactive whiteboard, if you have one. If your desks are arranged in groups of four, you might seat just two students at each group to minimize noise. By having some kids sit at

Math stations are stored in numbered clear plastic containers with lids on a countertop in a second-grade classroom.

A shelf unit on wheels holds numbered math stations with lids in a first-grade classroom.

Two children sit at a table to work at a measurement station. Their teacher observes and talks with them as they weigh plastic farm animals using a balance scale.

their desks and others on floor spaces, the noise in your room will decrease and will be distributed to make the room feel quieter and calmer. Also, children won't mix up their materials with another pair's seated at the table.

Sit at your small-group table and look around the room to be sure you can see every student at all of the math stations. If you can't, move furniture around to be sure you have clear visibility. You'll want to keep an eye on the students to check their engagement during times when you're working with small groups.

In this second-grade classroom, the teacher meets with a small group for math while the rest of the class works at stations around the room. Some use the computer station. Others work in pairs on the floor or at their desks.

Students work in pairs around the room with portable math stations materials. Some work on the floor. Others are at tables.

Working with Partners

Many teachers tell me their classrooms get too noisy when students are at centers. To decrease the noise level, try reducing the number of students working together. Pairing students reduces the amount of interpersonal work they must do. It's easier to take turns, share, and even discuss when there are just two people involved rather than three or four. Increased student engagement occurs with students in pairs, too. When there are just two students, each has to do a bigger share of the work (and the thinking). At the start of the year, pair students who get along well together. Later, you can try other flexible ways to pair children based upon need.

Sometimes, students will work in a parallel fashion, individually exploring or investigating a problem. But when playing partner games, you really need to require that partners sit side by side (instead of face to face) in order for them to view the numbers the same way while they work together.

Occasionally, you'll have an odd number of children. What do you do then? You have several options. Sometimes you'll have children who prefer working alone at times and actually do better working on their own. You might have individuals work on the computer. Or you could create a group of three students who work well together. Be flexible and work to meet the needs of all students in your classroom.

Using Instructional Materials

Instructional materials *previously* used in whole-group lessons go into the math stations. The idea is for the teacher to model how to use the materials first by using them with the students multiple times, then move them into the math stations for independent exploration and practice. Students need to play partner games several times in whole-group instruction with the teacher facilitating *before* moving those same games into math stations for independent work time. If you move materials too quickly into stations, students don't remember how to use them and then off-task behavior often occurs.

I used to make and use lots of games with file folders, but I found that the children who were most successful with them were usually those who didn't need the practice. Likewise, commercially made math centers usually don't produce the desired results for exploration and deeper thinking. Students often have trouble reading and following the directions on these products. They look very

tempting in the catalogs, but there is no quick fix for quality teaching and practice. In Chapter 8, you'll read about one team's struggle to move from these instant measurement *centers* to more thoughtfully planned measurement *stations*. You'll find out how they charted what to teach and how they built their stations based on their own classroom instruction. You may want to visit the opening of Chapter 8 now for an example on how to plan for stations that will directly connect what you're teaching to the stations you'll introduce.

Use things you're already teaching with and move those materials and activities into stations. If you use a core program for math instruction, you already have a storehouse of ideas for math stations. Use the partner games, suggestions for math workshop activities, software, and other materials that come with your series for independent work at math stations as well as in whole-group instruction.

Here's an example of moving materials from whole group to math stations for more independent work. Your teacher's edition recommends that, during whole-group time, you model with 3–D objects, such as a basketball (sphere), an oatmeal container (cylinder), a die (cube), and a crayon box (rectangular solid). Students also explore wooden

A second-grade teacher points to parts of a box as she teaches mathematical vocabulary like *edges, faces,* and *rectangular solid.*

Students work with 3–D wooden objects as part of a whole-group lesson on geometry.

3–D objects, comparing them to each other and to your examples while they learn new vocabulary, such as *cubes, faces*, and *solid figures*. After introducing and teaching with 3–D shapes over several days, move some of these materials to several math stations for further investigation. At this time, all the stations don't have to focus on 3–D shapes. Some of

them may contain materials for students to review mathematical concepts taught before your exploration of 3–D shapes. You don't teach new concepts or skills one day and move it to a station the same day for practice. Wait until you've taught and reviewed a math concept several times before moving it to stations for independent exploration.

After teaching with three-dimensional shapes, partners work at several geometry-related stations doing activities such as Guess My Shape, Shape Sort, and Shape Hunt, which are all described in Chapter 7, "Geometry Work Stations." Remember to look at your math curriculum documents for ideas, too.

Variety of Activities

Choice is an important feature in making math work stations successful. Over time, a station should include a variety of things for children to choose from, but there shouldn't be so many choices that the children feel overwhelmed. Aim for what I call "controlled choice." Provide just a few choices of materials or activities within a work station. For example, if you're using a core program such as Investigations or Everyday Math, integrate activities that you've used in whole-group work as choices. So, if you used color tiles or pattern blocks in a geometry lesson on symmetry, students should use those same materials at a station to further explore with them. You might also include small mirrors at this station and a picture book about symmetry. Any of the choices at a station should provide opportunities for exploration and/or practice, but allowing the child to choose the activity will enable him or her to learn more.

You might place in the station container two or three different things students can choose from that relate to the same topic. For example, in math station 2, I might put two counting games from resources I already have taught with (perhaps from a core math program or training I've attended where we made partner games), with each game in

Two students play Guess My Shape using 3–D shapes at a math station.

its own plastic ziplock bag, as well as a picture book about counting. In this way, children are thinking about those mathematical concepts throughout the entire work period at that one station. I've found it helpful to include all the materials students need for a math station's activities in that numbered container—spinners, dice, counters, pencils, paper, or whatever is needed to do those activities. This cuts down on interruptions and movement around the room to find materials.

Having a few choices at a station gets rid of the problem of the "early finisher." Students don't have to put away the station or get up and move about the room to find something else to do after playing one game because they're done. They can simply choose another activity from the same container. This minimizes interruptions such as asking the teacher what to do next or moving around the room to get more materials. It makes management a bit easier for everyone.

If the idea of putting two or three things at each station seems overwhelming, take a deep breath and relax. Remember that early in the school year, stations are introduced one at a time (see Chapter 3), so you won't need to worry about having ten stations with multiple activities in each to begin. At first, you will probably start with just one activity per station and layer on more as the year progresses. One of the choices at a station can be reading a math picture book that highlights the same concepts that are being reinforced by the games or activities there. Another way to simplify is to have the same activities at two or three stations.

Opportunities for Independent Exploration

The emphasis at math work stations is on giving children opportunities to explore and develop mathematical understanding through independent practice. It is a time for children to work with concepts already introduced in whole group. Thus,

activities placed at the math work stations can grow out of either your core math program or other resources that develop the mathematical concepts you're teaching.

Worksheets are not put into the containers and called "work stations." Students aren't just playing simple Bingo games or flashing fact cards to each other. There is real thinking, learning, and conversation about math going on. You will hear math talk as children make connections between their new learning and what they already know. While second graders work with 3–D shapes at a math work station, you might hear, "This sphere is like the basketball we use during P.E." or "This cone is different from the cylinder. Both are for food, like an ice cream cone and an oatmeal container." Students practice using new math vocabulary and pose questions and wonderings to each other. For example, in second-grade classrooms I've heard talk like this at a geometry station: "What is the name of that shape again? Oh, it's a pyramid." "How many faces does it have?" "How are these shapes different?"

At math stations, students work on tasks where they must solve problems and use reasoning skills. They are asked to represent what they are learning through drawing, writing, and even dramatizing or telling stories. At a station where they work with addition, they might make up stories using numbers and objects. In this case, the children pull materials out of a ziplock bag—two dice made from wooden cubes with zero to five dots on each face, a work mat made of a plain plastic placemat, five little plastic pigs, and five small plastic cows (from a bag of dollar store farm animals). One child rolls the dice and gets a 4. She picks up four little pigs. The other child rolls a 1 and picks up one cow. Together they make up a story about the farm animals: "Once upon a time there was a farmer. He had 4 pigs and 1 cow. They were friends. There were 5 happy farm animals." They draw a picture of their story and plan to share it with the class after math stations during sharing time.

Differentiated Math Instruction

While students work independently at math stations, the teacher may choose to observe individuals at work and gather data to inform decisions about meeting student needs individually or in differentiated small groups. Many days, the teacher will meet with one or two small groups during this time.

For example, a teacher may have been teaching *counting on* as a strategy for adding two numbers during whole-group instruction. During math stations time, she observes that there are still a few children who count all the numbers, beginning with 1. She will want to work with those students in a small group to focus on number sense and help them first identify the greater number and then count on the second quantity without having to count both amounts to find the sum. Likewise, after observing during math stations time that several other students are advanced in counting skills and are ready to count by tens, the teacher will want to bring them together for a small group and work with them using larger numbers and counting on using ten-frames.

As you observe children at math stations and/or in small group, collect valuable information about students' understandings and misconceptions by taking notes to plan further instruction. While observing, it's helpful to record what children are doing and saying. You might use an anecdotal note system (just like you do when teaching reading) to write down what you see and hear.

Many teachers have found that carrying a clipboard around the classroom helps them record their observations, which in turn aids planning. Index cards can be useful for this. Begin by writing each child's name on the bottom right-hand corner of an index card. Prepare a card for each student. Then, tape the first card to the clipboard so it is aligned with the bottom of the clipboard. Layer the second

A clipboard with an index card for each child taped onto it can be useful in assessment.

card over the first so that both the first card's name and the second card's name are visible. Continue taping cards to the clipboard until all are attached and each child's name is showing. If you use a clipboard like this during independent reading, keep a separate clipboard with cards of a different color for your observations during math stations time.

A teacher takes notes while observing students playing a domino game. Kindergartners match up dots to make a domino train.

Jot down notes about individual students' mathematical understanding. Be sure to date each entry and keep it brief. Just take notes on a few children each day. You might start by observing the students you are most puzzled about—the ones you're least sure how to help.

Here are some examples of what you might record:

- Improving one-to-one correspondence.
- Counted on fingers.
- Counted on from 10.
- Made and named ABC pattern with Unifix cubes.
- Using straws for place value is helping.
- Drew picture to solve addition problem. Groups of 5.
- Wrote 7 and 2 backward.
- Compared 3–D objects using correct vocab.
- Used objects to solve problem. Extended it, too.
- Confusing minute and hour hand.
- Used cubes for nonstandard measurement accurately.

After a child's card is full, simply tear it off and save it with your records for that child. Then replace it with a new card so you can continue to take notes throughout the year. It's important to observe students, and it's even more valuable if you record what you notice and use your notes for planning differentiated instruction.

When you observe students at work and use your observation notes to plan small-group instruction, each math small-group lesson should look a bit different from the other groups' lessons throughout the week. At times, you may want to use the materials from a small-group lesson for a station for independent practice for just the kids in that group (because other students don't need the practice). Those materials might be put in a ziplock bag with a colored dot on it for just that group. For example, with the struggling group described several para-

graphs ago, give them smaller numbers to work with. Put those materials in a container with a colored dot on it to show that it is just for their group.

Gradual Release of Responsibility in Math

The best way to guarantee success at math work stations is through lots of modeling both for conceptual understanding and procedures, with teachers gradually releasing more responsibility to the children. Pearson and Gallagher's gradual release model of instruction (1983) outlines this principle (see Figure 1.1). To best train students for math work stations routines, begin by modeling—showing students how to do something, such as how to play a new partner game from your core program or how to use the stamps at the pattern station. Show them how to get the materials out of the container and organize them on the table, one piece at a time rather than dumping the whole bag. Model how to place materials on a work mat to keep noise at a minimum and model how to play the game. Demonstrate how to clean up the materials so it will be easy for the next students to use them.

Remember that the best way to ensure student independence is to have modeled well with instructional materials before moving them to a station for practice. Students need to see and participate in several demonstrations of how to use materials or do tasks, such as playing partner games, before they can do them well on their own. Simply showing something once isn't enough for most learners, even adult learners.

Brian Cambourne's conditions of learning model (1988) identifies demonstration as an important prerequisite for language learning. Students will have math language to learn and experiment with at stations. Expect students to use "math talk" at stations by modeling this language with them and letting them know you want them to use these words as well. Throughout this book,

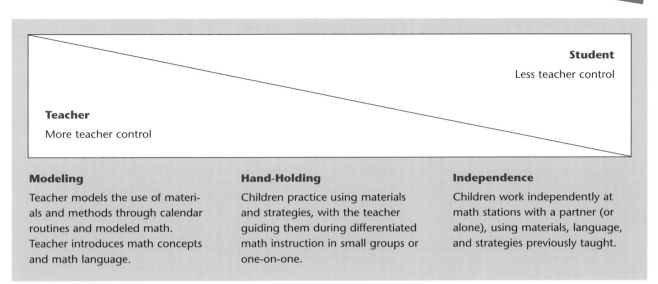

Modeling	**Hand-Holding**	**Independence**
Teacher models the use of materials and methods through calendar routines and modeled math. Teacher introduces math concepts and math language.	Children practice using materials and strategies, with the teacher guiding them during differentiated math instruction in small groups or one-on-one.	Children work independently at math stations with a partner (or alone), using materials, language, and strategies previously taught.

Figure 1.1 Gradual Release of Responsibility Approach (Diller 2003, adapted from Pearson and Gallagher 1983)

you will find many examples of math talk cards to teach with in whole group and move to math stations for practice.

When planning for math stations, be sure that children *can* do what is asked of them at the station. If activities are too easy or too hard, students will disengage (which also brings about discipline problems). Have high expectations but make them realistic.

A math talk card made from an index card provides math language support for an English language learner while she plays a counting game with a partner.

Math Work Stations Versus Traditional Math Centers

A math work station is fundamentally different from a traditional math center in several ways, as shown in Figure 1.2. The emphasis when using math stations is on teacher modeling and students taking responsibility for their own learning. In traditional learning centers, teachers often did too much of the work. They would, for example, think of ideas for the materials, make the materials, laminate them, cut them out, explain them, explain them again, and clean up after the materials were used. In addition, teachers would decide when to change the materials (usually *every* Friday afternoon!) and what would be done with them. In math work stations, students share in the decision making. They help decide when to change materials and they negotiate ideas for what they'd like to try at each station. No longer does the teacher change the centers weekly. This process is explained in more detail in Chapter 3.

There are many benefits to teaching with math work stations. My favorite is that *all* students get to participate in work stations daily. The natural result

Math Work Stations	Traditional Math Learning Centers
Materials are used by the teacher and students during instruction first. Then they are placed in the work stations for independent use.	New materials were often placed in the center without first being used in teaching. The teacher may have shown how to use the materials once, but they were often introduced with all the other new center materials at one time.
Stations do not change weekly. Instead, materials are changed to reflect children's levels of math understanding, strategies being taught, and topics being studied.	Centers were often changed weekly with units of study or even a theme.
Stations are used for students' meaningful independent work and are an integral part of each child's instruction. All students go to work stations daily.	Centers were often used by students when they "finished their work." Centers were used for fun and motivation, for something extra.
Materials are differentiated for students with different needs and levels of math understanding.	All students did the same activities at centers. There was not usually much differentiation.
The teacher observes individuals at work or meets with differentiated small math groups during math work stations.	If the teacher met with small groups, each group often did the same task.

Figure 1.2 **Differences Between Math Work Stations and Traditional Math Learning Centers**

of this is that the children will usually work harder because they are doing something they enjoy. No longer will you have bored students squirming in their seats or children popping up and down asking endless questions about how to do a worksheet. Nor will you have children speeding through their seatwork carelessly so they can go to centers. All students have equal access to the engagement that math work stations provide.

Another benefit is that math stations allow you to differentiate for the various levels within your classroom. Instead of assigning the same tasks to all children, you can suggest different activities or materials for particular children so as to better meet their needs at a particular station. For example, at station 7, which focuses on addition and subtraction, a blue dot stuck on one ziplock bag denotes differentiated materials to be used by the blue math group. These students have fewer numbers of dots on their dot dice to accompany the game they will play, because that is their level of mathematical understanding. The teacher simply reminds them to

use the blue-dot bag when they work at that station. Chapters 4 through 8 each include a section devoted to ideas for differentiation.

Improved student behavior is an additional plus that comes from math work stations. When students are involved with hands-on activities, such as playing partner games or creating and sharing stories involving math, rather than filling out math worksheets, they generally behave better and interrupt the teacher less often. Discipline problems arise when students are asked to work without the teacher's support on things that they don't find interesting or relevant. Skills students would traditionally practice with paper and pencil work can be made more manipulative at the work stations. For example, instead of having students fill out page after page of math worksheets individually, you might accomplish the same goal by having students work with a partner at a station. At that station, the students can utilize just one or two of the same worksheets on an overhead as transparencies and solve the problems using manipulatives. (Choose just a few of the best workbook pages for this adaptation.) Or they might use the SMART Board station, working with the same kinds of problems you did with them on an interactive whiteboard during whole-group instruction. For assessment, you can quickly glance at the board to see how they're doing and make note of any issues you need to address individually or in a small group.

Finally, students at math work stations internalize new concepts because they have a direct opportunity to practice a skill just as it was modeled. Children apply what they are learning by successfully completing tasks, which might include acting out a story with objects to represent dividing cookies among three friends or making a three-page math book about their schedule in school. Students get to connect old learning to new. They think back to what they learned during whole-group problem solving as they're working in stations. After a whole-group lesson involving bar graphs, students at a station might grab cubes out of a bag, saying, "We could show what we found by making a bar graph!" Best of all, students in work stations are constantly solving problems, reasoning, representing, communicating, and connecting while working with numbers and mathematical concepts. They practice using math vocabulary and interact with a partner to help cement this new learning. At math work stations, children are engaged learners.

Teachers sometimes tell me that they've tried centers in the past, and this approach just doesn't work. They say, "We used to do this many years ago. It didn't work then, and it won't work now." I challenge you to try something new. Think of work stations as a new twist on an old idea. Old ideas cycle around, but there's always a twist. I wore bell bottoms in the 1970s; they returned in the twenty-first century with a new name: "boot cut" or "flares." But they have a new twist—today they're made with Lycra. And what's not to love about that? Look for the Lycra in math work stations. There are many new twists that will engage your twenty-first-century students.

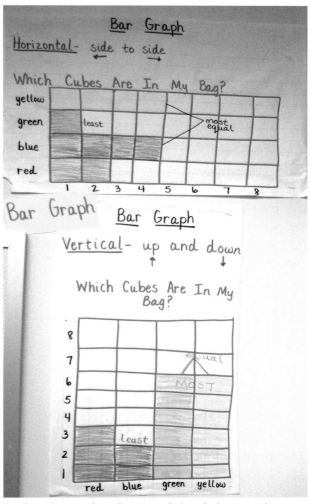

Students use anchor charts made in whole-group lessons, like these about bar graphs, when working at a math station. These visuals help kids remember what was taught. At this math station, they pull cubes out of a bag and make their own graphs.

As you read this book, you will find suggestions for managing time, materials, and student behavior in the first three chapters. Each remaining chapter (Chapters 4 through 8) focuses on specific skills, strategies, and activities that students might work on at math stations related to the National Council of Teachers of Mathematics (NCTM) and Common Core State Standards in your K–2 classroom. If you teach a higher grade level, you may be able to adapt the ideas in this book for your students too.

I organized the ideas for independent work around the following big ideas: beginning number concepts; addition and subtraction; and place value. These are all part of the Number and Operations content strand. There is also a chapter on geometry stations and one on measurement stations. These chapters all stand alone, and each is organized in the same way to make it easy to find what you need. Dip in and out of them depending upon your curriculum demands.

Instead of writing a separate chapter on algebra stations, I included ideas for exploring patterns as well as properties of arithmetic and equality throughout the book. Likewise, I integrated data and probability suggestions into existing stations in the beginning number concepts, geometry, and measurement chapters (Chapter 4, 7, and 8). This book is not intended to be a math program or curriculum. Rather, my intent is that it will support and extend the high-quality, standards-based math instruction that you are already doing in your classroom.

Reflection and Dialogue

To help you make the most of the ideas presented in this book, each chapter concludes with a list of ideas for discussion and questions for personal reflection. These may be used as part of a book study. Following is the list for this chapter:

1. Share your new ideas about math work stations with a colleague. Discuss the definition of math work stations provided in this chapter (on page 7).
2. If you are already using literacy work stations, what parallels did you see between literacy and math work stations?
3. Think about your students and their level of engagement during math. What specific things engaged them most recently? What ideas did you get from this chapter that you will try in order to increase student engagement?
4. How will what you teach in whole group impact the work students do at math stations? Share some examples of what you might move from whole-group math instruction to math stations.
5. Determine how and where you'll set up your math work stations. Use the pictures on page 9 for ideas and inspiration.
6. Discuss how math work stations can support differentiated math instruction.

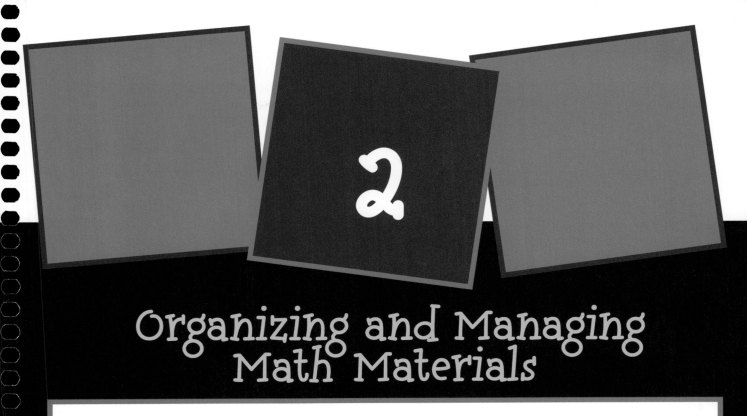

Organizing and Managing Math Materials

"I really want to use math work stations effectively in my classroom," second-grade teacher Jamila told me when I visited her room. "I have lots of materials we can use. Most of my math manipulatives are in one closet, but I know I have too much stuff." While working with Jamila (and many other teachers), I noticed that when our talk turned to math stations, it often turned to "stuff" and centered around the question, What stuff do I have that I can put out in tubs? We often find ourselves looking for premade materials that could easily work for independent stations practice. It seems like the fastest route.

However, in thinking about this question, another, better question emerged: How will I teach this math concept and what materials will I use? If we think about instruction *first* and then plan for stations practice based upon what we've taught using materials students are already familiar with, we will simplify the process and ensure that our students are developing conceptual understandings rather than just doing busywork.

This new question led Jamila and me to talking about improving the organization of her math materials so she could more easily access what she needed for teaching. Most teachers agree that math instruction should be hands-on to help our students understand the concepts we are teaching. But that requires math manipulatives with all those little pieces! If we knew (and organized) exactly what we had and started to plan instruction using those easily accessible materials, we could start to improve the quality of our math stations. Jamila had most of her math materials in one place, but they weren't really organized to maximize their use. We needed a system for storing and finding her stuff quickly. By having a system, she had whatever she needed right at her fingertips to maximize time on task and make planning and teaching simpler. She was ready!

Spring Cleaning: Math Manipulatives Makeover

As Jamila and I looked at her current math stations (mostly commercial games in tubs), she agreed to let me look in her math closet and help her create

Step 1: **Sort** your stuff. **Stay** put while you sort!	Start with just your math materials. Take everything off the shelves (one shelf at a time) and empty containers to see what you've got. Spread it all out. Don't walk away from this space! (You could get distracted.)
Step 2: **Purge** things you don't use for teaching.	Get a friend to help, if needed. If you haven't used it this year (and it is your personal property), don't keep it in your classroom.
Step 3: Put what you'll keep in **containers** (**containerize**) and place them in storage areas (**assign** a home).	Now put all those containers to use. Match containers to the size of materials to better utilize space. Label everything!
Step 4: Maintain your storage system. (**Equalize** every day.)	Every day, put things away. Get students to help you.

Figure 2.1 **How to Organize Your Math Manipulatives**

a system for all those materials. We decided to work on this project during spring break. It was a perfect time, because her students would not be in the classroom and we'd have a chunk of uninterrupted time. It was hard to carve out the time, but Jamila told me it saved her countless hours in the long run. If you identify with Jamila, you might plan for a time to get your math materials better organized. You might choose to do this in the summer or on a Saturday or even after school hours over the course of several days. Jamila found that when she could easily find what she needed for instruction, her teaching *and* her planning for math stations went much more smoothly.

In helping Jamila, I used a tried-and-true formula from Julie Morgenstern, an organizing expert and author of *Organizing from the Inside Out* (2004). It involves five steps that match the acronym SPACE: Sort, Purge, Assign a Home, Containerize, and Equalize. This procedure (see Figure 2.1) makes organizing all your math stuff (or even your closets at home) simple and doable. It's a system I have used successfully many times, both in my home and in classrooms.

Step 1: Sorting Your Stuff

The first step in sorting is to remove all the items from one storage area. Julie Morgenstern recom-

mends that you begin with just one shelf (or cabinet) at a time, and so do I. This makes the process manageable. If you experience success with one shelf, you will be motivated to try another. Caution: Don't leave this space! Sometimes we're tempted to start putting things away in another part of the room, and we get distracted. Commit to finishing this space before moving on to another. You'll find that when you get one small space organized, you'll be inspired to move on to work on another.

When we began, Jamila told me that all her math manipulatives were stored in one cabinet and all her literacy materials were in another. So we started in the math cabinet, only working with that space. We opened the doors of the math closet, pulled everything off the shelves, and put the contents on the floor and surrounding desks so we could see exactly what she had. Sometimes things were already in containers, but we took everything out and stacked the containers off to the side so we could really see what was there. Warning: It will look quite overwhelming with all that stuff everywhere, but it is the only way to really see what you have for math instruction. Work with a colleague to help you stay on task.

Jamila teaches in a recently constructed school in Houston, Texas, so closets and shelves were built into her classroom. Not everyone has a closet or

Step 1: Jamila and her student teacher remove all the contents of her math cabinet onto the floor and surrounding desks. Then they dust off the shelves.

Before the makeover: Materials for math were stored in one large cabinet (top) and also on built-in shelves beside this cabinet (bottom).

cabinet for storage, so you might use clear plastic stacking drawers or matching labeled dishpans on a shelf, or even see-through containers that stack out in the open so their materials can be accessed easily. In one district, each K–2 class was provided with ten uniformly sized dishpans with labels. The teacher then placed all manipulatives from the current adopted math curriculum and from the school's supplies in these containers and placed them on shelves where they were easily accessible for instruction. The ideas from this chapter can be adapted to these kinds of systems for storage as well.

Once we had placed all the math stuff on the floor where we could see it, we began to sort. It was easy and logical to sort things into piles according to the math topics Jamila teaches. For example, we gathered all the geometry manipulatives in one spot; objects used to teach about money went in another; and fraction materials were in yet another place.

Some of the piles were very large, such as those containing materials used for teaching about counting and place value. There were lots of counters, connecting cubes, Cuisenaire rods, and other materials for number and operations. In contrast, Jamila only had a few materials for teaching symmetry and a handful for data and probability. We used index cards to label each pile with its category so we could easily add to that group of sorted objects. The following is a list of labels we used (please adapt this list according to what you have):

- Number and operations
- Geometry
- Fractions
- Money
- Time
- Data and probability
- Symmetry
- Measurement
- Calendar

Of course, along the way we found stuff that wasn't used in math class in the mix, too. We simply sorted that into other piles away from the math materials. We had three of these nonmath groups: art supplies, science materials, and after-school tutoring materials that weren't used by the children in this classroom. We labeled each of these piles with an index card, too, to keep us sorting.

One caution while sorting: Don't get sidetracked! It is so easy to find something that distracts us and keeps us from the task at hand. For example, when we found hundreds of drinking straws (more than one teacher would ever need) with the math materials, we were tempted to start organizing the art supplies. Instead, we simply placed some of the straws with our geometry materials and put the extra straws on the pile labeled *art supplies*, which would become a project for another day. If we'd started working on the art supplies, we'd never have finished organizing the math supplies.

We did what I'd call a "big sort" first. We simply sorted everything into big piles according to a math

All the math materials have been removed from the shelves and sorted into piles according to math topics Jamila teaches.

These baskets needed to be emptied so we could see what was in them. Empty baskets were put aside with other empty storage containers to use later in the process.

concept Jamila would be teaching at her current grade level. We didn't worry about sorting through each item in each pile as we went. We just got everything sorted until all the math materials were in plain view. As we put geometry materials on a pile, Jamila said, "I just remembered that I have some more geometry things on that shelf over there" (not in the math closet). So we added those materials to the stacks as well. This happened several times, as seeing a certain material reminded this teacher that there were other hidden math treasures all over the classroom.

Step 2: Purging—Hard to Do, but Necessary

Sorting is fun; the brain is naturally a pattern seeker, so we don't mind this part of the process. However, the second step, purging, is a lot more difficult for many of us. If you are someone who has a hard time throwing things away (like me), get a friend to help you who does *not* have this problem. When you see the stacks of stuff, you'll probably realize that you may need to reorganize and possibly get rid of some things. I've found that once I get started with pitching old or unneeded materials, it feels so good to pare down to the essentials needed that I'm able to keep going. There is something cathartic about decluttering your space; I've found that it often makes room for new thinking and new ways of teaching. Jamila had received many extra sets of math manipulatives at trainings she'd attended over the years. As a result, she often had more manipulatives than she needed for one classroom.

You'll want to have a trash can and extra trash bags on hand for the purging step, as well as a space to put things that need to go to other grade levels or other teachers. Alert custodians, too, so they can check in periodically to empty the trash or put things in the recycle bin, especially if you're going through old files. (Custodians will often be more than happy to help. An uncluttered classroom makes their job easier too.)

Step 2: Jamila's student teacher throws away outdated materials (circa 1977) no longer needed for instruction.

One important note: Before you begin purging, find out if your school or district has a list of the minimal set of manipulatives that should be in your classroom for your grade level. Use this list as you're organizing, so you don't get rid of things you are expected to use for instruction. If you come across manipulatives you're not sure how to use, don't throw them away. Ask a colleague or math coach in your building for help on how to use them.

To start the purge, choose one stack and begin to go through it. Use the following questions to help you.

Ask Yourself: Should I Keep This?

1. Does this belong to the district or to me? If it belongs to the district and is currently in adoption, *don't* throw it away!

2. Is it something I will use in the future? Is it something I need help knowing how to teach with?

3. Is this something I might look over and use to improve my teaching?
4. Is this something that is taking up too much space and could be replaced easily?
5. Is this something I used to use, but I have something better now?
6. Do I already have enough copies of this?

"I can collect these as I need them and take up less closet space."

In Jamila's room, we began with the measurement stuff. We got rid of things she hadn't used in a year or so. She didn't throw away the extra items; she gave them away. But only things worth giving away. She shared things that were in good shape and had been published within the past ten years. In fact, her school was opening a math lab, so many of her extra materials went there. Figure 2.2 lists some of the measurement materials we purged and why.

Things We Purged	Why We Purged Them	Teacher Comments
Gallon milk jugs	These took up valuable closet space.	*I can collect these as I need them and take up less closet space.*
Duplicate balance scales	We didn't need seven of these; we kept three.	*This scale was from a school where I used to teach. It's missing the weights that go with it. How many scales do I own? I had no idea I had so many! I'll donate the extras to the math lab.*
Extra oatmeal containers	We only needed one of these.	*I need one of these while teaching about 3–D shapes. I can throw the others away.*
Lots of rulers	Some were broken; we only needed a class set, so we donated the extra ones to the math lab.	*Now I'm looking at all these rulers . . . how many do I really need? This is just greed!*
Special ruler for intermediate grades	This is not needed with second-grade standards; we gave it to the fourth grade.	*I have this but never used it. I should give this to somebody who can use it.*
Big boxes that commercial materials came in	Take materials out of boxes to see what's in there; throw away boxes and place materials in smaller, clear containers.	*What's in here? I don't think I've ever opened this box before.*

Figure 2.2 A Sample Purging Process

So, what measurement materials did we keep? Here's a list:

- Three balance scales and matching weights
- Liquid measurement containers (commercially made) for quart, cup, gallon, and half-gallon
- One set of plastic measuring cups and spoons
- One plastic funnel and one sieve
- Two commercially made measurement games
- Class set of rulers
- Fourteen tape measures (one per two children and two extras for stations practice)

Before: Measurement materials.

After: Measurement materials.

After: Measurement materials are now stored in the math closet, taking up much less space. Labels make retrieval and return a snap. And all the measurement stuff is in one convenient location. Clear plastic containers help us see what we have and remind us to use these materials for instruction.

Step 3: Putting Math Materials into Containers

After we'd determined which measurement materials were essential, we placed them in a large, clear plastic container that we found in Jamila's room. (We'd emptied it when sorting through all her math stuff.) We used a big container because many of the measurement things, such as the scales, were large. We wanted to put most of them in one container so we could easily retrieve them for use. I recommend using clear containers so you can see what's inside them and access them more easily. Adding a large label that says *Measurement* to the front of this container would help Jamila both find and return objects to their home after she'd taught with them.

Step 3: Putting related materials in labeled containers that are just the right size keeps them better organized.

Don't buy containers before you start organizing! Here are all the empty containers left over at the *end* of Jamila's math storage makeover. We didn't buy any containers before, during, or after this makeover.

We placed several oversize measurement items (for liquid measurement, and one scale) on the shelf beside the measurement materials and labeled that shelf *Measurement* too. After organizing materials for other math topics, we placed things for teaching data and probability next to measurement, because there was just the right amount of space for this in the newly organized math closet.

Interestingly, each time I help a teacher organize a storage space, we seem to find all the containers we need right in the classroom. We don't buy any containers before we begin. Start with what you've got. Many times we have materials stored in the wrong-size containers with lots of dead space. When we finished Jamila's math storage makeover, we had bunches of extra tubs.

Step 4: Maintaining Your Storage System

Once you've set it all up, keeping it organized isn't hard, as long as you have a home for every math item. Labels on everything will help you maintain your storage system. We made labels for the outside of each container, but we also made labels for ziplock bags inside the containers. That way the Jamila can easily return things to the right spot when it's time to put them away (instead of just shoving them back into the closet). I recommend 2-by-4-inch *removable* labels available at office supply stores. These are large enough to read easily from a distance and can be removed effortlessly if you decide to change labels. There's nothing worse than having to scrape an old label from a plastic container!

The old saying "A place for everything, and everything in its place" rings true. If you have a home for all your math stuff, it will be easy to put things away at the end of the day. Labels are like a physical address that will help you deliver items to their proper places instead of on your countertops or teacher desk. Take ten minutes at the end of each day and be sure all your math materials are returned to where they belong. Julie Morgenstern calls this "equalizing." The good news is that in your classroom you have twenty-plus little "equalizers" to help you. Teach children where math materials belong and how to put things away so they are easy to use.

For example, Jamila had many connecting cubes. She prefers smooth Unifix cubes that connect in only one direction to make number trains, towers, or pattern trains (rather than cubes that connect in many directions and can be distracting when used for these tasks). We sorted the Unifix cubes by color, because Jamila told me that she likes the students to use just one color of cube when they're working with number concepts. If she gives them a wide variety of colored cubes, some students fight over them or they make patterns instead of thinking about combining sets or solving problems. We linked the cubes together in groups of ten and stored them in clear plastic shoeboxes. Now they were ready to hand out to students during whole-group or small-group math instruction. We decided to teach the children to put the cubes back just like they found

Before: Unifix cubes.

After: The Unifix cubes for Jamila's second grade are now organized by color in groups of ten to save space and time, with one additional bag of loose, mixed cubes.

them (in sets of ten of the same color) at the end of a lesson to save time and effort in the long run. For Jamila in second grade, the cubes took up less storage space when put into groups of ten rather than being randomly tossed into plastic containers.

Step 4: Labeling materials makes it easier to find and return them to where they belong.

An alternate idea for organizing Unifix cubes is to snap them together in sets of five of one color joined to five of another color (in sets of ten). By doing this, students can easily count on from five when making number trains to show combinations. Many teachers also make up enough bags of Unifix cubes to be shared by two children at a time in whole-group instruction (loose, mixed, or sorted by color, depending on the focus during math instruction).

If you teach kindergarten or first grade, you may not want to store your Unifix cubes in the same way that Jamila did for second grade. You may simply have quart-size bags of cubes sorted by color stored in a large, clear plastic container along with another shoebox-size container of loose, mixed-color Unifix cubes for sorting with younger children. However you choose to organize connecting cubes, be sure to teach kids to return them to their containers the same way they found them.

Organizing Manipulatives for Number and Operations

Jamila had a lot of materials for number and operations, including the Unifix cubes described in the preceding section. She also had more base ten blocks than she needed for one class. Jamila had these stored in several places around the room and kept remembering she had more. When they were all gathered in one place, she was shocked at the excess. Some of them were still in their original wrapping! There were a bunch of yellow base ten blocks and a lot of blue ones too. Jamila decided to keep just the blue ones. She'd donate the yellow ones to the math lab her school was opening, so we put those near the door with a card labeled *Donate to Math Lab*. We were tempted to haul them off to another room to store them, but we stayed on task and returned to the blue base ten blocks.

To be sure she had what she needed, we sorted again—this time it was base ten blocks by ones, tens, and hundreds blocks. We put them into plastic ziplock gallon bags and labeled them *ones*, *tens*, and *hundreds*. Later, Jamila would get students to help her

organize the base ten blocks into small, individual bags so that each child would have his or her own place value kit (20–30 units, 18 rods, and 10 flats).

Next, we got to work on the dice. We put them put in a quart-size ziplock bag (instead of big gallon-size bags with lots of dead space). Using bags that match the size of the materials saves much-needed storage space. Another way to store the dice is to sort them by type and place them in smaller labeled ziplock bags (those with dots; those with numbers: 0–5, 1–6, 4–9, 10–20, etc.), and then store all the

Before: The dice are stored in several large ziplock bags.

After: The dice are in a much smaller space.

Before: Base ten blocks.

Jamila sorts the blue base ten blocks she'll keep.

In another classroom, dice are placed in smaller ziplock bags sorted by type and are stored in a clear plastic container.

bags in a clear plastic shoebox that's just the right size. If you have enough dice, you might place some with partner games that require dice. This saves time and movement of students across the room to get dice for their games.

Our next step was to look at the place value mats Jamila had created and gathered over the years. She'd just never looked at them all in one spot before. Now she could decide which were most useful, keep those, and purge the rest. She kept those that were easiest for students to read and that were in the best shape. She donated some and tossed others into the recycle bin. As we sorted, Jamila told me that one night she'd gone home and made place value mats only to find that she already had some at school the next day. Sounded familiar to me!

We narrowed the place value mats from eight down to four different kinds. Jamila already had a great wire sorter to store them in, so we placed it in her small-group teaching area. She was pleased to find how easy these were to access now.

Jamila kept these organizers because they were the easiest for students to use.

Old charts that are not needed are thrown away.

The place value mats and hundreds charts are now stored in the small-group area for easy access.

Jamila compared these hundreds charts to decide which to keep.

After: Number and operations materials are stored neatly in containers on one shelf in the math closet.

Organizing Geometry Materials

There was quite a pile of geometry materials, especially geoboards and tangrams. Again, we sorted into two piles: things to keep and things to donate. Jamila needed to store enough materials for only *one* class of students in her room. There just wasn't enough space for all that extra stuff. She kept enough geoboards so there was one for every student and a few extra for future replacements. (We got rid of geoboards with missing pegs, since these are frustrating for students to use.) Then we found a clear plastic container that

was just the right size in which to store the materials. It was on the pile of empty containers from materials we'd dumped out earlier in this makeover. Again, we didn't need to go out and buy new containers.

We sorted blue polygons into a clear plastic shoebox with a lid instead of keeping them in a ziplock bag. We did the same with pattern blocks. This way we could stack the two boxes on top of each other in the closet and save space. As we examined the geometric pieces in Jamila's room, we found some made of hard plastic and others of soft foam; we kept the soft pieces since they make less noise when students work with them. Also, we found a brand-new container of tangrams, so we gave a ziplock bag full of old tangram pieces to another teacher on her team who needed some. They were in great shape, but we liked the container the new ones came in. It fit perfectly in the math storage area.

Before: A jumble of geometry materials is piled on the floor.

After: The geometry materials are now neatly stored.

We took commercial math games out of their big storage box and put them with the appropriate math concept shelf in the math closet.

After: The geometry materials are now labeled and stored in the math closet on one shelf.

Jamila decided to keep a set of containers and objects that represented 3–D shapes and she put these in a cardboard box she already had. When it was time to put them back on the shelf, she said, "Let's put these in a clear plastic container so I can see what's in there." She liked the way this looked and thought she'd be more prone to put things away in the new system if she could more easily see what she had. It seems that when our containers "match" and look better, we are more apt to keep up with them. Strange, but true!

Jamila had a box of commercially made games, which we decided to empty and sort. We chose to store each game with its matching math concept rather than put the games all together in a separate place in the storage box they came in. This way Jamila would be able to more easily find (and remember she had) a geometry game while teaching geometry concepts. Also, we placed partner games for geometry in a gallon ziplock bag labeled *Geometry Partner Games* and put it on the geometry shelf in the math closet.

Organizing Materials for Teaching About Money and Time

When we looked at materials for teaching students about money, we saw a rather messy stack. It was littered with a bunch of old ads, a box full of large magnetic money, some games, and a nice cash register that contained plastic coins. All it needed was a little rearranging, and we condensed the materials in no time at all. We decided that Jamila could simply collect ads (and ask her children to bring some in too) when she was teaching students about money and not keep ads from year to year. Anyway, prices *do* change!

She took the large magnetic money pieces out of the commercial box they came in, sorted all the coins into small, labeled bags, and placed all the

Before: The money materials in a messy stack.

Jamila takes large magnetic money pieces out of the commercial box they came in to save space and throws away old ads.

After: The money materials are now condensed and stored neatly.

money materials in one clear plastic shoebox. We left the lid off so the money games would fit in. This container would now fit neatly and easily on a math closet shelf. We placed the cash register beside it so Jamila could access it easily when teaching about money.

Before: Too many clocks.

After: One set of clocks is stored in a small clear plastic container.

Jamila had several sets of student clocks. She chose to keep the little "Judies" and donated the others. Each child would have one small clock to use for working with time, and the clocks would be stored in a labeled container. Jamila also kept a larger demonstration clock to use for modeling in whole group and small group, as well as one clock stamp for use in small group or at stations.

Halving the Fractions Materials

"How many fractions sets do I have?" lamented Jamila as we looked at all those little pieces. "I don't need all these," she went on. "In fact, I like this set better. There are numbers on them, and the pieces are bigger. Let's give away these smaller pieces without numbers to a higher grade level. These are really better for older students." And so we divided the fractions materials.

As we searched through the materials, we discussed the best way to *teach* fractions concepts. Jamila decided she'd need one large magnetic set for teaching in whole group and another set with smaller-size pieces for small group. We also kept a favorite pizza fractions game with large pieces easy for primary children to handle.

In just a few minutes, we had halved the number of Jamila's fractions materials. Many fractions sets were donated to other classrooms in need of them. Fractions sets have so many little pieces, and Jamila could teach second graders to use paper to create their own sets, which could then be sent home for practice.

When I returned to Jamila's classroom two weeks after her storage makeover, she was starting to introduce fractions to her class. I immediately recognized the large set she'd reserved for whole-group modeling. She told me, "It was so easy to prepare to teach with fractions this year. Everything was in one easy-to-find container. This saved me so much time."

Before: Jamila had lots of little fractions pieces.

Materials for time, money, and fractions are all stored on one shelf in their own labeled containers, with room left over for symmetry, calculators, and problem solving.

After: Fractions materials are now condensed and stored in one clear plastic lidded box.

Modeling with large magnetic fractions pieces is easy . . . when you can find your materials!

Making Materials Accessible: Setting Up a Classroom Math Corner

When organizing materials for literacy, most teachers have a classroom library to give students access to books for independent reading and exploring. We set up a parallel structure in Jamila's room called the math corner. Figure 2.3 explains the similarities between a classroom library and math corner. It is a place to store manipulatives and graphic organizers being used to teach math concepts, rather than keeping them in a closet where they are out of sight. When working on investigations and problems during whole-group time, students may use a material from the math corner that the teacher may not have considered. This area may also be used as a math work station during independent work time.

Before the start of school, Jamila and I brainstormed materials her children would probably need in the math corner for the first nine weeks of school. After school began, she would also be flexible in adding materials that we might have overlooked. Throughout the year, materials in the math corner would be changed in and out, depending on what Jamila was teaching. For example, when she taught about money and time, she would add coins and clocks to the math corner.

Purpose	**Classroom Math Corner**	**Classroom Library**
Purpose	■ Independent use for problem solving and talking about math during math stations ■ Students may borrow materials to help them solve problems during independent math time in whole group.	■ Independent use for reading and talking about books during literacy stations ■ Students may borrow books to read during independent reading time in whole group.
Recommended Space	■ Corner or special space devoted to math materials for independent use ■ Can be part of a whole-group teaching area	■ Corner or special space devoted to books for independent reading ■ Can be part of a whole-group teaching area
Materials Needed	■ Math manipulatives, graphic organizers for math, problem-solving supplies ■ Store in labeled containers ■ Anchor charts for math posted nearby	■ Books and magazines for independent reading, graphic organizers for reading ■ Store all in labeled baskets ■ Anchor charts for reading posted nearby
Optional Items to Make This Space Inviting	■ A rug, lamp, low magnetic dry erase board, plants, clock, calendar, small table and chairs	■ A rug, lamp, plants, pillows or comfy chairs, stuffed animals

Figure 2.3 **Parallels Between the Classroom Math Corner and the Classroom Library**

To begin, we looked at her district math core curriculum for the first six weeks of school, which stated that students would do the following:

■ Learn and understand processes and procedures for daily problem solving and develop computational fluency.
■ Model, create, and describe multiple representations of numbers that show equivalence for addition and subtraction.
■ Begin to discover inverse relationships between operations and use patterns to develop strategies.
■ Build representations of numbers to 100 using concrete objects to give descriptions, make comparisons, and place groups of objects in order using place value.
■ Measure length using connecting cubes to approximate standard units.

We chose the following materials for the math corner for the start of the school year:

■ Colored plastic counters
■ 3/4-inch plain wooden cubes
■ Units and tens base ten block kits
■ Unifix cubes
■ Tens and ones place value mats
■ Popsicle sticks and straws bundled in tens
■ Ten-frames
■ Hundreds charts
■ Blank storyboards to be personalized
■ Missing number pattern strips

- Blank Frayer models for building vocabulary (Frayer, Frederick, and Klausmeier 1969)

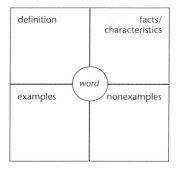

definition	facts/ characteristics
examples	*word*	nonexamples

- Addition and subtraction fact flash cards

For the math corner, we chose a space in the classroom that would be large enough for two children to work at independently during stations time.

It was centrally located, so students could easily borrow materials from here as they worked on problems during whole-group time. And, as an extra bonus, this space was located near the whole-group calendar bulletin board, which students could use as reference during math stations. We decided to use a corner, borrowing this idea from the setup of the classroom library. (If you don't have a corner, you might angle two shelves slightly to give the illusion of a corner.) Most elementary teachers create a special spot for the classroom library; we wanted an equally appealing space for the classroom math corner. Please don't despair if you don't have a usable corner in your room for this. Just create an interesting space around some shelves.

We anchored the classroom math corner with a bookshelf (you might use two if you have them) and a small rug to define the space. Math manipulatives were stored in labeled containers, and printed materials (graphic organizers, books, etc.) were placed in a labeled set of stacking trays. Two class notebooks were housed here, too, where students could record problems they generated for themselves and their peers to solve. We propped a

The classroom math corner is set up as an attractive spot in this second-grade room. Shelves hold math tools that children will use independently, including manipulatives, dry erase materials, and graphic organizers. The space is anchored by a small rug and has a low dry erase board on an easel, as well as a clock at eye level.

This stacking paper holder contains two problem-solving notebooks for the class to record problems they have devised and solved, blank missing number puzzle papers, and blank Frayer models. To the right, math manipulatives are stored in labeled containers. On the bottom shelf are dry erase materials, math books, and blank storyboards for problem solving.

large magnetic dry erase board on an easel on the floor for children to work at. We planned to add picture books related to math concepts being studied as they were read aloud over time, along with a variety of materials for problem solving.

If you set up a classroom math corner, you might add inviting elements, such as a lamp, plants, or even an awning overhead. Ours was made with a trifold project board. We hot-glued fabric to one section that hangs down and propped it open with metal door hinges from the hardware store, which we fastened to the cardboard with Gorilla Glue. We hung a clock at eye level on a cabinet in this corner, too. Over time, anchor charts for math would be posted on the cabinets and nearby bulletin board for student reference. Even if you don't have a large space available, you might plan for an area near some shelves or stacking plastic drawers to house your own classroom math corner.

Teaching with Manipulatives

Once you're organized, it'll be time for teaching with all those little pieces. The more you can think through what you'll need for each math lesson and how you want children to use the materials, the more effective and efficient your teaching will be. Be sure to build in some "exploration time" when introducing manipulatives to your class. The lesson that follows demonstrates how to use exploration as part of a whole-group lesson. Another way to include exploration time is by using exploration stations during the first few weeks of school, as described in Chapter 3.

The number of minutes for exploration depends upon your grade level. If you don't give them this time, children will play with the materials anyway, and you'll be tempted to take the manipulatives away from them. Young children, and many older ones, learn best when they can touch and handle concrete materials to help them develop ideas and concepts rather than just memo-

rize facts. Always begin with the concrete before moving to more abstract thinking.

In a classroom I visited, the teacher was introducing the children to money and wanted them to explore coins. She had the class sit near her on the whole-group carpet. She gave each student a handful of money and asked them to examine the coins. Before she knew it, there was money everywhere. Kids were rolling coins across the floor; some were trying to spin the coins; money was clinking in their hands; it was chaos. This teacher wanted to give her children experience with manipulatives, but it didn't go very well. She decided that coloring in workbook pages of coins would be a quieter, more manageable activity for the next day.

Unfortunately, this can be the reality for some teachers. But with careful planning and thought about how to prepare and introduce the manipulatives, children can have the rich experience of working with hands-on math materials rather than a slew of endless worksheets. So, what went wrong? First of all, the children had too many coins and no boundaries or explicit modeling. Instead of sharing only the coins that she wanted to introduce, the teacher brought out all of them at once and overwhelmed the children (and ultimately, the teacher, too). Next time, she might begin with just pennies. Starting small can create success.

Here are some suggestions for coin exploration. Before class, prepare snack-size baggies with six pennies in each. An even number of items promotes equal sharing and minimizes arguing. Put an assortment of pennies in each bag, including some dull and some shiny. Prepare enough for half the number of children in your class so you can have pairs of students work with each bag of pennies. This will reduce the number of coins to deal with in the lesson. Put the baggies in a container near your whole-group teaching area so you can easily access it during your lesson.

When it's time for math, gather the class on the carpet while you sit in a small chair in that area. Show them a large penny (these are available in plastic with magnets on the back). Talk with the children about the name of this coin, the color, the shape, and the value. You might even have a little poem or song about this coin that you teach them, such as the following (author unknown):

> *Penny, penny, easily spent,*
> *Copper brown and worth one cent.*
> *Nickel, nickel, thick and fat,*
> *You're worth five, I know that.*
> *Dime, dime, little and thin,*
> *I remember you're worth ten.*
> *Quarter, quarter, big and bold,*
> *It's worth twenty-five, I am told!*

Then have the class sit in a large circle, or along the perimeter of your carpet. You might tell them to "get in their circle spots." This lesson will have two parts: first the children will explore pennies and then they will use them for a specific purpose. Have one of the children be your partner to demonstrate what they will do with the manipulatives as they explore them. Be sure all the children are actively paying attention to you so they know what you expect. Sit beside your student partner and tell the class that when it's time for them to explore, they will work with a partner too. Show them a ziplock bag of pennies and a math mat (9-by-12-inch sheet of foam shelf liner or felt or laminated black construction paper) and explain that they will be working with a partner and getting these materials to share. Have your student partner put the math mat in front of the two of you as you sit side by side. Then model how to open the bag carefully with the zipper side facing up, so the pennies don't fall out yet. Show how to gently pour the pennies onto the mat so they stay on the mat. Next, demonstrate how to explore the coins; you might line them up, stack them, make a pattern, and so on. Tell the students they will have a few minutes to explore the

Children learn about pennies in whole group through a poem on a chart.

coins and then they will do some math work with the pennies. Tell them, "The pennies must stay in your hand or on the math mat. If they don't, I will take the pennies away."

Next, assign partners for the children and have pairs sit side by side. Give each pair one bag of pennies and a math mat. Set a timer for just one or two minutes and let the kids explore the pennies. You might as well as give them this time, because they will do it anyway. Watch closely. If anyone throws coins or uses them inappropriately, take the coins from them for the rest of the exploration time. This will usually stop the fooling around immediately. The student who has lost his or her pennies can sit and watch everyone else.

When the timer rings, ask children to place all their coins back on the math mat, put their hands in their laps, and look at you. Now that they have had a few minutes to explore, have them use the pennies for a specific purpose. Tell them that now you want them to look carefully at the coins and talk about them with their partner. Model this by looking at a penny and saying, "This penny is round and shiny. It has a one on it." Ask them to share what they notice about the pennies with their partner. Observe carefully as they talk about their coins with each other. Give them as much time as needed for all children to be engaged thoughtfully. Try to end the activity before they tire of it.

After students have discussed their coins, it's time for them to share with the whole group. Ask them to put their coins back on the mat and tell the class what they noticed. Be sure to have them speak in sentences when they share. You will probably find that they are very interested in this kind of exploration and come up with all kinds of things. In one classroom, I heard the following:

- One penny was really shiny. Most of them were dull.
- All the pennies are round like a circle.
- They all have the same man on them. That's Lincoln. They have words, too.

- Mine says 1998 on it. Another one says 2000. Those are dates like on the calendar.
- The penny says "one" on the back. There's a picture on the back too.

After they have shared, have students put the coins back in the ziplock bags, push the air out of the bags, and then zip them up tightly, making them as flat as possible. Collect the math mats and baggies. A student can help you. Ask students what they learned about pennies. Suggest that they look for pennies at home and when they're outdoors. Tell them that sometimes they might find pennies on the sidewalk or playground or even in the car.

On another day, repeat this lesson with another coin, such as the nickel or quarter. Once you've introduced several coins, make baggies with only three like coins in each. Then give each pair of students a baggie of pennies and a baggie of nickels.

Two students examine a quarter during a whole-group lesson on money.

Have them examine the coins and compare and contrast them.

After you have taught several lessons with a variety of coins, students will know how to use them and can work with them independently. When opening a math station with coins, I recommend keeping the numbers of coins small. Use about the same number you used in the whole-group lesson. For example, have three pennies in one bag, three nickels in another, three dimes in another, and three quarters in the last baggie. Children will repeat the activities they did previously in whole group (only after you have modeled with each type of coin several times). When you introduce this station, model and have students remind you how to use the materials—everything from how to open the baggies, to how to pour them gently onto the math mat and keep them on the mat, to how to put them away, push the air out of the baggies, and zip them shut so they lay flat.

Note: It is not recommended to have students explore coins on desks. This will be too noisy, and coins may accidentally drop and roll off the desks. Use coins with math mats on the floor. Also, if children are seated on the floor near you, you can better engage them and see what they are doing.

Remember that children will play with any manipulatives you give them (coins, tangrams, pattern blocks, etc.). For that reason, be sure you give them a bit of exploration time before you try to teach a lesson with these materials. Use a timer so you don't let this go on too long. While exploration through play is valuable, you'll want to spend the bulk of your time with children engaged in guided practice using math manipulatives.

Other Considerations for Using Manipulatives

Chapters 4 through 8 each contain a special section on troubleshooting. These sections contain tips for managing materials specific to the part of the math curriculum discussed in the chapter. For example, Chapter 7, "Geometry Work Stations," has ideas for using pattern blocks and geoboards. The measurement chapter (Chapter 8) has tips for measuring rice and beans, using rulers and string, and managing scales and objects to weigh.

Here are a few other general considerations when using math manipulatives:

- Whenever possible, limit amounts of manipulatives you give to students to simplify management. For example, if you want children to make AAB patterns, give each child just two colors of Unifix cubes to keep this simpler. Don't give them a huge container of Unifix cubes and expect they will sort out just two colors. Give them about ten of each of two colors, rather than fifty of many different colors.

- Let children explore the manipulatives when you first introduce a new type. In kindergarten, you may have several lessons early in the year in which students explore new manipulatives. I call these exploration stations. Likewise, you might provide first and second graders with free exploration time using manipulatives during the first week of school before the stations are introduced. You'll want to set expectations during this time (e.g., stay at your place and don't move around the room; pieces stay on the mat and may not be tossed around). During exploration time, let students build that tower of Unifix cubes or make the longest snake they can. Then teach them how to use the materials for math time. If they don't get to explore with them now, they will play with them during stations time.

- Be explicit about your expectations for how to handle math manipulatives. Show children what they may do, and make it very clear what they may not do. If you don't want them to build towers with cubes, tell them that is not okay. Model, model, model. Have kids sit on the floor near you when you demonstrate so you have their full attention. You might even make a chart of how to use the materials and add photos showing children doing the right thing.

■ Be consistent. Once you've established how to use materials, hold students accountable. If a child is playing around or using materials incorrectly, remove the manipulatives from that student (not the whole class) immediately. Let the child try again when you think he or she is ready to use them the correct way.

■ If you have foam manipulatives, use them. They are so much quieter than hard plastic. Foam dice and pattern blocks are two essential items to add to your math supplies.

■ Don't make paper manipulatives unless you have no other alternatives. All those little pieces of paper can be nightmarish to manage. Yes, paper is quiet, but it's much better for children to have geometric solids (cones, cylinders, spheres, etc.) to hold, count, measure, and explore. Foam or hard plastic shapes, rather than paper ones, are also easier for students to manipulate, put away, and not lose.

■ If you don't have much money and need counters, consider getting small fun items for math from a dollar store. Or ask parents to clean out the toy box at home and send small items that will fit in a sandwich-size baggie. See the "junk hunt" parent letter for collecting milk jug lids, buttons, old keys, and so on, on page 220 in the appendix (adapted from *Mathematics Their Way*). I've found it's best to have lots of similar items so kids don't fight over who gets what.

■ Use math mats. When students are working alone or with partners, have them keep their materials on a 9-by-12-inch mat. The boundaries set by the mats will help a lot with management, because they let children know what you expect. Mats can be made from cut pieces of foam shelf liner found at dollar stores, colored "fun foam" available at craft stores, or

A student uses a math mat on his desk while working with manipulatives to make this activity quiet and manageable. The mat is made of foam shelf liner, which is available in home goods departments and dollar stores.

black construction paper that's been laminated. Paper is not as soft and is a bit more slick than the other mats, but it will work. Foam mats will last for years (and can be laundered), but paper mats may only last one school year. Another alternative is plain foam placemats cut in half, which you may find at a dollar store. If you use foam placemats, be sure they're solid and not decorated with a vivid print or pattern, because these designs may cause visual confusion when a student is working with manipulatives.

■ Set the purpose. Let children know why they are using a type of manipulative and how it will help them learn a concept in math. If they know *why* they are doing something, they may be less apt to play with the materials.

■ After children have worked with a manipulative, ask them how it helped them learn a math concept. Ask for their feedback whether this manipulative helped or if there's another manipulative they think would better help them. Be open to kids' ideas.

■ Don't take away manipulatives because you feel they are a "crutch." If children need concrete objects to help them learn math concepts, let them use them. When students no longer need the teddy bear counters, they will stop using them. The same thing applies for fingers. Fingers are the most concrete manipulative of all. Children always have them handy! Asking a child not to use fingers or cubes is taking away a strategy that is working for that student. Provide a new, more efficient strategy, and ask the child to try it. Keep trying until you find a scaffold that will move the child to thinking more abstractly *over time*. It takes a lot of practice with manipulatives to connect the concrete to more abstract thinking. Math facts are a good example of this. Kids may be able to memorize 2 + 2 = 4, but until they can manipulate four counters to show this relationship, it is just an abstraction.

Reflection and Dialogue

1. Which ideas in this chapter on organization did you find most helpful? Share your favorite three ideas with others at your grade level, and commit to trying at least one of them in the next two weeks.

2. Create a plan for organizing your math materials. Where will you begin? What's your goal? Who might help you? Start small.

3. Which math space do you want to organize first? Choose one. It could be a cabinet, a set of shelves, a large math bin given to you by your school, or a "junk table." Work with a colleague, following the steps in this chapter to sort materials, purge, containerize, and equalize the space. Take before and after pictures to share with others at your school. You might do this as a grade-level team, sharing ideas and successes.

4. Which categories of math manipulatives do you have too many of? Not enough? How can you work together to get the materials you need for teaching math?

5. Make plans for a classroom math corner. Look for a special place in your room to set it up. Do you have an unused corner or one you could clear out? A bookshelf and clear plastic containers? Work with a colleague and help one another set up your math corners for students to use. Then invite others to visit your new space for math. Watch the idea grow throughout your building!

6. Think of a lesson you've taught in which use of manipulatives went really well. What did you do that made this lesson successful? Then think of a lesson when manipulatives were a nightmare. What went wrong? How could you restructure that lesson to improve it, and still use manipulatives?

7. What tips on using manipulatives will you try from the end of this chapter?

3

Getting Started with Math Work Stations

Now that you've decided to set up math stations and have organized your materials, you may wonder how to get started. Questions may be circling in your mind: How can I use math work stations most effectively in my room? What about cleanup? How many stations should I have? What do I put in them? How do I introduce them? Most of these questions relate to management. But surprisingly, many of the answers involve thinking about *teaching* effectively before moving activities to work stations for independent practice. I've found it helpful as I set up a math station to think through exactly what I'm teaching and what I want students to explore more deeply at the station.

In this chapter, you'll learn a variety of steps taken by different teachers to ensure that math stations run smoothly. The key is to model, model, model, and think clearly about how you want students to work in each station before you even begin them. Of course, you will probably not use *every* suggestion included here. This chapter is intended to offer you choices of things you might try to help your stations time work well. If you are new to math

stations, you'll probably want to start small. From year to year, you'll find that different groups of children need varied levels of scaffolding to support their independence. As you read, look for tips that resonate with you and feel doable. Those will offer you a starting place.

When and Where Do I Begin?

In first and second grade, I recommend starting to introduce math stations in the second week of school. You'll need the first week or so to begin to get to know your students and teach basic procedures as well as to do some review of familiar math concepts. Things children already know how to do from previous school experience will make up the base of your early math stations and provide a safe ground for students' independent work. Don't worry if you're reading this book later in the year. You can start math stations at any time. Of course, it's best to start early in the year so procedures will be firmly in place and allow you to meet with small groups all year long. But if it's December or even April and you're reading this book, you can start tomorrow.

If you teach kindergarten, you may take a slightly different approach during the first three to four weeks of school. Instead of introducing math stations, I like to start with having children do exploration stations, in which they explore a different type of math manipulative each day. One day you might show the class connecting cubes and discuss what they may and may not do with them. Then let all students work with a partner using connecting cubes. On another day, repeat the procedure with teddy bear counters. Have half the students work with teddy bear counters and half work with connecting cubes (unless you have enough teddy bear counters for the whole class to use), then flip-flop. Add a new material each day (buttons, pattern blocks, wooden cubes, etc.), and by the end of a week or two there will be plenty of materials for students to explore with a partner. This isn't quite math stations, but it's a start. Exploration stations can be used for investigation of materials for the first few weeks and will be replaced by math stations as you introduce them. You might also take this approach with first graders in the first week or two of school.

While children are working at exploration stations, carefully watch what they do with the materials. Ask your students what they notice. Within a short time, you will probably see them begin to make patterns with materials. This is a signal to move the materials into a more structured type of work, which will become their first math stations. For example, in kindergarten you may notice kids sorting buttons into piles after just a few days. At this point, talk with them about ways to sort (by color, number of holes, size, fancy/not fancy) and add sorting cards with word and picture clues. They might use plastic desktop sorting circles to structure their sorts as this becomes math station 1.

After just a few days, kindergarten children begin sorting buttons at this exploration station.

Kindergarten children work with exploration stations early in the year.

By adding sorting cards and a desktop sorting circle, this exploration station with buttons is converted into math station 1.

As you introduce math stations (beginning in week two for first and second grade, and about week four or five for kindergarten), launch only one new station a day. This way you can be clear and explicit so students will remember exactly what you expect. Here's a process you might use when introducing stations to your class:

Introducing a New Station

1. Gather all materials for the new station and place them in a labeled container. (Be sure you have *taught* with these materials first.)
2. Show the materials to the whole class and discuss what students can do at this station. (If you've taught well, students will usually give great suggestions.)
3. Make an "I Can" list together if you think children will benefit from this support to help them remember what to do with the materials to deepen their mathematical understanding. "I Can" lists are discussed later in this chapter.

During the first weeks of school when introducing the idea of math stations, you will be circulating, observing, and giving assistance to students while students investigate with materials at stations. (Small-group math instruction should begin *after* your initial investment of time teaching routines for the first four to six weeks of school, so you know your students and they know your expectations.)

At some point in these early weeks of school, you might brainstorm with the class what math stations time should look like, sound like, and feel like. This helps both the teacher and the students clarify the expectations at stations, which increases the likelihood that they will run more effectively and not just be busywork. If you choose to brainstorm these expectations, list students' ideas on a chart, using language they understand. Here's an example from a second-grade classroom:

In Our Room Math Work Stations Should . . .

Look Like	Sound Like	Feel Like
Kids are working with math ideas.	Quiet voices so others can learn	I can do it!
Kids are taking turns nicely.	Using math talk	I like to solve problems.
Kids are talking with their partners about math.	Talking with just your partner	Calm
Things are put back in their places.	Making choices together	I like math!
Kids are on task.	"Let's try this together."	
Kids are using materials like the teacher showed.		
Teacher is not interrupted while working with a group.		

Display the chart in a prominent place in your classroom so students can view it as a reminder of what they should do during math stations time. You might want to take digital photos of students working on tasks at stations and post these pictures

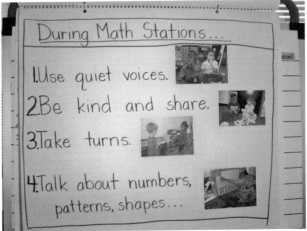

A kindergarten class uses this chart as a reminder of appropriate behavior in math stations.

around the chart as a border, adding more over time. If you teach kindergarten or first grade, you might post these photos beside the corresponding print describing what the photos show. This visual reminder can help students remember the behavior they will exhibit while they work on their own.

Another option is for the class to come up with three or four agreements or rules for stations time. Again, use photos for support. In a kindergarten class, the chart could be made when introducing exploration stations.

Math Work Stations Progression: A Daily Routine

Math stations usually follow a whole-group lesson for math. After you teach the math lesson, students move to their independent stations for further investigation. Don't introduce new concepts or skills and move them into a station the same day. Add the station after you've taught the concepts

over time and when you feel students are ready to use the materials and explore the ideas on their own. To facilitate student independence, many teachers find it best to use a three-step approach that I call the "Math Work Stations Progression." (See Figure 3.1.) By including all three parts of this approach, you will find that there are fewer discipline problems and interruptions when you are teaching in small group, and children will work more productively at their stations.

As needed, use a brief stations mini-lesson (suggestions follow) to show students exactly what you expect during math stations time. Mini-lessons for stations should be included daily early in the year as you introduce math stations and may be used on selected days once stations are established. Following the stations mini-lesson, students read the management board and move into math stations to work with a partner using the materials provided to expand their mathematical thinking. They usually go to one or two stations for fifteen to twenty minutes apiece. The teacher rings a bell or

Steps	Purpose	How Often/How Long
1. Math Stations Mini-Lesson	To make sure students understand exactly what to do at stations	■ Daily early in the year when introducing math stations ■ As needed to introduce/review what kids will do at math stations (possibly several days a week) ■ About 3–7 minutes per mini-lesson
2. Math Stations Time	To enable students to investigate math concepts with a partner independent of the teacher, and to enable the teacher to work with a small group or observe/interact with partners as they work at stations	■ Every day, if possible ■ 15–20 minutes per station ■ 1–2 stations per day
3. Sharing Time	To allow students to share with the teacher and their classmates what they explored and/or learned that day in math	■ Daily, if possible ■ 5 minutes max

Figure 3.1 Math Work Stations Progression

gives a signal so kids know to move to their second station after the allotted time. Following their last station, students return to the whole-group area for a brief sharing or reflection time. This sharing time lets them know you value what they did and gives you helpful information about what is working or not working in the stations.

Mini-Lessons for Math Stations

Starting math work stations time with a brief stations mini-lesson, or model, will provide focus and direction to the day's independent work and will make students' work more meaningful. During a math stations mini-lesson, you can show students exactly what you expect them to do at a math station. Whenever you introduce a new task or tool, take a few minutes to show and tell kids how they can use it at the work station. The key to successful

mini-lessons is making them *short* and *focused*—no more than five to ten minutes in length.

Please note that these are not mini-lessons to teach math concepts and ideas, although you will certainly want to include those in your whole-group math instruction. Instead, stations mini-lessons are used to ensure smooth management of stations practices, including treatment of materials, on-task behavior, and working with a partner. After the first few weeks of using math stations, you probably will not need to conduct a math stations mini-lesson every day. Use them as you see fit. You likely will find that there are three different times when a mini-lesson for stations is helpful:

1. When you are first introducing the math station
2. When you are adding something new to a station
3. When you're reviewing (or re-modeling) a work station activity

A teacher introduces how to use materials in a stations mini-lesson during the first weeks of school.

I have sometimes mistakenly assumed that I can show students something once and have them do it successfully, especially in today's classrooms, where it seems as though there's so much to teach and so little time. My experience has taught me that students often need several models and exploration on an ongoing basis when they are building understanding of a concept or learning a new skill. Fewer activities revisited multiple times at stations are more effective than having children try out a different game every other day and playing it only once or twice before it disappears.

Stations Mini-Lessons at the Start of the School Year

At the beginning of the school year, the stations mini-lessons you conduct are different from those you'll do later in the year. You might teach one of the mini-lessons suggested in the following sections daily for the first two weeks or so of school. (For more ideas, refer to the sections titled "What the Teacher Needs to Model" in Chapters 4 through 8.) Do not assume that students who have used work stations in first grade will know exactly what you expect them to do at stations in second grade.

Start mini-lessons by having students sit close to you on the floor to engage their attention. Tell them and model explicitly what you expect them to do. Then have two children role-play while the rest of the class watches. Have the observers tell what they notice. Use *familiar* materials that you've already taught with during whole-group math instruction so this lesson goes quickly. You are not teaching a concept here; you've already done that before moving this activity to math stations for further exploration and/or practice.

Here's an example of creating story problems at a math work station. Again, you would introduce this station only after you have taught several lessons to students about story problems and they are familiar with this concept. To introduce this station, model and explain to your class how they will tell,

act out, and record a word problem using the following materials:

- Story mats (preprinted or mats that children have made previously)
- Connecting cubes
- Small dry erase board and markers or class math journal

I say something like this: "We have been learning how to tell number stories using story mats and cubes. Today we will start to use these during math stations. You and your partner should choose a mat and make up a story about the place pictured on the mat." I then choose a student, Travis, to assist with the modeling in this mini-lesson and explain, "Travis and I will be partners and show you what this might look like. We'll work together and use cubes to show what happens in our story. Which mat do you want to use, Travis?"

Travis chooses the farm mat and says, "Let's tell a story at the farm. There were 4 cows." He places four black cubes on the mat.

I add, "And there were 2 pink pigs," and put two pink cubes on the mat. "Together there are a bunch of animals." (Travis and I count the cubes together.) "Six farm animals are on the farm. We can write our story for others to read too."

Next, I have two other kids show the rest of the class how they would work together to tell a story, act it out, and record their word problem. These two students choose a mat with a beach scene and work together to tell a story: "Juan sees 3 blue fish," one student says. "Cedric sees 2 red fish," says the other. As they talk, they put three blue cubes on the mat and then two red cubes. Then they say, "Together they see 5 fish." They draw and write on a dry erase board to show the work they did.

When the two students are done, others give feedback and tell what they thought the partners did well. It sounds something like this: "I like the way they worked together. They didn't fight. They were nice and used quiet voices. They drew a picture

Two students tell and act out a story problem for the rest of the class.

Students place teddy bear counters in egg carton "ten-frames" while playing a collect, group, and count game.

and showed their work." This helps students *own* the activity and clarifies what they should do. Don't always pick the top students in your class to do the modeling. By having a variety of students do the modeling, they all get to have ownership. Plus, you'll see if you skipped something in your directions (perhaps you didn't give sufficiently explicit directions or forgot to put certain materials in the tub), and will be able to correct it before students start to work on their own at this station. Assume nothing; model everything!

You may want to use simple games for these first introductions to stations. Look in the teacher's guide for your core math program for ideas. If you have taught students to play a "collect, group, and count" game in whole group like the one that follows, it would be a good one to have two students model for the rest of the class as one of your first station activities. For this game, you'll need the following:

- Four empty egg cartons to be used as ten-frames (simply cut each egg carton into two rows of five sections each)
- Buttons or cubes or teddy bear counters to fit in the egg carton sections
- A die

In this game, two children take turns collecting a number of counters equal to the toss of a die and placing the counters left to right in their egg carton sections. Whenever one section of ten becomes full, they begin filling a new section. Partners must "tell how many before you take your turn," describing the groups of ten and leftovers and the total. For example: "I have 1 group of tens and 4 leftover ones. That's 14." The first to collect twenty wins. To add a challenge, have partners add the sum of two dice to determine the number of counters earned each turn, and use more egg carton "ten-frames," extending the goal to 50 or 100.

As demonstrated with the preceding two sample mini-lessons, it's a good idea to start with simple stations that don't require much prep (other than good teaching) to make it easy for you to introduce them and for students to be successful in using them. Find the chapter in this book that corresponds with the math concepts that you'll be teaching first, and choose ideas from that chapter to open your first math stations for the year. Also, if you're using a core math program, incorporate ideas from it.

The following are some mini-lessons you may want to conduct as you introduce math stations. Each is accompanied by some suggested wording for your explanations:

■ *How to use the equipment/materials.*
"When you use the dice, be sure to roll them on the mat. That way they won't make too much noise or roll far away." "While playing with the cards, turn them face up like this, one at a time. At the end of the game, shuffle them so they're ready to play with again." "Spin the spinner carefully. If it lands on the line, spin it one more time."

■ *How to share materials.* "There are plenty of materials, but you will have to share." "If somebody wants something that you want too, use a problem-solving strategy." "Don't take too much of something, or there won't be enough for anyone else." "Braden and Emma, pretend that you are at this station investigating patterns and you both want to use the same stamp. Show us what you would do to share the materials there."

■ *How to take turns.* "You will be working with a partner, so you will have to take turns. Decide who will go first and who will go next. Switch back and forth. If one of you goes first in one game, let the other one go first the next time. To decide who goes first, you might play Paper, Rock, Scissors, or roll the dice. Cassidy and Joseph, please show us what it would look like if you were having trouble taking turns and solved your problem."

Two students use Paper, Rock, Scissors to decide who will go first while playing a game at a math station.

■ *How to decide what to do at a station.*
"There may be several things to do at each station. Work with your partner to decide what to do together. As a class, we will write an 'I Can' list with ideas of what to do at some stations. Read it with your partner and pick something you both want to do. If you can't agree, you might each do something different and then show each other what you did when you are finished. If there's a partner game, it will be best to play it together, though. You'll have to work it out, because if I am at the table working with a small group, I won't be available to help you. I know you will be able to figure out what to do on your own, because the ideas on the 'I Can' list are your ideas. Gabrielle and Lexi, you are partners today. Show us how you will choose what to do when you work with the counting materials at station 3."

■ *How to solve a problem.* "Sometimes a problem will come up at your work station. Maybe you are missing some pieces to a game or someone doesn't play fairly or someone doesn't want to do what you want to. What do you do? There are many ways to solve a problem. If you can't find some game pieces, put the game in the 'Missing Pieces' basket. If I'm working with a small group, you might write a sticky note telling what is missing so we can be on the lookout for those pieces. Or you can tell the class about the missing piece during sharing time. If someone isn't playing fairly or uses mean words, tell that person that his or her words or actions are hurting you and to please stop. If that child doesn't stop, you might go to your desk and write me a note so I can talk to that person after group is over. If your problem has to do with taking turns, remember the ways we have to solve that problem. If I see that two students are arguing and cannot resolve their problem, I'll have both of them sit out for the rest of the station." As part of a mini-lesson, have two chil-

A "Missing Pieces" basket holds little things that may have been put in the wrong place. Students can also put a note in here to tell about a station that may be missing a piece.

dren role-play solving problems that may come up (before you see a need for it during stations). If we teach children to be proactive, they will learn to solve problems on their own.

■ *Where can I go for help?* "If you need a pencil or more paper, you can help yourself. You know that we have a tray with blank paper and a cup with sharpened pencils. If you have trouble with the computer, ask the Computer Expert [a role that you can assign to a computer-savvy student]. If you don't know how to work a math problem at the station, ask your partner. Please do not ask me for help if I'm working with a small group. You don't like when someone interrupts your group. Patrice and Luis, please pretend that you are at your station and just ran out of paper. Show us how to help yourselves without interrupting the teacher."

■ *How to put things away.* "It's important to put things away neatly and carefully, so the next people can find and use them. Everything has a special place where it should be put away when you're done. Put things back in the ziplock bags and zip them up. Push the air out of them before closing them, so they will fit easily into the math tub. Put the lids back

tightly on the dry erase pens; listen for the click so they don't dry out. Remember to put things back like you found them. Levon and Jayden, please show us how to put things away at station 7, where you work with addition materials."

■ *How to switch to the next work station.* "I will ring a bell to let you know it is time to clean up. When you hear the bell, please stop and begin to tidy up. Be sure to make things neat enough for the next group to use them. When I ring the bell the second time, you'll hear three dings in a row. That's the signal to switch to your next station. Quietly walk to your next math station. Use the management board to check where to go, if you need to. When you get to your next place, get to work right away. Sandra and Quincy, show us how to switch stations. Show us what it would look like to find your next station at the management board." An alternative to ringing a bell is to teach a predetermined signal, such as clapping a pattern and having the children repeat it. Some teachers sing a little song to let the children know it's time to move to the next station, and others ask everyone to stand up wherever they are in the room. The important thing is to teach a signal and use it consistently.

A teacher rings a bell at the end of small-group time to signal to the rest of the class to clean up and move to their next station.

Creating an "I Can" List During Mini-Lessons for Stations

To help students focus on what to do at each station, I've often found it helpful to make a list of what students *can* do there. I call it an "I Can" list, a positive term to remind students of what they should be doing while at that station. We usually *tell* students what to do at a station, but writing it down helps them remember over time. Also, there will normally be several things to choose from at each station, so the "I Can" list reminds students of what they might do there. It may be tempting to make the list on your own after school, but you'll find that when students give their input they are more apt to use the lists to guide their work.

To make an "I Can" list, gather the children close to you on the carpet and show them several materials you've been teaching with that they might use at a particular station. Name each item to

"plant the seed" of what they might do there. Then give them a minute to think about what they can do while working at this station and tell them you'll write it down. Next, record their ideas on a 4-by-6-inch card or an 8½-by-11-inch piece of white paper. I like these sizes because they usually fit in the math stations container, where the list will be placed for student reference. (I often tape an "I Can" list inside the lid of the stations tub.)

Jot down students' "I Can" ideas one at a time in kid-friendly language. You might add a simple sketch or a digital photo to help students "read" and remember the list. This can be especially helpful for children just learning to read, English language learners, and autistic students who understand pictures much easier than words. Remember that you can duplicate a station. If you make an "I Can" list to go with a station that has a duplicate,

In second grade, the "I Can" list for fractions practice uses words and pictures. It is also taped to the inside of the math station lid so students can access it easily. A sample of the Fraction Cubes activity is stored in a ziplock bag with matching materials at this station. The children suggested we add this sample, because they sometimes forgot what to do with the materials.

A kindergarten "I Can" list for counting includes photos and words brainstormed with the whole class. It is taped inside the lid of the math station container for easy reference.

be sure to provide a copy of the list at the duplicate station.

The key to using "I Can" lists is to keep them simple. Spend just a few minutes developing each list with your class, as needed, for stations where you think the extra support will help students remember what and how to practice.

Not every math station will need an "I Can" list. If students already know how to play the games in a station, there may be no need to list the games or directions there. However, I've found that when I notice that students are unsure about what to do or how to use materials at a station, the "I Can" list is worth a few minutes to develop with the class for both review and reference.

Making a Math Talk Card During Mini-Lessons for Stations

While observing children at stations, I noticed that they sometimes forgot the math vocabulary we'd been teaching and would use vague terms to talk about what they were doing or learning. For example, at a station for measurement, they'd say, "Give me that thingy" instead of "Let's use the measuring cup." One goal at math stations is to provide opportunities for students to talk about their math learning using appropriate math vocabulary. In order to support this talk, I decided to periodically make math talk cards *with* the class to use at selected stations.

We gathered together as a class on the carpet and spent a few minutes to make a math talk card. (Don't take too long doing this, or kids won't have any time to go to math stations.) First, I explained to the children the purpose of the card and why I wanted their input: "Today we're going to make a special math talk card to use while at the fractions station. We want to practice using math vocabulary so we'll learn these new words and think and sound like a mathematician. Let's brainstorm some words we've been learning that we can use at the fractions station." Next, I drew a big speech bubble

on an 8½-by-11-inch piece of white cardstock to remind students they'd use these words while talking. Near the top of the bubble, I wrote *MATH TALK . . . fractions.*

I gave the students a minute to talk with a partner about some possibilities for the list of fractions words, and they shared their ideas with the whole group. This was a great opportunity to review what they'd been learning and clarify concepts. They came up with words they'd been exposed to but weren't necessarily using as they worked on their own at stations. As one child said, "Fraction bar," I asked, "What could I draw to show that?" They suggested I write ¼ and draw an arrow to point at the line separating the two numbers. I wrote that term and a matching picture inside the speech bubble. Following that interchange, another student suggested the words *numerator* and *denominator*. Again, I added an illustration using ¼, and drew an arrow pointing to the number 1 for numerator and 4 for denominator.

Several children then named specific fractions, like *one-fourth, one-third,* and *one-half*. I wrote just *one-fourth* on the chart so it wouldn't be too crowded. This example would remind them to use other fractions, too. From there, they suggested *parts* and *whole*, followed by *half* and *equal parts*; I added each of these to the card.

Before placing the new math talk card in the station, we had two children model what it would look like to use this support. They decided to read the card together first to remember to use the words. They took turns reading the words and talked about their meanings. Then they took out some of the fractions materials in that station's tub and showed the rest of the class how they would use the pieces to build a whole from parts while using some of the words on the math talk card. It sounded something like this:

Child 1: Let's use some of our new words.
Child 2: Okay. Here are some *parts* to make a *whole*. Let's use *fourths*.

Child 1: We'll need four *fourths* to make a *whole*. And they're *equal parts*. (Looks at the chart and points to these words.)

Child 2: Let's write the fraction *one-fourth*. Mrs. Diller, we need to add a dry erase board to the station and some markers so we can practice writing fractions, too.

Later, as I observed students at this station, I found them using the math talk card for fractions and practicing with this academic vocabulary. In kindergarten and early first grade, you can adapt this idea by brainstorming just a few words to go with selected stations. For example, for a station about shapes, the card may say, *circle, square, triangle, round, curve*, and *side*. Include a picture clue to go with each word and remind students to use the picture and the first letter's sound to help them read the words on the card. Or you might want to include a simple sentence frame on the card using high-frequency words they know, such as, *This is a _____. It is _____. It has _____.*

Follow the lead of the children by asking them about the words they think they should practice. Remember that this is not a time to introduce new

Children at station 2 refer to words on the math talk card to use as they work with fractions at this station.

vocabulary, but a time to review what you've already taught. If you have not taught these words previously, students won't add them to the list or use them during stations time.

By adding supports like the "I Can" list and math talk cards at stations, you'll find that children's work will be more productive and focused. The addition of these supports at stations along with quality math instruction will increase rigor in the math exploration that students do. Taking the time to periodically develop these during stations mini-lessons yields great returns in the long run.

Work Stations Time

Daily, following a brief mini-lesson as needed, let students review the management board and move right into their work stations, going to one or two for fifteen to twenty minutes each. Children should know what to do and get busy right away because of the modeling done during stations mini-lessons. Remember that at the beginning of the year, while students are learning to work at their math stations, you'll want to walk around, observe, and assist students.

I recommend that you not meet with small groups for math until about four to six weeks into

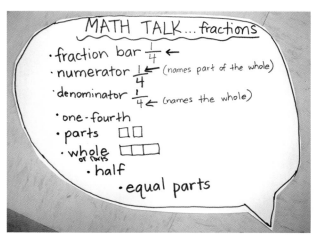

This math talk card focuses on fractions, a topic the class has been studying at the end of second grade. We brainstormed this list in whole group. Drawings and arrows help clarify terms we want children to use while at a station focusing on investigating fractions. A copy of this card is put in that station for reference.

the school year in first and second grade (and a few weeks longer in kindergarten). Only when management is under control will you be able to focus on good small-group teaching for math. You are wise to invest the first six weeks of school in teaching routines and watching your students explore at math work stations, so that you *will* be able to work with small groups in the following months.

Once you have begun small-group instruction, you must still keep aware of what students are doing at work stations. You will want to observe at stations some days so you can note what they're doing as they investigate concepts more deeply on their own. Chapters 4 through 8 each include a section on assessment with suggestions specific to that chapter's topic.

Commonly Asked Questions About Math Work Stations Time

There is not one right answer to any of the questions that follow. Management styles are as varied as the teachers in classrooms. There is not one ideal way of managing math work stations that will solve all problems. However, taking a commonsense approach does seem to work.

How many students should work together at a work station?

When analyzing what kinds of problems occur during work stations, I have found that most of them are *interpersonal*. The troubles are usually among the children working there: kids don't share; they argue; they get too loud; they push or use hurtful words. Most teachers I've worked with have found that by only having *two* children work together at a work station, noise levels and behavior problems are dramatically reduced. The old saying "Two's company, three's a crowd" seems to ring true in the classroom too. When children work together in pairs, there are often fewer problems during work stations time. Also, when only two students work together, each has to be more engaged. It's easy to

let someone else do the work if there are four or five of you in a group.

If you have an odd number of students, you might group together three kids who can work well together at a station that lends itself to three children (usually not a partner game scenario unless the game can be expanded to accommodate three players). Recently, I heard a teacher say to a student whose partner was absent, "Would you like to work alone today or with two other kids?" The child wanted to work with some friends. So the teacher offered two or three choices of stations where she knew the child could be successful (because they could support three children working together in a pinch). If you have three computers, three kids could easily work at the computer station.

Occasionally, you might have a child work alone during math stations. Some students *prefer* working alone at times. Often these children possess what Howard Gardner (1993) calls "intrapersonal intelligence." They may march to the beat of a different

In this classroom, there is an odd number of children. Two boys play a counting game at a station practicing the concept of *more* and *less*. One rolls the dice; the other spins the spinner. If they land on more, they add to the stack as many cubes as the number they rolled. If they land on *less*, they take away that many cubes. In the background, another child works alone on a problem-solving activity at a table.

The teacher has assigned three children to this station, but only two are playing the game. The third child is supposed to be the scorekeeper, but isn't getting much of a chance to think mathematically. This station would work best for a group of two.

drummer, and seem just to work better alone. Christina was one of those kids. Some days she could be very gruff or impatient with others and would actually thwart her partner's practice. But when she was alone, she could focus better. Her teacher would watch Christina carefully and make decisions on partnering based upon the day.

Most students like working with partners, and this structure works well for math stations, especially when you use partner games from your core curriculum. Over the years, I've worked with teachers who used to have four or five students work together during this time. But as they've made the transition to having students work in groups of two, they've seen increased student engagement and focused exploration at stations.

How do I decide on who works with whom?

There are many ways to pair students. You should decide on your purposes for the grouping before making decisions on who will work together. For example, if you want students to practice activities on the cutting edge of their development—if you want them to do things that have just a little bit of challenge but are within their range of doing them

on their own—then you might pair students who work at a similar level in math and who need practice with the same concept or skill. If two children are deepening their understanding of numbers from one to five and you'd like them to work with these numbers, then it makes sense to pair *them* at a counting station rather than pairing them with students who are working with larger numbers. Two other students in this same classroom may be investigating numbers to twenty and would be more engaged working together.

Some teachers pair students heterogeneously so they can help each other. This has its place, too, at times. If you feel that a student might be able to help another child understand a concept he or she has had difficulty with, then you might pair those two children. At times, students learn better with a peer tutor. However, don't always use high-low pairing. You may find that the child who is more advanced in mathematical understanding just does the work for the student who is struggling.

Occasionally, some teachers allow students to choose their own partners. This may motivate some children because of the added choice provided. Again, there's not one right way to choose partners. Think carefully about how you set up your partners at work stations, and don't stick to only one way of doing this. Vary partners occasionally to keep interest high.

When should I change partners?

I have found that there are several times when you might want to change students' partners. If you're pairing children who are working in small group at a similar level of understanding for a math concept, then change partners if you move them into a different small group for math. Another time to change partners is if you see that certain children aren't getting along well or aren't working productively together; a new partner may help them stay on task. Finally, when students move or are absent, you'll want to help students find a new partner, even if it's just for that day. Be flexible. Don't worry if a child "misses" a station. You can always rearrange where kids will go using your management board.

How many work stations should I have? How often should I change them?

You must decide how many stations you and your students can handle. Many teachers have eight to ten math stations set up. Each station is used for several weeks, depending on how long you'd like students to investigate particular mathematical concepts. The stations are not changed out every Friday (unlike mine as a young teacher in the 1970s!). The independent activities that get moved into the work stations are things that students have already learned to do with the teacher *during* instruction. Students are exploring them over and over again during math work stations. A variety of work stations keeps interest high. And because there are quite a few of them, they don't need to be changed out as often.

If the idea of ten stations sounds overwhelming to you, start small. Introduce just five stations and duplicate each. Or have half your students work at their seats doing independent work while the other half of your class goes to math stations.

When making decisions about when to change out materials at a math station, here are some things to consider. If the answer to a following question is *yes*, it's time to change out some materials at that station.

- Have children mastered the concepts this station provides opportunities to investigate?
- Are the numbers children are working with too small for them at this time of year? (They may need larger numbers.)
- Are students getting tired of this activity?
- Are kids finishing at this station too quickly? (They may need something more challenging or need more variety.)

- Are kids complaining that they need more time at this station? (The concept they're working at this station may be too hard or too involved for stations time.)
- Are children arguing or not using materials properly at this station? (You may need to add an "I Can" list or write directions with them. Or you may have too many materials here.)

You will probably want to keep some "old stations" out for review as you add new stations. For example, when you teach children about measurement, many of your stations will include materials for making comparisons about attributes, such as longer/shorter and heavier/lighter. Students may be using informal units like drinking straws or unsharpened pencils to measure objects around the room. But some stations may still contain materials for concepts taught earlier in the year that you want children to continue investigating. You may want to keep a station or two related to counting open throughout much of the year. The materials and numbers students explore can change over time, as they are ready to handle more sophisticated work. Likewise, you may have a patterns station that is a constant. Again, materials and concepts there may expand across the school year.

How long should work stations time last? How many days a week should students use work stations?

In first and second grade, we usually have students spend about twenty minutes at each math station. In kindergarten, children work at each station for about fifteen minutes. I've observed stations time in many classrooms and find that discipline problems often increase if teachers let their kids stay too long in one work station. It's a good idea to keep an eye on the time and change students to a new activity before trouble starts. Many teachers keep a timer at their small-group math table and set it for fifteen to twenty minutes. When the bell rings, the students automatically clean up and get ready to transition to the next station.

Most teachers let students work at two work stations a day for a total of thirty to forty-five minutes a day. Of course, at the beginning of the school year, math work stations time might last only ten to twelve minutes, and students might work at just one station.

My recommendation is that students use math stations most days, not just on Fridays. If stations time is part of their everyday routine, students will be more likely to know what is expected and settle to work quickly. You probably will want to observe children at stations or meet with small groups for math during this time, and it may be easier to be consistent with small-group instruction when your class is in the groove of using math stations every day. Of course, some days you might schedule a longer whole-group problem-solving session or investigation, and you will confer with individual students rather than meet with a small group. On those days, students will not go to math stations. But this is probably no more than once a week. Aim for a balance of some whole-group and some small-group instruction on most days.

Should kids write something at every math station? Where should they put their work?

No, students don't need to write at *every* math station. But sometimes they will use recording sheets. For example, at a station where students are solving word problems, you will want them to use numbers, pictures, and words to represent their thinking. This usually involves writing and drawing pictures. At another station where they are estimating length before measuring with nonstandard units, children will record their guesses and results. In these cases, you'll want to look at their work. It is easiest to manage if students have a special place to store stations products. There are several ways to store written work:

- If you want a central storage place to collect everybody's work, you might keep a box or

Two community math journals are placed at this "Multiplication Celebration" station (named by second graders late in the year). They create arrays and write about them in the journals.

tray labeled *Finished Work* into which students place completed products. The teacher can then simply pick up work at the end of the day to look at it.
- Or you can collect students' work at each station where you expect something written. You can have a "Finished Work" folder at each station that has a recording sheet. This way the products are already presorted.
- If you want a storage place for each individual, a pocket folder for each child works well. Students can place completed work or work in progress in the pockets of the folder.
- Or you might use community math journals at some stations where pairs of kids can record what they've done. Everyone uses this journal at this station, so there's only one journal for the teacher to look through. You'll need to teach kids to initial and date their responses if you use this option.

What if students misbehave during math work stations time?

It is a reality that children sometimes don't do what they're expected to do during work stations time. They should know ahead of time what they are supposed to do and what will happen if they break the rules. I use the "one strike and you're out" rule during math stations. The stations time of the school day is highly motivating to the children, and they don't like to miss it. So, if they know the teacher means business, they will be more likely to do what is expected. I simply tell students, "This is what you may do at the stations. This is what you may *not* do. If you break the rules, you will have to leave the station at once." I don't give idle threats or warnings. I tell them what I expect and then I follow through.

Many teachers have found that simply having a chair or two next to their small-group math table for children who have not followed the rules works best. When I sent students back to their desks to put their heads down, they still acted out and wanted my attention. If I sat them near me but didn't involve them in my lesson, they tended to pay attention to what the other students were doing and may have even learned something from this vicarious learning experience. If one child from a pair is removed from the station, be flexible. Either have the remaining child work with another pair or do something alone at that station.

One teacher shared with me a sure-fire method for discipline in her class during math work stations. If kids had to be removed from stations due to poor behavior, she had them take a piece of paper

A girl who misbehaved during math stations sits in a student chair near the small-group math table. She watches the lesson and thinks about how her behavior will change when she returns to stations.

and *draw a picture* of how their behavior would change when they returned to that station. Notice that she didn't ask them to write, nor was she "punishing" them. She was simply asking them to reflect on their behavior in a nonthreatening way. She said that many times students began writing spontaneously about their behavior after they drew. In fact, she got some of her best writing samples from some of her "behaviorally challenged" students this way.

If the same students have to be removed from work stations day after day, take a closer look at those students' needs. You may want to design an individualized plan for them to help them get back on track.

How can I encourage children to clean up? They don't put things away properly.

The best place to begin is by organizing materials so they can be easily put away. Use the suggestions in Chapter 2 to create a place for everything, so children know where to put things. I like to use clear plastic containers with lids for math stations, with a number on the front of each, and stack or line them up in numerical order. If there are little pieces that go with a game, I put those materials in a ziplock bag and label the bag with the name of the game. Then place the bag in the station tub. Each station has several activities for kids to do, so there could be two of these bags in one container along with a picture book. If you put lots of little pieces in a big tub, things get lost and it's hard for students to access what they need easily.

When introducing a station to the class, you'll want to model *how* to clean up materials and return them to the right place. Be explicit, saying things like this as you demonstrate: "Only get out the materials for the game you will play first. For example, at this station I'm going to use the Go Fish game first, so I'm only taking out the ziplock bag that holds the materials for that game. Play the game and when you are done, put all the pieces back in the bag they belong in, like this [show the

Two first graders clean up their materials by returning pieces to a ziplock bag and placing them in the stations tub to return to the shelf.

kids how to neatly put the pieces back in the bag and zip it up]. Then get out another game and play it. Clean it up before you read the book in this station. If you put things away as you use them, cleanup will be easy when I ring the bell to switch to the next station." Be sure to have two students model for the rest of the class what it will look like to play the game *and* clean up quickly.

When it's time to have kids switch to their second station, I've found it useful to have children "tidy up." That way the next pair of students can get to work quickly. If you have them neatly place materials in the spot where they've been working, the next partners can move there and get to work quickly. I don't expect students to put everything away and return the container to its storage spot unless nobody else will be using it on that day. When stations time has ended, then have children clean up fully and put all the materials away.

Should the children decide or should I choose which stations they will go to?

Research has shown that choice helps motivate students (Patall, Cooper, and Robinson 2008). When it comes to classroom management, many teachers do best initially giving children "controlled choices" at math work stations. It is generally easier to start the year by assigning students where you'd like them to go and eventually turning over more of the choice

to them than to begin by letting everyone go wherever they'd like and ending up with chaos.

Early in the year, you will probably only put out one activity at each station, because stations time is shorter when you first begin. Do provide choice over time at math work stations by including in each container two or three activities from which children can choose. This allows students to have some choice in a controlled way, which will help establish a predictable routine. And it prevents "early finishers." For example, when a child goes to station 5, an addition station, he or she may choose to play an addition game, read a picture book about addition using manipulatives to work out problems in the book, or write and solve an addition story problem. Don't worry if students don't get to do all these things during their first time at this station. They will visit the station more than once and will have a chance to try something else the next time. Likewise, at station 4, a place to practice graphing, there may be two different graphing games or activities from which to choose.

In one classroom I visited, the teacher had assigned only one activity for students to do at each station. She wondered why they were finishing too fast and why she was having discipline problems. When she added another choice or two within the stations, her problem with early finishers disappeared.

Again, teachers must know their students and what they need in order to decide which math stations children go to. Management of math work stations is a very personal teacher decision.

Management Boards

There are a variety of ways you might want to manage who goes to which work station. I've found that stations time is generally more successful when a teacher uses a management board, although some highly skilled teachers can run classrooms without them. The key is that students must know where they're supposed to be, when, and what they're supposed to be doing.

The easiest management board that I've found is a basic pocket chart, because it offers so much flexibility. (See the examples pictured.) Make a name card for each child and display them on the board. Write each child's name on a card in black ink large enough for the child to read and add a picture of the child, if possible. Students love seeing their photos on the chart. It makes the chart personal and shows you value them.

Place two name cards side by side in the top row of the pocket chart on the left-hand side to show who will work together. Continue to place name cards for partners in the pocket chart, two at a time, row by row. Then beside each pair of name cards, put numbered icons showing where those children should go during math work stations. (Or, in classrooms where children choose their own stations, they should take turns placing icons on the board.) I like to use numbers for math stations; each icon card simply has a numeral from 1 to 10 (or more or less, depending on the number of stations available). Icons to use on your management board are included in the appendix on pages 221–223.

If students are going to just one station that day, place one numbered icon beside each pair of names. If kids are working at two stations per day, put two icons beside the partners' names. Instruct

students in how to read the management board and how to remember where they are going that day.

At the end of each day, move each pair of icons down to the next space so their activities change for the next day. You don't have to worry about students "getting all the work stations done" in one week. Simply rotate kids from station to station, and they automatically get to do everything over time.

As mentioned, I recommend you start by having each child go to one work station daily. Eventually, you might have students go to two a day. To show this, make two copies of each numbered icon. Place the icons beside the pair of students' names to show where they will go first, then second. Children read the board and automatically know where to move

This management board is set up for literacy and math stations, which are scheduled at two different times of day. The literacy stations are on the left and use picture icons, and children are going to two per day. Different partners work together and are posted on the right for math stations. Numerals show which math stations students are to go to. When the teacher works with a small group, she posts a "Meet with Mrs. Thrash" icon to show who she will meet with. On this day, she is not meeting with small math groups, but will observe during math stations time. Her students are only going to one math station a day.

Before math stations time, students read the management board to see which stations they'll go to. The teacher dismisses them several at a time, and they get right to work.

when you signal them to go to the next station. Again, the icons are simply moved down to the next row beside the next pair of names daily.

There are, of course, a variety of other types of management boards and different ways to use them. Some teachers use pocket charts and cards; others use sticky notes or magnets. The key is to find a system that works for you. I've described the

This teacher moves cards for the next day's work at math stations using a management board I created for the company Really Good Stuff. Partners' photos are on the left. Two numbered icons are to the right of each pair of kids' pictures. They read the orange numbered card to find out their first station, and go to the station number on the yellow card in their second rotation. The teacher is observing children in this class today and not working with small groups for math. The opposite side of this reversible pocket chart shows where students go for literacy work stations.

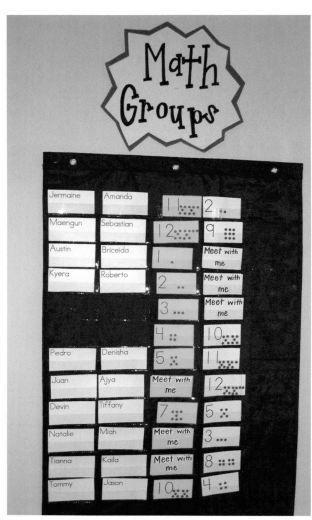

Students using this management board go to two math stations per day. The teacher is meeting with two small groups on this day. The first rotation is noted by the yellow numbered icon on the left. The white numbered icon on the right shows which station kids will use in the second rotation. The "Meet with Me" cards show which students will meet in small group with the teacher that day.

system that I've seen many teachers use easily and with success.

It's important to note that you should be flexible as you move students from one station to another. If you use a simple rotation system, as described here, you must still be flexible enough to move the icons to provide the right kind of practice for each student. Some teachers assign the first station and let children choose their second station. Find what works best for you and your class.

Sharing Time

Following work stations time, I have found it useful to have a brief sharing time with the class. This provides an opportunity for students to reflect on what they've done that day to deepen their learning. While gathered with your students on the floor, lead a short, focused discussion about what they did and learned in math that day. They may include examples from math stations, small group, or whole group. Sometimes, children will want to show things they've made. Be sure they tell about what they did and learned as they show the rest of the class. Limit sharing time to about a total of five minutes, so time doesn't get away from you. If everyone wants to share, have them turn and talk to a friend about what they did. Then call on just a few to share with the whole group. You might find it useful to have one or two specific questions to reflect on each day. Here are some possibilities:

- What did I do at math stations today? And what did I learn?
- What did I enjoy doing at math stations today? Why?
- What didn't I like doing at math stations today? Why?
- How did I solve a problem today?
- How did I help someone else solve a problem today?
- How did I represent or record what I learned?
- What else would I like to do at math work stations?
- What do I think we should change at math work stations?
- How did I collect and use data today?
- What math connections did I make today?
- What math talk did I hear or use today?
- What did I do to become a better thinker/problem solver today?

These and other questions may be copied onto cards, secured with a ring, and used to lead the sharing time discussion. See page 224 in the appendix for black-line masters of these cards.

In kindergarten at the beginning of the school year, you will have to model how to answer these questions. For example, you might say, "We're going to talk about what you did at math stations today. This will give you some ideas of what you might try when you work at them tomorrow. Today I saw Skylar taking turns while playing a game. She helped Michael and used kind words. I watched Van and LaShonda making patterns. They each made their own pattern, labeled it, and then showed each other and explained their pattern. Who can tell me something they investigated at math stations today? I'll call on three children today, and tomorrow we'll do it again and more of you will have a turn to tell what you did."

Early in first and second grade, sharing time may resemble the following scenario:

Teacher: What did you like doing at math stations today?

Brianna: I liked working with you in small group. We got to build and break apart ten-trains to learn about all the ways to make six. Nobody interrupted us and I learned a lot.

Teacher: Thank you for doing such a good job of working independently at math stations today. While you were working, the students in our group did learn a lot today. Keep up the good work of solving problems on your own. That way everyone can learn.

Marcus: I liked reading the book about patterns. Kevin and I talked about all the patterns we saw in the book. Nature is cool. Like the caterpillar's pattern was AB.

Teacher: That is an interesting book with all those nature photos in station 3. Naming the patterns, like AB, is a great way to practice what we've been learning about patterns.

Maria: We made up math stories at station 6. Here's a picture we drew to go with our story. (Both children show drawing and tell their addition story.)

Teacher: I hope more of you make up stories like this at station 6. Telling stories helps you understand what we're learning about addition. Look at the numbers Maria and Emile wrote to help tell their story, too.

During sharing time, two children show and tell about the graphs they made at a math station.

Solving Ongoing Problems at Math Work Stations

When students mention problems they had at work stations during sharing time, the problems can become the next day's stations mini-lessons. For example, when a student in one class told us that he couldn't find the pieces he needed for a partner game at station 4, we decided that on the following day we would, with the class, make a list of materials that should be stored in the ziplock bag holding that game. We wrote the short list (with picture clues) on an index card and taped it to the inside of the bag. Now, students know exactly what should go where. We also decided to label a plastic basket *Missing Pieces* and put it in the classroom math corner so students could place pieces that didn't belong

in their station there. Having materials easily accessible allows the teacher to work without interruptions during small-group math time.

Although good teaching should head off many problems, trouble will still brew from time to time. When a problem arises at work stations, begin by looking at what might have caused it. The first place to look is your own teaching. Ouch! I admit that I used to prefer looking at the students when there was a problem, but then I realized that the trouble at hand was often related to my instruction. Consider the following questions:

- How did I model this new task or use of materials? Did I model enough? Should I re-model?
- Have children had enough experience with the concept during whole-group instruction before I placed the task or game at a station?

■ How long has this material been in the work station? (It might be time to replace it to keep interest high.)

■ Are the materials at the work station well organized and easy to use?

■ Have I recently changed partners? Is it time for new partners? Would someone work better alone?

■ Is there an "I Can" list in the station? Does it need to be updated?

■ Is there enough for students to do at this station? What materials need to be changed out or added?

■ Can the child do this activity on his or her own?

■ Is the activity interesting and meaningful to the child? If not, what can I change to make it so?

In one first-grade classroom I visited, the teacher told me that math stations were closed. When I asked why, she replied, "They just don't know how to use them correctly, so I shut them down." Out of frustration, we are often tempted to simply close down stations. I talked with this teacher about what the students had been doing at the station. She said that some students were playing around with the manipulatives and not doing what they should be. They weren't doing quality work at stations.

I brainstormed with her about how she could reopen math stations. First, we looked at a few of the stations. In some cases, the activities were too easy and had been the same for months. We discussed what she was currently teaching in math and how we could change out some of the stations to make the work a bit more interesting to the students. She had not yet tried the "I Can" list idea with her class, so I modeled how to make one of these. When she reopened math stations, there was a different feel in the classroom.

In a kindergarten class I worked with, the teacher said that the children loved the station where they got to make patterns, but they were doing the same thing over and over again. I asked her if I could meet with the class and talk about this station. She agreed. Before meeting with the kids, I watched students use this station. They had several materials to work with—stamp pads, stamps, Bingo markers, white paper strips, a variety of different colored connecting cubes, and colored beads to string. They were happily stamping dots and stringing beads, but there was no talk about patterns.

When I met with the class, I showed them the tub materials they'd been using to make patterns. Then I asked them what kind of patterns they could make. I wrote some of the pattern names on individual index cards: *AAB, ABCD, AABC,* and *ABB*. I asked a child to model how to use a card to label the pattern he made. The children had been learning about money, so we decided to remove the stamps and stamp pads and substitute coins at the station. Two students modeled how to make patterns with coins and label the patterns on a small, handheld dry erase board. (We added the dry erase board to the station also.)

We ended by creating a new "I Can" list for the station:

I Can . . .
■ Make and label patterns.
■ Make patterns with dots.
■ Make patterns with beads.
■ Make patterns with money.
■ Talk about the patterns I make.

We added photos to go with each item on the list. The use of the "I Can" list and the new materials revitalized this station and added rigor.

Scheduling for Math Work Stations

The last question teachers usually ask me is, "I think this will work and I want to do it, but how can I make it all fit into my already-crammed schedule?" My answer is twofold: (1) you may have to get rid of some old things to make room for the new, and (2) you may have to multitask. Whenever we bring home a new piece of clothing, we need to make room for it in our closet. If we keep buying and never throw anything old away, we will soon run out of space. Our daily schedules are just like that. If we keep adding new routines but don't do away with something old, we'll run out of time in our day.

Look honestly at your lesson plan book. Put a star beside each thing your students did last week that truly helped them become better mathematical thinkers and problem solvers. Don't mark things you *hoped* would help them. Mark things that you know worked because you saw a high level of engagement, interest, and motivation. Now look at the unmarked items. What could you get rid of? Or what could you change to make it more engaging, interesting, and motivating? Perhaps it could be integrated into math work stations for further exploration or practice. An activity from your core math program that you used to do always in whole group might be moved into work stations since the class now has experience with it.

After you've gone through your daily schedule, carve out a block of time for math work stations (and small-group math instruction); usually this will follow your whole-group math lesson. Most schools allocate sixty to ninety minutes for math instruction daily. You'll need about thirty to fifty minutes of that time for math stations and small group: five to ten minutes for the stations mini-lesson (on selected days); fifteen to twenty minutes for each math station/math small group math rotation; and another five minutes for sharing. Be sure to teach math concepts in whole group and not rely just on stations to do your teaching. Math stations are for *reinforcement and extension* of concepts and skills you have already taught. Many kindergarten teachers also have a second "centers" time for traditional kindergarten centers, which might include block building, housekeeping, and the sand table, as well as the option to revisit literacy *and* math work stations.

Commit to trying your new schedule daily for several weeks. If you only have math stations once a week, students won't work efficiently or effectively at them. They need to have clear, predictable routines to help them learn. A special time devoted to math work stations is one of the best routines you can provide to engage your students in meaningful independent practice that will lead to better mathematical thinking and problem solving.

Reflection and Dialogue

1. Think about what math work stations time should look like, sound like, and feel like in your classroom. Be as specific as possible. You might brainstorm with a group of colleagues who teach your grade. Then try it with your class. Share their list with your colleagues. What did the students come up with that you hadn't even thought about? How did this exercise help you and your students?

2. Plan several stations mini-lessons with a colleague. Think about everything that kids might possibly *not* do right, and include those things in your mini-lessons. That way kids will know *exactly* what you expect. You might videotape a mini-lesson and share it with teachers from your grade level. Discuss how this mini-lesson helped your students.

3. Choose a math work station from your classroom that didn't go as well as planned. Brainstorm with a colleague what to do to improve upon this station.

4. Make sharing time cards for math stations (pages 224–229 in the appendix). Try doing sharing time regularly. Discuss with other teachers how the use of this reflection time is going. What are you learning from the children?

5. With your class, make an "I Can" list for one station that needs this structure and share the results with a colleague. Discuss what you learned from this experience and how you will

implement this as part of your stations time. Do the same with the creation of a math talk card for a station where you want students to practice new math vocabulary.

6. Work with another teacher to develop a plan for behavior at math work stations. Let students know exactly what will happen if they don't follow the rules. On a weekly basis, meet with your colleague to discuss your plan until behavior is well established. Readjust your plan as needed.

7. Create a management board and a place to store work stations products. Go on a "field trip" to other teachers' rooms to see their management boards and storage ideas.

4

Beginning Number Concepts Work Stations

Beginning number concepts provide a strong foundation for all the mathematics your students will do. Let's visit a classroom to see quality beginning number concepts stations in action. No matter what grade you teach, think about how these examples could be applied to your classroom.

In a kindergarten classroom, the teacher has used Kathy Richardson's (1998a) dot cards (from *Developing Number Concepts, Book 1, Counting, Comparing, and Pattern*) to help her children think about numbers in fast, fluid, and flexible ways. She displayed dot cards one at a time to the whole class and then had children tell her as quickly as possible in a quiet voice the number of dots they saw. The class did this activity for a few minutes daily until they could recognize the number of dots instantly. She also asked her students, "How did you know that?" to get some insight into how they were thinking about numbers. Here are some of the children's responses:

"It's 4 because 2 and 2 is 4."
"It's just 4 because my mom taught me."

"It's 6. I counted them. 1, 2, 3, 4, 5, 6."
"There are 8. I counted 2 at a time."

Now the teacher has moved the dot cards and matching numeral cards to a pocket chart for children to use independently. They "play teacher," with one child pretending to be the teacher and the other the student. Today Sophia is the "teacher" and flashes a dot card for her partner, Jason. He says the number quickly and matches a numeral card to it, placing both cards in the pocket chart side by side. They take turns being the teacher and student at this number-related math station. When they have finished matching the cards, they turn over the dot cards to check the numerals on the back. (The teacher has written the matching numeral on the back of each dot card so the children can self-check.)

They can also make their own dot cards at this station. Students use Bingo markers and large index cards to copy spatial patterns like those on the dot cards. Their child-made dot cards can be sent home so students can practice there.

Students match numeral cards to dot cards.

At another station, two children are reading counting books together. Because this is a kindergarten class, the teacher includes simple books kids can read on their own at this station—wordless counting books or books with just a numeral, a few words, and an illustration that matches the number of objects on each page. Today Jason pulls out Eric Carle's *1, 2, 3 to the Zoo* (1996), which has been read to them in whole group, and says, "Let's read this book." Early in the year at this station, partners just read the book and talked about how many animals were on each page. Now, they match a cube to each animal on the page and make up a number sentence to go with the picture. For example, on the page with three giraffes, they place a black connecting cube on each giraffe and together say, "Two and 1 is the same amount as 3." They are exploring beginning number concepts as they work together at math stations.

At another station in this classroom, two children are playing a counting game adapted from *Developing Number Concepts Using Unifix Cubes* by Kathy Richardson (1984). They take turns rolling a numeral cube (with the numerals 1 to 6 on it) and a cube with a different colored dot on each side. Using connecting cubes of the same color they roll with the second cube, they "build" the number that they roll with the first cube. For example, if they roll a 5 and a

Two children match a cube to each animal on the page of this counting book and say a number sentence: "Two and 1 is the same amount as 3."

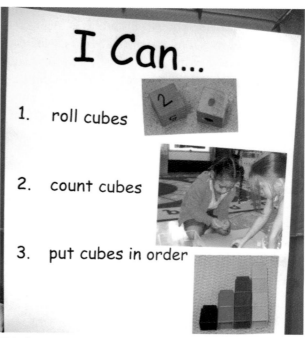

This "I Can" list made with the class supports student independence.

blue dot, they join together five blue connecting cubes. The goal of the game is to be the first to build five trains (cubes lying down) in sequential order (one cube followed by two cubes followed by three cubes, and so on). If a duplicate number is rolled by a child, he or she loses a turn. The game continues until one of the partners has five trains in order: one cube, two cubes, three cubes, four cubes, five cubes, six cubes. For support in playing this game, partners use the "I Can" list the class had brainstormed for this station. This station is duplicated so that several pairs of children can have this experience.

For yet another station, several big books—classroom originals—about counting are set up at the big book easel. The books are kept in a tall laundry basket. The teacher has put the math big books that the class made in the front of this basket; big books for literacy work stations are stored in the back of the basket. Children work with only the books the teacher has already taught with. One of their favorites was made at the start of school and is called *Our Number Book*. Each page features a photo of objects found in the classroom that kids can count and read about. For example, the first page says, "We have 1 big carpet" and has a picture of the class meeting rug. The next page shows two children at a math station, with these words at the bottom of the page: "We have 2 kids at a math station."

Children love reading these big books over and over. They develop both counting and reading skills at the same time. As they read, they count the objects on each page.

Throughout the year, these counting stations will change. At the big book station (station 12 in this classroom), new big books will be added to those the children are now using. As a class, they will make a big book of position words, a big book about the 100th day of school, and big books about 2–D and 3–D shapes. But children may always choose to read an old favorite, like the one they are reading today.

The number work students do will grow more complex. They may still roll number and color cubes, but they will build bigger numbers and graph their results. The dot cards may be used for adding numbers as children take two cards and determine the sum. Or they may use the cards for part-part-whole work. In this case, students will choose one card, such as a 4. They then use two different colored cubes and place a cube on each dot to show the parts of the quantity. For example, they might place three green cubes on the dots of a 3 card and two yellow cubes on the dots of a 2 card, and then state the number sentence, "Three and 2 is the same amount as 5."

A big book on counting that was made with the class is used at a math station.

Two boys work with dot cards, matching two different colored cubes to the dots and saying, "Three and 2 is the same amount as 5."

These beginning number concept stations will change and grow in complexity throughout the year. Some old favorites may be available, too, to provide opportunities for spiral review. Rich instruction will lead to meaningful math stations work that engages children and allows the teacher time to work with a small group or observe and take anecdotal notes to help her prepare for differentiated instruction.

Key Beginning Number Concepts

What will children work on at stations related to beginning number concepts? Counting and number recognition are certainly two things that come to mind, but there is so much more. Rote counting is something many children learn to do before they come to school, just like they learn to sing their ABCs. But just because children can recognize and name *t*, they don't necessarily deeply understand this letter. So we help students learn to apply *t* in both reading and writing. In essence, we add *meaning* to letters.

Likewise in math, children may learn to recognize the numeral 5 or hold up five fingers to show they are 5 years old before they understand what *five-ness* really is. As we help them explore and understand *five* more deeply (its quantity—that when counting to *five*, *five* includes all of the set and not just the last one; that *five* is one more than four and one less than six; that there are various spatial patterns that show *five*; etc.), students can then apply this number when skip-counting by fives to tell time, counting money (including nickels), and adding, subtracting, multiplying, and dividing with five over time. In this chapter, we focus on math stations that attach *meaning* to numbers as quantities.

As you think about the math stations you'll want students to use to develop beginning number concepts, it is helpful first to consider what you want children to know and understand about num-

bers and their relationships at your grade level. Meet with colleagues both at your grade level and in vertical teams to be sure you know exactly what is included in your state and district standards. Use ideas from curriculum guides, planning documents, your core program, and other resources your school provides to plan for what you will teach, including instruction related to counting, comparing, and number patterns.

Here are some of the beginning number concepts students learn in the primary grades. Key concepts are listed here with examples of benchmark numbers. Adjust these as necessary to meet your district's standards.

In kindergarten, children will . . .
- Touch and count objects using one-to-one correspondence, and produce sets of given sizes (up to 20).
- Read, write, and represent (in pictures, objects, and numerals) numbers from 1 to 20.
- Compare and order sets and numerals from 1 to 20.
- Quickly recognize "how many" in sets of objects to 5 without counting.
- Count forward by ones, beginning with any number less than 30.
- For any set to 10, name the quantity one more and one less.
- Name ordinal positions in a sequence, such as first, second, third, etc.
- Compare two or more sets of objects (up to 10 objects in each group) and identify which set is equal to (same number as), more than, or less than the other.
- Use objects, pictures, numbers, and (oral) words to make combinations to 5.
- Describe part-part-whole relationships for sets to 5.

In first grade, children will also . . .
- Count by ones to 100 fluently and accurately.
- Read, write, compare, and order numbers to 100.

- Estimate quantities of objects to 30.
- Count by groups (twos, fives, tens) to 100.
- Apply number patterns to properties of numbers and operations (such as even and odd numbers).
- Name one more/one less and two more/two less than any number to 10.
- Decompose numbers from 6 to 10 as 5+ combinations, using real objects (i.e., use blocks to explore and understand 5 + 1; 5 + 2; 5 + 3; 5 + 4; and 5 + 5).
- Use "broken counting," shifting from counting the groups to counting the leftovers (e.g., 5, 10, 15, 16, 17 when counting the value of 3 nickels and 2 pennies or 17 minutes past the hour on an analog clock).
- Count by tens off the decade (14, 24, 34, 44, 54, . . .).
- Represent counting numbers (1, 2, 3, . . .) on a counting tape or hundreds chart.
- Describe part-part-whole relationships for sets to 10.
- Name the missing part when given the total and one part for sets to 10.

In second grade, children will also . . .

- Count on and off the decade and on and off the century, forward and backward by ones, tens, and hundreds.
- Read, write, compare, and order numbers to 1,000.
- Count in multiples of twos, fives, tens, and hundreds.

What the Children Do at Beginning Number Concepts Stations

To make these stations meaningful to children, plan for opportunities in which students will count *for a purpose*, just as we plan experiences for them to read for a purpose. You will probably find many ideas for beginning number concepts activities in resources you already own, such as partner games from *Every Day Counts Partner Games, Grade K, Grade 1*, and *Grade 2* (Gillespie and Kanter 2005a, 2005b, 2005c). But to get your creative juices flowing, I've included

Beginning Number Vocabulary (Kindergarten)

- more
- less
- fewer
- same as
- equal
- (number words from one to ten)
- set
- one more
- one less
- first, second, third, fourth, fifth, sixth, seventh, eighth, ninth, tenth

Taking It Further (Grades 1–2)

- compare
- numeral
- least
- greatest
- greater than
- less than
- (number words from *eleven* to *one hundred*)
- order
- skip-count
- odd
- even
- pattern
- before
- after
- between
- number line
- whole numbers
- estimate

a variety of suggestions for these kinds of math work stations. The list that follows is by no means exhaustive. Consider it a menu of choices to help you think about which independent experiences you'll provide for your students.

I've started with stations ideas (rather than whole-group teaching lessons) since stations are the focus of this book. But remember that great stations are preceded by strong whole-group teaching (and then materials are moved to a math station for practice and reinforcement). Also, be sure to consult the section in this chapter titled "What the Teacher Needs to Model" to guarantee better success for your students at these stations.

■ *Play counting games.* You might use simple board games like Hi Ho! Cherry O or Chutes and Ladders (or make your own using game boards from your math resources). Children take turns rolling a die or spinning a spinner and counting that many spaces on the board. You can change the game by substituting a number cube (with numbers on it that match the counting levels of your students) for the die or spinner. You can also make and add a spinner with four sections that are labeled: *1*

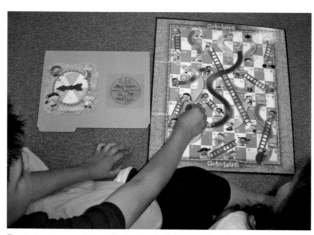

Partners use two spinners to determine how many spaces to move in this counting game that uses a Chutes and Ladders board. After they spin a number from 1 to 6 (on left), they use a second spinner to find out if they move 1 or 2 more, or 1 or 2 less than that number.

more, 1 less, 2 more, and *2 less.* Students roll the die and then spin the spinner to determine how many spaces to move. For example, if a child rolls a 4 and spins *1 less,* he or she would move just 3 spaces.

Encourage children to work together rather than to compete while playing these games to help them think about number concepts (rather than just who will win). Have them continue playing until both of them reach the end.

■ *Use dominoes for counting and comparing.* Dominoes can be used for counting explorations and games. Begin early work with dominoes using those that have dots on just one end. Children simply match dominoes to numeral cards (included on page 230 in the appendix) with those quantities. Partners can also place dominoes facedown and take turns flipping them over, one at a time. They then compare to see whose domino has more dots, saying, "My 6 is more than your 5."

Over time, young children can turn this exploration into a Battle game. Each child turns over a domino, and the child with the larger number of dots (on the domino) keeps both dominoes. If they both get the same number of dots, they each keep their own domino and go again. As they play, encourage them to use the math talk *more, less,* and *same as.* A variation over time would be to have them also state *how much* more or less one domino is than the other.

After students become proficient working with dominoes with dots on just one end, give them dominoes with dots on both ends to do this activity. Now they must use the total number of dots to play. When using dominoes with dots on both ends, they can also create number sentences about combinations of dots on the dominoes as they look at the parts that make a whole. For example, when examining a 3 domino, they might say, "Two and 1 is the same amount as 3."

Young children play Battle with dominoes and talk about who has more or fewer dots using the math talk card for support. Whoever has more wins both dominoes.

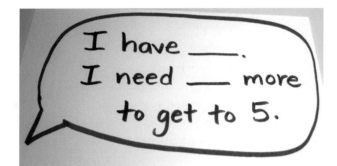

A math talk card made with a 3-by-5-inch index card can be used with Five Frame Fun.

Some students will be ready to play traditional Dominoes, matching ends of dominoes showing the same number of dots to each other. An advanced option of this game is to have them play "One More" Dominoes, in which they can only make a match if the domino they turn over has *one more* than the domino they are matching to. For example, if a child flips over a 6 domino, it can only be matched to a domino with 5 dots, since it has *one more* than its match. Similar games can be played matching *two more, one less,* or *two less,* which develops algebraic thinking down the road.

■ ***Play Five-Frame Fun.*** Each pair of students gets 3 five-frames (as found on page 231 in the appendix) and 2 ten-trains (ten connecting cubes joined together make a ten-train) of two different colors, such as one blue ten-train and one yellow ten-train. They also need a numeral cube with 0 to 5 on it. To play, the first child rolls the cube and places that many connecting cubes of one color on one of the five-frames. Then he must tell how many cubes he has on his five-frame and how many he needs to fill that five-frame. The second child then takes a turn and follows the same steps.

The players must fill each of the five-frames with just two different number rolls (a 4 and a 1, a 3 and a 2, etc.). For example, if the first child rolls a 4, he places 4 yellow cubes on a five-frame and says, "I have 4. I need 1 more to get to 5." (Provide a sentence frame written on an index card or sentence strip to support math talk.) One of the players will need to roll exactly a 1 to fill in that five-frame. However, there are two more five-frames to fill in as well. Whoever fills in a five-frame scores a point.

Now the other child takes a turn. She begins filling in the second five-frame with blue cubes according to her roll, which is a 2, following the same rules.

Play goes back to the first child, who rolls a 3 on this turn. Since he needs a 1 to fill in the first five-frame, he must now start to fill in the second five-frame, which holds 2 blue cubes. He places 3 yellow cubes on the second five-frame, stating, "I have 3." Three and 2 is the same amount as 5." He scores a point. Using two different colors helps the child see two-number combinations that add up to five, which is the goal of this game. To be sure children focus on these part-part-whole relationships, teach them that after the first roll, they can fill the remaining spaces only with a roll of the exact amount needed. In other words, if the frame has been started with 2, it can only

Two students play Five Frame Fun. One child rolls a 0 and cannot place any cubes on a five-frame, saying, "I have 0. I need 3 more to get to 5."

be filled with a roll of 3, not three rolls of 1, 1, 1, or a 2 and then a 1. Play continues until all the five-frames are filled. Whoever has the most points wins.

This game can easily be adapted for play using ten-frames. To do so, provide a second numeral cube with 5 to 10 on it. The language of the game changes to "I have _____. I need _____ more to get to 10." (Adapt the sentence frame on the math talk card accordingly for support.) Students decide which numeral cube they want to roll on their turn.

- **Play Memory or Go Fish matching games.** Children love playing Concentration or Memory. There are many variations they can play. They can match dot-card patterns (or dominoes) that are the same. Or they can match a dot-card pattern to a digit card. Or they can do a three-way match that includes the dot-card pattern, a digit card, and a number-word card. Students can also match digit cards with cards that say *odd* or *even*.

Still another option is to play with a focus on one more/one less or two more/two less. For example, a match is made when the second card turned over is one more or one less than the original card. There might be leftover cards, but the game ends when there are no more matches to be made.

Have students play with a set of game materials that matches their needs. Be sure not to give them too many cards at a time. Teach them how to line up the cards in rows while playing.

Most of these matching games can be played as Go Fish. Each player gets 5 cards. They put the rest of the cards face down on a stack. Players take turns asking the other player for a card to make a match. For example, a child who holds the digit card for 5 might ask her partner, "Do you have 5 dots?" If the other child has the dot card for 5, he must hand it over. The match is laid down. If the other child doesn't have the requested card, he says, "Go fish," and the first player takes the top card off the deck. You may find that it causes less disruption always to have children take turns rather than have them go again if they get a match.

- **Play comparing games.** Comparing games can be played with a variety of materials. If students are working with single-digit numbers, you might use playing cards, numeral cards, Ten Grid cards (from Great Source), or even dominoes. Kids can play Bigger Number, where each child draws one card and compares it to the other player's, or they can play Who Has Less?, with the winner being the one with the smaller number.

Playing cards visually represent quantities, which may help young children picture *how many* as they read the number on the card and compare it to another. Ten Grid cards have the added advantage of helping students picture 6 to 10 as 5 + 1, 5 + 2, 5 + 3, 5 + 4, and 5 + 5. If young children have already worked with seeing the set of 6 to 10 as 5 and _____ more, they will be more likely to invent "pulling out fives" when adding addends 6 to 9 in the future.

Dominoes can be used for the same purpose (working with numbers from 6 to 10). Use only dominoes that have 5 dots on one half. (You'll need to pull dominoes from several sets.) Or make your own domino cards on 3-by-5-inch index cards with these representations. Students place dominoes facedown and take one at a time to compare to one another's.

Bigger Number and Who Has Less? also can be played with two-digit numbers, as pictured with the following example. One player chooses two cards and uses those to make a two-digit number. For example, if a child picks 8 and 7, that's 87 (or 78). Then his partner chooses two cards and makes a two-digit number. Whoever has the bigger number (or the smaller, depending on the game being played) keeps all four cards. Avoid using playing cards for these two-digit games, since these cards picture quantities. If students choose an 8 card and a 7 card, as in the preceding example,

they see eight objects on one card and seven on the other. They may think that represents 87, when in actuality it shows 15! Using any card with a quantity (even flash cards) can create confusion for children when playing these games. To make numeral cards for two-digit comparing games, simply write *0* to *9* on separate index cards. (You'll want multiple copies of each numeral.) Be sure that the emphasis is on the digits.

■ ***Grab and graph objects.*** Provide a "grab bag," a small colorful gift bag. Inside the bag, place several small treasures, such as teddy bear counters, plastic insects, or little toys from a dollar store. Be sure to include several of each item. To play, a child reaches in the bag and grabs a handful of items. Partners work together to sort, count, and graph the objects. When graphing, children should simply line up the like objects in rows. They can then compare amounts using these sentence frames: "There are more _____ than _____." "There are fewer _____ than _____." "There are the same number of _____ and _____." On the next turn, the other child grabs items from the bag, and again the partners work together to

First graders play **Bigger Number** using numeral cards from 0 to 9. Each child draws two numbers and makes a two-digit numeral. They use the math talk card to help them tell who has the bigger number. Whoever has the bigger number keeps all 4 cards.

A pair of students plays **Grab and Graph**. They take turns grabbing a handful of objects from a bag and lay those materials out one to one to see which they have more or fewer of. Over time, they may also graph the results on paper. Math talk cards with pictures remind children how to talk about the math in this game.

sort, count, graph, and compare. Over time, students may show their findings by creating graphs with paper.

If children need to count smaller numbers, put bigger objects in the grab bag. If they need to count bigger numbers, let them take two handfuls.

■ ***Create and complete surveys.*** This is a favorite of young children. They fill in the blank on a survey sheet template to create a question (see page 232 in the appendix for a sample). Then they place the sheet on a clipboard and circulate around the room, asking their classmates the survey question. As students answer the question, the surveyors record their names in the appropriate column, and then count and record the results.

They can ask yes/no questions to begin. Over time, they can make graphs, compare results, and tell how many more and less. They can make pictographs or create bar graphs using 1-inch graph paper. Second graders can create keys to go with their graphs.

Kindergartners ask classmates the survey question, "Do you like strawberries?" and record their data.

■ ***Read and write counting books.*** Picture books provide meaningful contexts for counting. Use the "Literature Links" section of this chapter for suggestions of counting books to read aloud to your class. You might also con-

sult resources like *Math and Literature* by Marilyn Burns and Stephanie Sheffield (2004) or *Math Memories You Can Count On* by Jo-Anne Lake (2009) for ideas. After you've read some of these counting books aloud, put some of students' favorites in a stations container along with objects to count.

You might also want to teach your children how to write their own counting books. This can be modeled during writing workshop. Read aloud several counting books and then have children examine the features of these books to find out about the text structure of this genre.

During writing workshop, make an anchor chart with your class about how to make a counting book.

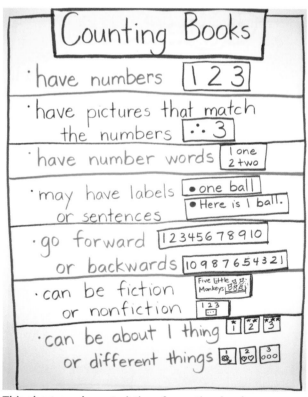

This chart on characteristics of counting books was made over several sessions during writing workshop. Students use it at a math station to make their own counting books.

Put a copy of the anchor chart at the math station where children will make their own counting books. You might also include at this station a chart of number words and several sample counting books for support.

If your children are working with combinations to 5, have them make "Ways to Make Five" books. Have them write the words and draw pictures to illustrate a different way to make 5 on each page. English language learners might need the following sentence frame for support:

I have _____ _____ and

_____ _____.

I have 5 things in all.

This book idea can be adapted to include "Ways to Make Six"; "Ways to Make Ten," and so on.

You might label a basket in your classroom library *Counting Books.*

■ ***Make big books about beginning number concepts.*** To learn about math concepts, young students love reading big books over and over again that they have helped make. To make a "More, Less, and Same" big book, have children help you find objects that have the *same* amount around the classroom. Also have them locate things there are *more* of and things there are *less* of. Take pictures of these items to compare numbers, and label each picture on a page of the big book. Use text like this:

☐ There are the *same* number of chairs and desks.

☐ There are the *same* number of clocks and calendars.

☐ There are *more* boys than girls.

☐ There are *more* windows than doors.

☐ There are *less* computers than boys.

☐ There are *less* easels than big books.

To make a "Five Plus" book, take pictures of a child's hands to illustrate one page and tally marks on the opposite page so that you have two illustrations for each 5+ combination. The pages of the book may have text like this:

☐ There are 5 fingers and 1 more. 5 + 1 is 6.

☐ There are 5 tally marks and 1 more. 5 + 1 is 6.

☐ There are 5 fingers and 2 more. 5 + 2 is 7.

☐ There are 5 tally marks and 2 more. 5 + 2 is 7.

☐ There are 5 fingers and 3 more. 5 + 3 is 8.

Continue up to combinations of 5 + 5.

Note: If you have rekenreks, provide one at this station so children can build number combinations. These wonderful math tools help children easily see 5+ combinations. (For more information on how to use them, see the resource by Barbara Blanke (2008) provided by The Math Learning Center at http://www.mathlearningcenter.org/media/Rekenrek_0308.pdf. Or, check out Catherine Fosnot and Maarten Dolk's *Young Mathematicians at Work* [2001] for ideas on using rekenreks and constructing students' number sense.)

Partners read a class-made "Five Plus" book and use a rekenrek to build 5+ number combinations.

■ **Play Odd and Even** (adapted from *Every Day Counts Partner Games, Grade 1* and *Grade 2* by Janet Gillespie and Patsy Kanter [2005b, 2005c]). Make one laminated ladybug for partners to share. Label one half of the ladybug *odd* and the other half *even*. (See page 233 in the appendix for a pattern.) Partners take turns rolling two dice (or they can roll two numeral cubes and add them). With each turn, the partner rolling must prove if the roll is an even or odd number by placing that number of black cubes on the ladybug, in a paired arrangement. If the number is even, all the cubes will be paired; if the number is odd, there will be a leftover cube. After the even or odd designation has been proven, the numeral is recorded on the appropriate side of the ladybug with a dry erase marker by the child who rolled that number. Children work together to see which "side" of the ladybug wins. You might include a book about even and odd at this station, such as *Odd and Even Socks* by Melanie Chrismer (2006).

Two children play Odd and Even on a laminated ladybug mat. They roll two cubes and add them. Then they place that many black cubes in a paired arrangement on the odd or even side and record the numeral accordingly with a dry erase marker. Which side will win—odd or even?

■ **Play How Many to 20?** Make two oak tag boards with 20 dots on each of them. Place the dots close to the edge of the board in two colors (red and blue) by fives (see photo).

Give each player 20 wooden clip-type clothespins. Color-code one set of clothespins with red tips (use a marker to color the ends as shown). Make the other set blue. Partners take turns rolling a die and placing that many clips on their board, matching one to one. At the end of the roll, the child should say how many she now has and how many more to 20. To promote math talk, you might provide a sentence frame on an index card that says, "I have ___. I need ____ to get to 20." Encourage students to look at groups of five to count rather than count one dot at a time. The first player to reach 20 wins.

Partners play How Many to 20? by rolling a die and placing that many clothespins on their dot board. Note the dots in groups of five to help them count by fives and consider 5+ combinations.

■ **Use ordinal numbers to tell and/or retell a cumulative story.** Children can match their photos or colored paper cutouts to ordinal numbers (*1st, 2nd, 3rd*, etc.) and digits and/or ordinal number words (*first, second, third*, etc.) using a pocket chart. As they do so, they can tell a story: *First, there was a pink bear. Then a second bear came along. It was purple. The* *red bear was third. Soon a fourth bear joined them. The fourth bear was orange . . .*

A cumulative tale like *Move Over, Rover!* (Beaumont 2006) is a great book to use for retelling using ordinal numbers. Read it aloud to your class several times and have students tell what happened in order using animal pictures and ordinal number cards arranged in a pocket chart. At a station, students use the same book and cards to retell the story in order on a pocket chart. See the "Literature Links" section of this chapter for other suggestions of books for retelling with ordinal numbers.

An "I Can" list of choices for a beginning number concepts station in kindergarten.

A student puts colored bear cutouts, digit cards, and ordinal number cards in order on a pocket chart.

■ *Use Caterpillar Counting mats and task cards.* Students can work with these mats and task cards in a multitude of ways. In addition to a laminated Caterpillar Counting mat for each child, this station needs a dry erase pen and eraser, a way to get a number (either by rolling a die or by choosing a numeral card), and a set of Caterpillar Counting task cards. (See the templates for the Caterpillar Counting mat and task cards on pages 234–236 in the appendix.) If you use numeral cards instead of a die as a way for students to get a number, include cards with 0 to 9 on them. For two-digit numbers, students pick two cards; for three-digit numbers, three cards. The task cards can have the following directions written on them: *count forward, count backward, count by 2s, count by 5s, count by 10s, count by 100s,*

A child chooses the numeral card 36. She counts by tens and writes numerals on the Caterpillar Counting mat, using the hundreds chart to check.

count by even numbers, and *count by odd numbers*. Include only the task cards appropriate for what your students need to practice.

A student begins a turn by rolling the die or choosing a numeral card to get a number. Then, the student picks a task card to decide which numbers to write on the Caterpillar Counting mat. Teach children to write on the caterpillars from left to right, just as they do in reading and writing. This can minimize confusion. For example, if a student gets the number 17 and the *count backward* task card, she would write *17, 16, 15, 14, 13, 12, 11, 10, 9 . . .* on the caterpillar from left to right. They can check one another's work using a hundreds chart for support.

■ *Practice writing numerals.* Use a large chart to teach children how to form numerals. Then provide a station or two where they can practice writing numerals. At one station, they can roll a numeral cube and then write the number they roll on a graph. Each time they roll that number, they write it again in the appropriate column on the graph. They can also use a tape recorder and headphones to listen to how to form numerals as they write them. Be sure the correct model of the

A pair of students does the Number Dice Toss activity. They roll a numeral cube and write the numbers they toss to create a graph.

numeral is clearly visible and displayed close to the station. See pages 237–240 in the appendix for the Numeral Dice Toss and Numeral Writing Practice recording sheets.

■ *Establish an estimation station.* At this station, provide three clear plastic containers filled with small objects. Label the containers *A*, *B*, and *C*. Fill each container with fewer than thirty objects. Put a different number of things in each. You might use little toys, such as plastic firefighters, bugs, or jewels from a dollar or craft store. Or use pennies or marbles or teddy bear counters. Students start with container A. Using a recording sheet (included on page 241 in the appendix), each student writes his or her estimate of how many objects he or she thinks are in that container. Then partners work together to count the objects in that container. Encourage students to organize the items by groups (twos, fives, or tens) to make counting easier. Have them then record the actual number of objects in the jar. Encourage them to use numbers, pictures, and words to represent what they find out. Over time, children can determine the difference between their estimates and the actual count. For example, a student might conclude, "I estimated 25 and there were 18. There were 7 fewer objects in the jar than I thought." You might include Stuart Murphy's book, *Betcha!* (1997), at this station, too.

■ **Count money.** Working with coins is a meaningful counting experience for young children that can be provided in a variety of ways. It's best, if possible, to use real money so students have an authentic experience and become familiar with real coins. Plastic coins can be used, but they don't look or feel quite the same.

At a simple level, children can sort coins on a sorting mat and decide which type of coins they have the most of, least of, or the same number of. They use coins and cards naming coins and their amounts, along with cards that say *most, least,* and *same.* (Include two cards that say *same.*) Students can graph the result of their coin sort, lining up the coins in one-to-one correspondence or using a graphing mat. At a more advanced level, students can count the money to find the totals in each part of the mat, and then count the

Coin	Value
penny	1¢ 1 cent $0.01
nickel	5¢ 5 cents $0.05
dime	10¢ 10 cents $0.10
quarter	25¢ 25 cents $0.25

This anchor chart using real coins was made by the class for reference as they count money. Note the different ways to write the value of each coin and the highlighted *s* in *cents.* (Many kids were saying *5 cent.*)

mixed coins to find the grand total. If needed, they can refer to a chart listing the value for each coin.

Also, you might set up a store with real items to "buy." Put price tags on each item; use prices that match the numbers your students can work with. Provide coins and coin stamps along with blank grocery lists. Have children list each product they bought and use coin stamps to record its cost. You might also have students write the price with dollar and cents signs. See page 242 in the appendix for a sample recording sheet.

Children will enjoy playing money games like Coin Battle and Piggy Penny, too. In Coin Battle, they each choose a card with coins

Partners sort coins and then read a book about money.

To play Piggy Penny, partners take turns spinning and placing pennies on their pig. The first to cover his or her pig is the winner. To add challenge, they can tell how many more they need to have ten cents.

stamped on it. Whoever has the larger amount of money keeps both cards. Play continues until all cards are gone. The player with the most cards wins. In Piggy Penny, children use a spinner with pictures of one, two, or three pennies in each space. They also each get a pig

Students shop at a "store" station that houses real objects and coins. They use coin stamps to record what they bought and the cost of each item.

cutout with X's, arranged in two rows of five, stamped on it. (See page 243 in the appendix for a reproducible pig cutout.) Students take turns spinning and placing on each X the number of pennies they spun. The player who covers up all of his or her X's first is the winner. This game can be adapted by stamping different coins on the spinner. For example, if dimes are stamped, players count by tens; if nickels are used, players count by fives.

One more game is Coin Combinations. Provide two number cubes. One should have 1 to 6 on it; the other should have 4 to 9. To play, each partner rolls a number cube. The two numerals are put side by side to create a two-digit numeral representing cents. For example, if one child rolls 9 and the other rolls 5, the amount of money is 95 cents or 59 cents. Students decide which quantity they want to represent. Then they work together to create as many combinations as they can to make this amount of money. (You may want to limit the number of pennies to nine or fewer.) They record their ideas using stamps or pictures on a recording sheet, as provided on page 244 of the appendix. If students have trouble with broken counting, include at this

Two children play Coin Combinations by tossing two numeral cubes to create a two-digit number and then showing how many cents with coin combinations. They record their thinking on a reproducible sheet.

station an anchor chart on how to count money. If you don't have money stamps, children can draw a circle representing the coin and record the value of the coin inside the circle.

Coin Combinations

① **Make a table of the coins.** Choose which coins you want to use:

(H) = Half Dollar

(Q) = Quarter

(N) = Nickel

(D) = Dime

(P) = Penny

② **Roll a number generator** and combine the number in any order.

③ **Make as many combinations as you can with that number.**

Directions for how to play Coin Combinations were made with second graders at this counting- and money-related station.

■ ***Measure and count.*** Please see Chapter 8, "Measurement Work Stations," for ideas that combine measuring and counting.

Materials

To teach beginning number concepts, you will need a variety of materials for counting. Because there are so many different kinds of math manipulatives available, I've included a Picture Glossary of Math Materials at the end of the book for your reference. Consult this glossary as needed while reading about what students do at beginning number concepts math stations (and all other kinds of stations).

I recommend placing each different kind of material in a labeled container to make it easy for both you and your students to easily access what is needed for counting explorations and stations work. Use what you have on hand, and vary the objects to add novelty to counting activities. Young children love small objects and will enjoy working with them. You might use toys from a dollar or craft store, such as plastic firefighters, bugs, or jewels. Most schools provide commercial manipulatives, such as connecting cubes and clear plastic counters. Be sure to give children opportunities to "play" with these little objects before teaching with them and using them at math stations. If you don't, you may find children marching bugs or firefighters all over the floor rather than counting and comparing them.

In addition to these concrete objects, you'll want to use paper items, such as cards, cups, and mats, to help organize children's counting and beginning number explorations. Here's a list of materials you might use for counting and beginning number concepts stations:

■ dot cards
■ small counters or blocks
■ connecting cubes (in several colors, including black) or Unifix cubes
■ numeral cubes

- dot cubes (wooden cubes with a different colored dot on each side)
- cards and/or spinners that say *more, less, same*
- calculators
- math mats on which to build patterns
- dominoes
- playing cards (use for games working with single digits only, not double digits)
- numeral cards (from 0 to 9)
- Ten Grid cards to develop number sense around sets to ten
- five-frames
- ten-frames
- small objects for counting (counters, little toys, plastic coins, cubes, etc.)
- hundreds charts
- coins for sorting
- coin stamps
- sorting mats
- cards labeling names of coins
- bookmaking supplies (paper, stapler, markers, optional digital camera)

What the Teacher Needs to Model

Here are some things to model to help your students get the most from their time at beginning number concepts stations:

How to touch and count objects using one-to-one correspondence. Many children come to school already rote counting. Help them attach meaning to those numbers by giving them many opportunities to count things with you. Model how to touch and/or move each object as you count from 1 to 9. Count objects around the room, count children for a variety of purposes, and count manipulatives such as cubes, buttons, and teddy bear counters. Help children understand that the last item they touch and count tells how many objects

there are in all. This may take many experiences for some children and just a few for others.

You can tell a lot about students' understanding if you do a "give me" activity. Present a pile of objects or counters and say, "Give me 5." Do they count 1 to 5 or can they quickly grab 5 objects? Then ask, "How many are there?" Some students will have to recount just to be sure they do have 5. Others know that they have 5 and won't need to count again.

How to read, write, build, and order numbers from one to nine (and above). Use dot cards or dot plates with sets to five as flashcards, and have students quickly tell how many dots they see. Have them tell you how they know. Young children will be able to instantly identify 2, 3, 4, and 5 dots without counting; this is called subitizing.

Every day as you work with the calendar bulletin board, such as the one from *Every Day Counts Calendar Math, Grade K, Grade 1,* and *Grade 2* (Kanter and Gillespie 2005a, 2005b, 2005c), you have opportunities to help children develop the date and the number of days in school. They may help you read the number, write the number, and build the number with items such as paper clips or tally marks. By using a counting tape (each number is written on a sticky note and added daily side by side), you can give children practice in finding the missing number and thinking about the order of numbers.

A kindergarten teacher flashes dot cards to help children instantly recognize "how many."

$4+10$ (14) $100-86$
$7+7$ $200-186$
$10+4$ $21-7$
$14+0$ $300-286$
$9+5$ $24-10$
$8+6$ $17-3$
$12+2$ $20-6$
$13+1$ $1000-986$
2 groups of 7
2×7 $28 \div 2$
7×2 number of
14×1 days in 2 weeks

This chart made by a second-grade class as part of their "number of the day" routine in whole group shows what they know about the number 14.

Children work with ways to make 5 in small group. This builds a foundation for addition and subtraction over time.

Some teachers have children work with a "number of the day" as well. Students read the number, represent it with objects or by having that many children stand up, and help their teacher make a list of things related to that number. For example, if the number of the day is 6, they might look at a 6-dot card, show 6 fingers, have 6 girls stand up, have 6 boys stand up, and find 6 things around the room (there are 6 chairs at a table; we have math station 6, etc.). The emphasis is on attaching meaning to the number. Look for opportunities to count in meaningful ways all day long.

How to develop concepts of five and ten. Having flexibility around these "friendly numbers"

allows children to develop mental math strategies organized around fives and tens. So spend lots of time helping children really understand these two numbers. Start with a five-frame in kindergarten (a reproducible is included on page 231 in the appendix). (Once children understand five, move to a ten-frame and build understanding of the number 10. From there, have students work with two ten-frames and numbers to 20.) Tell students that only one counter is allowed in each space on the five-frame. They should build on it from the left to the right. Ask children to use their counters to show 2 on the five-frame. (You can model on the overhead or with a projection device.) Then have them tell what they notice, which might include the following:

- There are 2 counters. 1, 2.
- It's like 2 eyes.
- I see 3 blanks.
- There are 3 white spaces.
- There are more spaces than counters.
- Two and 3 is the same amount as 5.

Do similar work with ten-frames.

How to form numerals. This is a handwriting skill, but it is important for children to learn so they can write numerals fluently. I like to use a poetry

Children recite a rhyme in whole group to learn how to correctly form their numerals.

chart, with a rhyme that helps children remember how to make each numeral. Have students write the number in a variety of ways—in the air, on the carpet, on your hand, on a dry erase board, on paper with chalk, markers, or crayons, and so on.

Most activities you use for teaching children how to write letters can be used to help them practice writing numerals. One difference is in the types of strokes they'll use. When writing letters, the basic strokes are top to bottom and left to right. When writing numerals, this rule no longer applies. The numerals 1, 4, and 5 all start with top to bottom movements, but 6, 8, and 9 all begin with right to left movements. Be explicit in helping children learn to write numerals, and this may minimize confusions over time when they add and subtract (and can't read the numerals they've written).

How to play counting and memory games.
Consult your curriculum materials to find counting and memory games to use with your students in addition to the ideas from this chapter. When mod-

eling games, show the whole class how to play a game first. You might model with a child as your partner. I like to seat the children in a circle or U-shape so they can all observe. Or if you have a projection device, use it to model how to play the game so all children can see at once. Be explicit, describing *each* step of the game, one step at a time, as you play. Teach children to sit side by side rather than face to face, so both partners will be able to view the numerals they are working with from the correct angle.

You many need to model a game several times to be sure students understand how to play it. Sometimes, if the game is simple and doesn't involve many materials, it may be possible for all students to try that game in pairs while you walk around and observe them. However, many times this may require too much preparation or too many materials, and you'll want to play the game in small group with children who need extra support to check for understanding before they play on their own.

At times, you might work together as a class to write directions for how to play the game, adding picture cues to help students remember. Write directions on 8½-by-11-inch white paper, slip the sheet into a clear plastic sleeve, and include it in the station container with materials to play the game.

A teacher and one child model how to play Coin Battle. They compare how many pennies are on each card. The player with more pennies gets to keep both cards.

How to compare numbers. In whole group, demonstrate how to compare and label two quantities. Begin with concrete objects, numeral cards within your students' range, and cards labeled with the words *more*, *less*, and *same*. Start by modeling how to make two small numbers with connecting cubes and then label the buildings with the word cards. For example, if you choose 8 and 12, join together eight blue connecting cubes; make a separate train of 12 red connecting cubes. Show students how to compare the two trains by placing them side by side. Then think aloud as you place the appropriate word cards by each building, saying, "I'm putting the *less* card here, since there are only 8 cubes and there are not as many blue cubes as red; the red train has 12 cubes, which is *more* cubes than the blue train, so I'm labeling it with the card that says *more*."

Then have students work with partners to practice. Give each pair a set of comparing cards (*more, less, same*) and connecting cubes in two colors. Choose two numeral cards and have students work together to build and compare quantities with two different colored cubes, telling which has more and which has fewer cubes. Ask, "How do you know?" and "What would you need to do to make them the same?" Over time, ask, "How many more?" or "How many fewer?" Second graders could use bundling sticks or base-ten blocks to build larger numbers. Also, in second grade have students use the <, >, and = signs.

To teach children how to compare numbers, you can also give each child in whole group a numeral card. Call two children to the front of the class and compare their numerals or put them in order. Then have them choose the card that tells whether they have more or less than their partner. In second grade, children can be holders of the <, >, and = signs on cards and insert themselves between the two number-holding students to complete a number sentence. Help students see that the inequality sign always points to the lesser number and opens up toward the greater number.

Second graders take turns comparing big numbers for the rest of the class, using numeral cards and cards that have <, >, and = signs on them.

How to make counting books. Read aloud counting books. Use the "Literature Links" section in this chapter for sample titles. In writing workshop, analyze some of the students' favorite counting books and make a chart with students that tells what should be included in a counting book. Make a counting book together. Provide a sample at this station, along with materials for making simple books about counting. Include paper, a stapler, counters, blank five-frames, blank ten-frames, crayons, and pencils.

How to work with ordinal numbers. Start by connecting ordinal numbers to the grades students are in. For example: "We are in first grade. Some of your brothers and sisters might be in third grade. Our reading buddies are fifth graders." Children's literature is also a good anchor for this work. It can attach meaning to ordinal numbers. See the "Literature Links" section for book ideas. Have children use ordinal number cards to tell what happened *first, second, third, fourth,* and so on in a story. Encourage students to use ordinal numbers math talk. Have them label or talk about the order of things around the classroom. For instance, they can look at photos of the class in a pocket chart and name who is in which position using ordinal numbers. Or ask them to do the same when they're lined up for lunch: "Aiden is the *first* child in the lunch line today. Maria is *second* and Roberto is *third*."

How to think about number patterns. The brain naturally looks for patterns. Arthur Hyde, in *Comprehending Math* (2006, 10), states that "Mathematics is the science of patterns." Children love to find, create, and extend patterns. Use calendar time to start a discussion about patterns and give students opportunities to look for number patterns as often as possible. When children count by ones, twos, fives, or tens, it is important to discuss how much is being added each time. When working with a counting pattern of two, you might ask the children what it takes to get from 2 to 4 or from 4 to 6, encouraging them to make observations about this counting pattern. Be sure to go past 100 in late first grade and into second grade. When counting by ones, many children count *100, 200*, because they haven't had enough exposure to numbers above 100.

You might also show cut pieces of a hundreds chart that display numbers vertically (showing 11, 21, 31, 41, 51, 61, 71, 81, 91, for example). Use the overhead or another projection device. Ask children, *What patterns do you notice?* Continue to display strips like this, one at a time, until you've built the hundreds chart. Have children look for patterns horizontally as well as vertically. Wikki Stix can be used to highlight patterns, such as odd numbers or even numbers.

How to count money. This is a complex skill. There is much for children to think about when counting money. To scaffold the learning, provide a chart listing each coin, its name, and its value. You can make this coin anchor chart *with* the class to help them remember this important information.

A first-grade teacher makes an anchor chart about coins with her class as they learn about money.

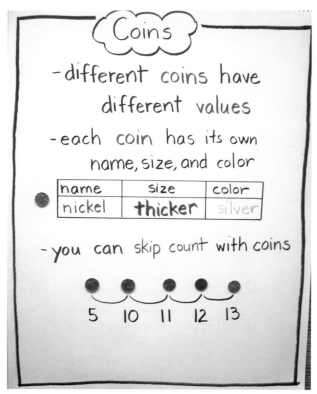

This anchor chart about coins was made with a second-grade class.

Connections to Problem Solving

To help your students engage in problem solving, begin by doing investigations about number with your class. For example, give each student seven coffee stirrers and have them show different ways to arrange them. Circulate around the room and ask them about their thinking. Ask them to draw a representation of their work. Here is a conversation between a young child and her teacher:

Student: I'm making a window.
Teacher: What do you notice about the window?
Student: It has little rectangles.
Teacher: How many?
Student: There are 6 rectangles.

A young child uses 7 coffee stirrers to make a window. She records her designs by drawing them on paper.

You will want to give all children opportunities to solve problems that require higher-level thinking at some of your beginning number concepts stations. These problems should encourage children to think in divergent ways. For example, there should be multiple ways to figure out the answer. Or use open-ended questions. Here are a few activities to get you started:

Create problems to go with a number. In the middle of a big piece of paper, write a number from 1 to 5, such as 3. Label the top of the page with the question, *If the answer is 3, what is the question?* Students write all around the 3, showing their thinking in pictures, numbers, and words.

First graders write questions that go with the answer *3* on a large sheet of paper. As more children come to this station, they can add more ideas.

Play Guess My Number. Student 1 attaches a number from 0 to 10 on a visor with a clip-type clothespin and places it on the head of Student 2 (see next page). Student 2 asks Student 1 questions about the number, and Student 2 tries to guess the number. Larger numbers can also be used with children who can handle a bigger range of numbers. If needed, a prompt card including questions brainstormed with the students might be included here. It may include questions like *Is it less than _____? Is it greater than _____? Is it odd?* and *Is it even?*

Provide problems on cards that children may work together to solve. Label each card with a letter (if you have six cards, each is labeled with a letter from A to F). Students write the letter on the top of their paper and put their initials on it. They work together to problem-solve and record their thinking using pictures, numbers, and words. If you've set up a classroom math corner, this would be a great place for students to sit and think together. You might

One child wears a visor with the numeral 23 clipped to it. He asks his partner questions from the index card and records his guesses on a dry erase board until he guesses the number.

provide a clipboard or a community math journal where they can place their work for others, including the teacher, to examine. Here are a few problems to get started (Adapt the numbers to match the needs of your students. Include some of their names in the problems to personalize them. Include real-world examples related to your classroom whenever possible.):

- There are twice as many birds as rabbits in the garden. How many of each might there be?
- There are only 2 colors (red and blue) in a crayon box. There are 10 crayons. How many could be red? How many could be blue?
- How many kids are here today? Could we all have a partner at math stations? Show your thinking.

Literature Links to Beginning Number Concepts

There are scores of great picture books on beginning number concepts available today. Read aloud lots of these to your class, and then move their favorites to math stations for rereading and retelling. You might want to make one of your stations into a counting books station. Place three or four favorite counting books there for children to interact with. I often include counters so children can match them up to the illustrations on each page to "act it out." Be sure you've taught students to say the numbers as they count and to pay attention to the numbers in the stories.

Another possibility is to include at each station a beginning number concepts book that reinforces the station's concept. The book becomes one of the things children can choose to do at that station. For example, they might play a game *and/or* read a math book at a particular station. Here are some of my favorite beginning number concept titles:

Betcha! by Stuart Murphy. HarperCollins, 1997.
The Cheerios Counting Book by Barbara McGrath. Scholastic, 1998.
Chicka Chicka 1 2 3 by Bill Martin Jr. and Michael Sampson. Simon and Schuster, 2004.
Count Down to Clean Up by Nancy Elizabeth Wallace. Houghton Mifflin, 2001.
Counting Crocodiles by Judy Sierra. Scholastic, 1997.
Counting in the Garden by Kim Parker. Scholastic, 2005.
Counting Kisses by Karen Katz. Scholastic, 2001.
Fat Frogs on a Skinny Log by Sara Riches. Scholastic, 2000.
Fish Eyes: A Book You Can Count On by Lois Elhert. Voyager Books, 1990.
Five Little Monkeys Sitting in a Tree by Eileen Christelow. Sandpiper, 1993.

The Gummi Bear Counting Book by Lindley Boegehold. Lorenz Books, 1997.

Hide and Seek by Brenda Shannon Yee. Orchard Books, 2001.

Just Enough Carrots by Stuart J. Murphy. HarperCollins, 1997.

Look Whooo's Counting by Suse MacDonald. Scholastic, 2000.

Odd and Even Socks by Melanie Chrisman. Children's Press, 2006.

One Duck Stuck by Phyllis Root. Scholastic, 1998.

One Is a Drummer by Roseanne Thong. Chronicle Books, 2008.

1, 2, 3 to the Zoo: A Counting Book by Eric Carle. Scholastic, 1968.

The Oreo Cookie Counting Book by Sarah Albee. Little Simon, 2000.

Roar! A Noisy Counting Book by Pamela Duncan Edwards. Scholastic, 2000.

Rock It, Sock It, Number Line by Bill Martin Jr. and Michael Sampson. Scholastic, 2001.

Teeth, Tails, & Tentacles: An Animal Counting Book by Christopher Wormell. Scholastic, 2004.

Ten Black Dots by Donald Crews. Greenwillow, 1995.

Ten Dirty Pigs: An Upside-Down, Turn-Around Bathtime Counting Book by Carol Roth. Scholastic, 1999.

Ten Little Ducks by Franklin Hammond. Scholastic, 1987.

Ten Little Fingers and Ten Little Toes by Mem Fox. Harcourt, 2008.

Ten Little Fish by Audrey Wood. Scholastic, 2004.

Books for Using Ordinal Numbers to Retell

The Hat by Jan Brett. Putnam, 1997.

Henry the Fourth by Stuart Murphy. HarperCollins, 1998.

The Mitten by Jan Brett. Putnam, 1989.

Move Over, Rover! by Karen Beaumont. Harcourt, 2006.

Seven Blind Mice by Ed Young. Putnam, 2002.

10 Little Rubber Ducks by Eric Carle. HarperCollins, 2005.

The Very Hungry Caterpillar by Eric Carle. Philomel, 1979.

Young children use an "I Can" list with pictures to focus their counting work using books at station 7.

Technology Connections

There is no replacement for hands-on counting work for young children, but technology can provide immediate feedback as well as audio and visual support for learning about numbers. Many schools have interactive whiteboards they use for teaching math. If you have this technology in your classroom, partners can work at an interactive whiteboard station using the same programs you modeled with.

You might also search the Internet for interactive counting games for your students to play and place these in a bookmarked folder labeled *Math Games* at computer stations. Be sure to teach children explicitly how to access this folder and play each game. I like to write directions *with* the class on how to find and use the math games for independent practice, and then post this list near the computers where students can easily access it. A few games for kindergarten can be found at www.learningplanet.com. You might also check out http://pbskids.org/curiousgeorge/games/#1. There you'll find Bring It, a spinner-type game that reinforces counting and beginning number concepts.

Another technology resource is the National Library of Virtual Manipulatives at http://nlvm.usu.edu/en/nav/category_g_1_t_3.html. If you look under the K–2 resources at this site, you might investigate Number Patterns (for second grade, although the examples have a few with negative numbers) and Spinners, where students spin a virtual spinner and count how many times a particular color comes up. Spinners includes a graphing tool to record the spins as well.

To add meaning to counting, do an online search for *citizen science* projects. These programs allow your students to be biologists in their own backyard. Organizations, such as the Audubon Society, have outlined ways to involve students in counting nesting birds in their communities (perhaps even outside your classroom window!).

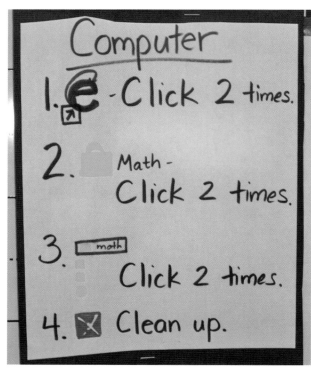

Directions for how to find and open a bookmarked file of math games on the computer is made with the class and displayed by the computer station.

Children love using the overhead projector to play Look, Make, Fix at a math station, even if it is rather low-tech. At the station, provide transparencies with a domino dot pattern (from 1 to 9) on each. Children take turns flashing the pattern on the overhead for a few seconds and look at it. Then they race to make the same pattern using a 4-by-6-inch index card and plastic counters. Finally, they turn the overhead on again to check their work and fix their pattern if they need to. Remind them to count the number of dots on the overhead and on their pattern. This helps children with *conservation of number*, or understanding that the number of objects remains the same when they are rearranged spatially.

One more technology tool children might use for counting is a calculator, which you can get from a dollar store. Young children just learning to count might use calculators to practice counting from 1 to

Partners play Look, Make, Fix on an overhead. They *look* quickly at a dot pattern on a transparency, *make* the pattern on an index card with plastic counters, and then check and *fix* their work if needed.

10 and back, as they can see the numerals while counting. Students can also use a calculator to count by twos, fives, or tens by adding that number to 2, 5, or 10 and making a prediction of what the next number will be.

Troubleshooting at Beginning Number Concepts Stations

Young children love to count little objects, and you'll want them to have many meaningful opportunities to do so. So to keep from losing your mind (and all those small manipulatives), here are some troubleshooting ideas for beginning number concepts stations:

Possible Problem	Troubleshooting Ideas
It's taking too long for some children to clean up at counting stations.	■ Place everything that's needed for a station in a lidded, clear plastic container. Have a ziplock bag or lidded plastic storage cup for each kind of small object students will need there, and include a picture of that object on the bag or cup. Limit the number of materials used at the station to make play and cleanup easier.
Children get confused with the counting sequence while they're counting.	■ Cut up hundreds charts to give children the scaffolds they need. Some students might need just 1–10 or 1–20, while others might need 1–50 or 1–100.
Students lose track when counting a large group of objects by ones.	■ Teach them to place objects in groups while counting (such as twos, fives, or tens).
Students forget how to play counting games, or play them incorrectly.	■ Model, model, model! Play a game with students multiple times before releasing them to play it on their own.
	■ You may want to play the game in small group with children who are having trouble remembering the directions.
	■ *With* the class, write simple directions with pictures or photos to help them remember how to play. Include this in the station container.
Children play a game once and announce they are "done."	■ Encourage students to play a game several times and see who wins the most. Place five "tickets" along with each game children might play. Each time

continued on next page

	someone wins, he or she gets to keep a ticket. Whoever gets the most tickets is the final "winner." Tickets go back in the bag with the game at the end of station time, so you don't have to keep replacing them.
Students misuse dominoes, teddy bear counters, or other manipulatives.	■ At the start of the year, remember to place manipulatives at exploration stations so students can play with them for a while. Soon, they will be ready for more formalized games and explorations. Be explicit about how they may use materials. If anyone throws manipulatives, he or she is immediately removed from that station.
Students don't stay in one area with their station.	■ Call them "*stay*-tions," and remind them to *stay* there. Number the areas around the room to match the number on the stations container. Be sure that stations aren't too close to one another and that students *can* do what's there so they don't wander away. See Chapter 2 for work station setup and management suggestions.
Children aren't writing numerals correctly.	■ Teach children how to *write* numerals, much as you teach them how to write alphabet letters. Post a large chart with rhymes to help them remember how to form each numeral. Set up a station that focuses on how to write numerals, knowing that it is more a handwriting station than a math station. Be sure they have a model to refer to right beside them.

Differentiating at Beginning Number Concepts Stations

The simplest way to differentiate at beginning number concepts stations is to change the range of numbers for children based upon their needs. Some children may need to work on 1 to 5 while others may be ready to move into 6 to 10. Still others may be able to work with numbers above 10 or above 100, depending on the age and developmental levels you work with. You might provide color-coded ziplock bags containing numeral cubes, dot cards, or digit cards that match the number range of a particular group of students. Let children know they need to choose the bag with the red dot or the green dot.

Most likely, you'll differentiate for your struggling students and more advanced ones first.

Be sure students have a solid understanding of counting by ones before having them skip-count by twos, fives, tens, or eventually hundreds. Provide stations that match their counting needs by being sure there is something *each* student in the class *can* do at that station before asking a child to work there. Don't just depend on a more advanced student helping the needier one. Often, the task is too easy for the more advanced child and too difficult for the child below grade level.

There are several things to consider when planning which numbers children will work with at beginning number concepts stations. It's easier to

Cards with numerals and dots provide support for children who are just learning the names of the numerals.

count forward than backward, and it's easier to identify more versus less. Adjust as needed to match the needs of your students as you place different task cards for them to use at particular stations.

If children need help with numeral recognition, have them work with numeral cubes or digit cards rather than dot cubes or dot cards. You might make cards that have both the numeral and dots on one side, or have dots on one side and the matching numeral on the back, so children can use the cards that best match their needs. Using numeral/dot cards that have both in view at once helps children who sometimes forget the names of numerals; they simply count the dots if they forget the numeral name. Students that need to practice writing

numerals might be assigned to work at stations where they get extra practice doing this.

Ways to Keep Beginning Number Concepts Stations Going Throughout the Year

Your beginning number concepts stations should reflect what students need to practice or explore more deeply. Therefore, they will change throughout the year. At the start of the year, the tasks will be simpler and use smaller numbers. Once children can count to 10, you'll want them to start working with numbers to 20. If students can compare two-digit numbers successfully, you can move to having them compare three-digit numbers.

Throughout the year, counting games may come and go, depending on students' needs. Over time, students may tire of playing the same old game. Novelty will keep interest alive. If you choose to put a game away for a while, it can be reintroduced later in the year with a new twist as students need the opportunity to play it again. For example, in first grade students might play a game comparing numbers early in the year. After three or four weeks, you may be able to tell from their behavior that they've become tired of this game. Plus, they've told you during sharing time that they would like to play a new game at this station. Now is the time to either revamp the game or replace it with something more relevant to student needs at this time. Here are a few ways you might keep beginning number concepts stations interesting all year long:

- Change numbers to match students' needs. Be sure that the work isn't too easy or too hard. Just a little bit of challenge engages the brain and holds students' interest.
- Occasionally, vary materials to keep interest high. Replace a cube with a spinner, or vice versa. Or substitute playing cards for numeral cubes.

- Change counters over time to provide novelty. Only change these out when students seem to tire of what they're already using. Try some of the following: cubes, clear plastic counters, buttons, beans, plastic jewels, teddy bear counters, pennies.

How to Assess/Keep Kids Accountable at Beginning Number Concepts Stations

To assess students' understanding of beginning number concepts, it's helpful to maintain checklists of important concepts as you periodically circulate around math stations. For example, in kindergarten, check to see who is using one-to-one correspondence as they count. Which numbers are they able to work with? Numbers to 5? To 10? To 20 or more? Expect to see students counting and recounting.

In first grade, listen for who can easily count by groups of twos, fives, or tens starting at different multiples of these numbers. By second grade, you might be observing for understanding of off-decade counting of larger numbers. As you observe, record on notes which students still need extra support so you can work with those children in a small group.

Check in with students at stations and ask them to tell you how they figured out which number comes next. Do they make reasonable estimates about the size of a group of objects? Do they change their estimate after they begin to count a few items?

Ask questions such as the following:

- What number is one more? One less? Two more? Two less?
- What can we do to make both groups the same? (When looking at two groups of objects.)
- How many extra are there?
- How many more? How many less?

Look at recording sheets children use. Check to see who needs help with numeral formation as well as who needs extra reinforcement with counting. During sharing time, ask children to tell about their favorite counting stations and what they learned at math stations that day. Use this information to help you determine when it is time to switch out stations. Students will tell you they are tired of an activity if they know you respect their opinions. Usually, this will be coupled with observations you have made during stations time and/or by looking at student work.

Kindergarten Considerations

Working with five-year-olds is quite different from working with children in grade two, so I've included this special section, "Kindergarten Considerations" at the end of each chapter. Young children operate on a more concrete level and are not ready to take on the abstract thinking that they will approach upon entering third grade. Because of the distinct needs of young children, here are some things to think about if you are a kindergarten teacher:

- Even though we want children to learn to rote-count, it's not our end goal in kindergarten. Be sure to provide *meaningful* counting experiences for young children, such as those included in this chapter.
- Consider the developmental sequence of learning to count:
  - ☐ Rote counting from 1 to 10
  - ☐ Counting objects to 10 with one-to-one matching
  - ☐ Introducing numerals 0 to 9 (name, match quantities, etc.)
  - ☐ Introducing how to write each numeral (Don't teach all the numerals at once.)
- Help kindergartners establish one-to-one matching in counting, as well as in reading. Note the relationship between the two in your

students. Give students strips with colored dots on them and blocks or counters to push onto each dot as they count, much as we do for teaching children to point to words as they read them.

■ Start with smaller numbers of objects for counting before building to 20. For example, work with having kids count 5 objects before moving to having them count 10, and so on.

■ Use dot cubes at first, then replace these with numeral cubes. Children may also benefit from using cards with both dots and numerals on them to help them connect quantities to numerals.

■ Counting forward is easier than counting backward. Attach these counting experiences to meaningful events in your classroom. For example, in unison, count how many students are eating school lunch as they line up to go to the cafeteria. Then count how many are carrying a sack lunch. Use counting backward as a signal to change activities from time to time, but only from 10 or less. Vary the number you start with. For example, you might say, "Let's count backward together from 8. By the time we're done, you should be in your seats."

■ Young children understand the concept of *more* much easier than the concept of *less*. It is easier to think about what *is* there rather than what is *not* there. Provide extra opportunities for children to think about *less*. Instead of always asking *Who has more?* try to ask *Who has less?* or *Who has fewer?*

■ Take the time to teach kindergartners how to form numerals, just as we teach them how to form letters. Realize that the strokes are different for writing numerals, though. There are two main strokes used when forming letters: top to bottom and left to right. Not so in writing numerals. See the ideas in this chapter on how to help students write numerals, and understand that, technically, this is handwriting. Fluency with writing numerals will help

them later when they are doing more traditional mathematical operations, just as fluency in writing their letters helps children become more fluent as writers by second and third grade.

Reflection and Dialogue

1. What investigations and partner games can you use or adapt from your core program or trainings your district has provided to develop beginning number concepts stations? Use what you've already got! Share resources with your team members, so everyone is not reinventing the wheel.

2. What kinds of counting opportunities do your children need next? How can you make these experiences with number meaningful and authentic?

3. What beginning number concepts stations are currently in use in your classroom? Which are most effective? Why? How do you know?

4. Observe your students at beginning number concepts stations. Take notes about what you see children doing. How does this help you plan for small-group instruction? Whole-group instruction? Additional stations work?

5. What math talk are children using at beginning number concepts stations? What would you like to hear that you're not hearing? How can you support students' use of math talk? Make a math talk card *with* your class and bring it to a team meeting to share.

6. What is something new you'll try as a result of reading this chapter? Give it a go. Then bring evidence of what you've tried to a professional learning community meeting. Talk about what went well, what didn't, and how you might adjust this station in the future.

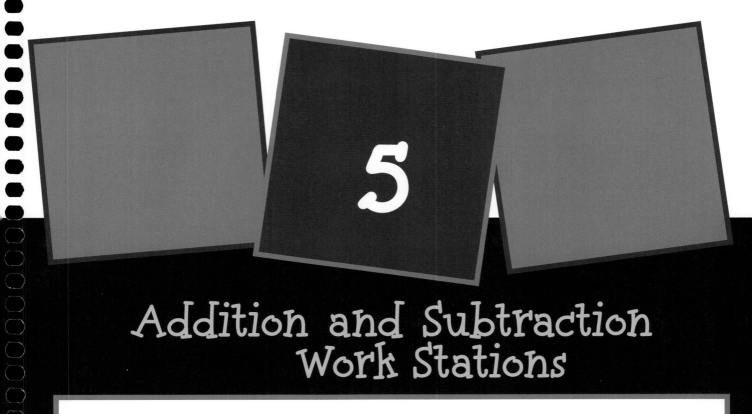

Addition and Subtraction Work Stations

Elaine and Alexis sit side by side at two desks, working together. They choose one of the *Character and Setting* index cards from a ring and smile as they read their card: "Frog and Toad . . . park." (Students brainstormed this set of cards in whole group using familiar characters and matching settings from books their teacher has read aloud to them in their second-grade classroom.)

Next, they pull two cards from the *Number Card* pile and get 55 and 92. (They've been learning about two-digit numbers and place value, and each student in the room wrote a number from 20 to 99 on an index card to place in a baggie at this station. Later in the year, they may work with three-digit numerals and use a place value mat with hundreds, tens, and ones columns.) Then they work together to make up a story problem using information on the cards. Alexis starts: "Frog and Toad collected 92 dandelions."

Elaine adds on, "They blew 55 of them." Then they create a question to end with: "How many still have seeds on them?" The girls work together writing their math story on a page in a class book called "Our Story Problems." The book is made of 8½-by-

11-inch plain white paper stapled together and it will be shared by all students in the class. Each new story problem is written on a clean page. The girls decide that Alexis will write two words, and then Elaine will write the next two words. As they write, they check one another's work.

After they've finished writing, they use a tens and ones place value mat and blue connecting cubes to solve the problem. First, they place 9 ten-trains (ten connecting cubes joined together make a ten-train) and 2 ones on the mat to represent 92. As they subtract, they remove 5 ten-trains, but at first hesitate about what to do when they have to take away 5 ones since there are only 2 cubes in the ones column. Then Elaine says, "Oh, we just take these 2 from the ones side and then 3 more from this ten-train." She snaps off 3 from one of the ten-trains, and since this is no longer a ten-train, moves the 7 leftover ones to the ones side.

Alexis says, "We have 3 tens and 7 ones left. The answer is 37. That was cool."

Finally, they draw a representation of their thinking showing the tens with sticks and ones with

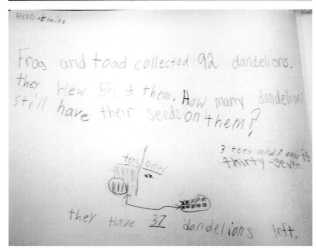

Two second graders work together to create a story problem using character and setting cards brainstormed with the class. They write their problem and solution in a class book for others to read and check.

dots. They write a number sentence, too. The next students that come to this station can read Alexis and Elaine's story in the "Our Story Problems" book as well as create and solve a problem of their own.

Down the hall, a first-grade class is also at math stations, and some students there are working at addition and subtraction stations. Because these children are in first grade, they are working with smaller numbers than the second graders, but they, too, are creating story problems. One station contains simple props so that children make up problems about apples on a tree, related to their study of fall harvest in science. They choose two friends' names and place small paper apples on the tree storyboard while telling the story. A simple sentence frame is provided to help them with storytelling, since many children in this classroom are English language learners:

_____ has _____ apples.
_____ has _____ apples.
How many apples in all? _____

They write their story on a piece of paper and then draw a picture and write a number sentence to show their thinking. They use plus and equal signs in their number sentences.

Two first graders make up a story about apples on a tree using number cubes and names of classmates. They have a sentence frame for language support.

Over time, this sentence frame will be changed to expose students to other types of addition and subtraction problems. For example, the sentence frame might say:

_____ has _____ apples and gets _____ more.
How many apples altogether? _____

Other versions of the sentence frame could be:

_____ had _____ apples and gave _____ to _____.
How many apples are left? _____

_____ has _____ apples and _____ has _____ apples. How many more does _____ have?

The sentence frames are a temporary scaffold. Over time, these will be removed, and children will be encouraged to make up problems on their own.

Today in kindergarten at this same school, the children are learning how to act out addition stories. The teacher begins by telling a story about the playground and has several children dramatize it for the class. Then she shows how to use a storyboard with a playground drawn on it and cubes to represent the children in the story. "Emily, Isabella, and Rachel were climbing on the slide," She says as she places 3 yellow cubes on the sliding board on her storyboard to represent the 3 girls. "Then 2 more friends joined them on the playground. Walter and Anthony wanted to play, too." She adds 2 green cubes on the storyboard. Then she asks, "How many friends were playing together on the playground?"

Many of the students answer, "Five!"

Some children have counted each cube; others started with 3 and counted on 2 more to reach 5; still others instantly recognized the set as 5. The teacher ends this story by telling a number sentence while pointing to the groups of cubes. "We could say that 3 and 2 is the same amount as 5."

The class responds, "Three and 2 is the same amount as 5." They have been learning about number sentences (orally, since it is early in the year, not written as in first grade) as they look at the number of the day in whole group. They are familiar with the concept of looking at parts to make a whole. On this day they are learning how to tell a part-part-whole, or "collection," addition story.

The teacher then gives each child in the class a storyboard with a playground drawn on it. She tells a few more stories about the playground while students act out the stories using cubes on their storyboards. Some even make up their own stories for the class to try: "Two kids were on the swings. Two more kids joined them. How many kids are there now?" After they practice telling stories together in whole group with a variety of storyboards (classroom, playground, ocean, etc.) over the course of many lessons, these materials will be moved to a math station for students to use with a partner. Children will use storyboards, picture cards, dice, and cubes to tell their stories. They will record their stories with pictures and numbers.

Kindergarten children act out problems using connecting cubes on their playground story mats. At first the teacher, and later the children, make up stories about kids playing on the playground.

Key Math Concepts to Teach for Addition and Subtraction

You'll want to plan for addition and subtraction stations using your state and district standards as a guide. If you are using a core math program, you are probably already integrating the NCTM standards and Common Core State Standards for mathematics for number and operations. Work with your colleagues to look at what you need to teach, materials you already have, and what you want your students to investigate and practice at math stations. Then use those ideas along with ideas from this chapter to plan for addition and subtraction stations. Some concepts you'll want to include at these math stations follow.

In kindergarten, children will . . .

- Understand that addition is putting together (parts to whole) and subtracting is taking apart (whole to parts), as in "take away" and "find the missing part" situations.
- Add and subtract using concrete objects and real-world situations with number combinations up to 10 (using pictures, numbers, and words).
- Decompose (or take apart) numbers to 5 in two different ways (such as 2 and 3; 1 and 4).

In first grade, children will also . . .

- Write number sentences to go with the story problems they write and solve.
- Use objects and pictures to apply basic addition and subtraction facts to 9 + 9 = 18 and 18 – 9 = 9.
- Use and explain addition and subtraction fact strategies, such as counting on to find a sum, counting up to find a difference, counting back, doubles, pulling out fives to make a ten for addends 5 to 9, turn around facts, and so on.
- Use addition and subtraction facts to 10 with fluency.

- Solve addition and subtraction problems with one and two-digit numbers to 100 without regrouping.
- Add 3 one-digit numbers.
- Understand that addition and subtraction have an inverse relationship.
- Understand properties of addition (commutative, associative, and additive identity of zero).
- Understand that subtraction is also finding the difference between two amounts in "comparing" situations.

In second grade, children will also . . .

- Add or subtract two- or three-digit numbers with regrouping.
- Use and explain fact strategies, such as doubles plus one and making a ten, and subtraction strategies, such as taking out of the ten.
- Use addition and subtraction facts to 18 with fluency.
- Select addition or subtraction to solve story problems.
- Estimate to determine if solutions for addition or subtraction problems are reasonable.
- Show how to multiply and divide with concrete objects in equivalent sets.
- Use a variety of methods and tools to compute, including objects, mental computation, estimation, paper and pencil, and a calculator.
- Mentally compute sums and differences of multiples of 10 as well as find 10 more or 10 less than any number less than 900.

What the Children Do at Addition and Subtraction Stations

In the opening examples of this chapter, students in primary grades were working with addition and subtraction using stories. This kind of work imbeds basic facts and bigger numbers into meaningful tasks that children enjoy and can connect to.

Basic Addition and Subtraction Vocabulary (Kindergarten)

- add
- in all
- subtract
- take away
- are left
- compare
- how many more
- how many fewer
- is the same amount as
- parts
- whole
- story problem
- number sentence
- join
- separate
- count all
- count on
- count back
- one more than
- one less than

Taking It Further (Grades 1–2)

- addition
- subtraction
- addends
- sum
- equal sign
- difference
- plus sign
- minus sign
- regroup
- equivalent
- fact family
- combine
- doubles fact
- turnaround fact
- equation
- strategy

Whenever possible, help your students engage in authentic, real-world applications of addition and subtraction. Lead discussions, encouraging students to talk about their thinking to deepen understanding (Chapin, O'Connor, and Anderson 2009).

You may be using a core program that includes independent choice time activities for addition and subtraction. If so, adapt the ideas that best meet the needs of your students for work at math stations. Choose things that support what you're teaching. You might make an "I Can" list with your students to give them options on what to do at an addition or subtraction station. Some of the games and explorations included may not take the full fifteen to twenty minutes of a stations rotation to complete, and providing options will solve the problem of the early finisher.

An "I Can" list reminds students of their choices at this addition station. This gives children the opportunity to do a variety of things in the fifteen to twenty minutes they have to work at this station.

I Can play...

- Chutes and Ladders with addition facts

- Combos to 10

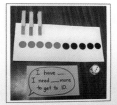

- Read and act out facts in an addition book

I've divided ideas for the work students might do at addition and subtraction stations into three categories: solving story problems; learning basic facts; and adding and subtracting bigger numbers. Please note that many of the following stations ideas can be adapted easily to include three-digit experiences.

Solving Story Problems

Tell, act out, and record addition and subtraction stories using objects or pictures and story mats. Children enjoy working with story mats representing a variety of scenarios familiar to them. See pages 245–247 in the appendix for samples. Encourage them to create stories using these settings (i.e., park, swimming pool, beach, forest, ranch, amusement park, zoo). Use story mats you already have, or ask students to make their own. Young children can use 4½-by-6-inch white construction paper and crayons; have them draw a different background on each side.

Provide counters (Unifix cubes, teddy bear counters, or little toys) for children to use in acting out stories on their story mats. Some children may like to use picture cards for ideas for their stories. One class of kindergartners brainstormed the following for picture cards: an owl, caterpillar, squirrel, and bird for a playground scenario, and a book, crayon, scissors, and glue for a classroom setting. Their teacher used Google images to create the cards. (You can also use clip art.)

To make up a story, partners take turns rolling a numeral cube and acting out and telling a story

using that many objects or characters on a story mat. They may also use picture cards for ideas. For example, one student picks a picture of a book and rolls the numeral 2, and then says, "There are 2 books on the table." Another student picks a second card picturing scissors and rolls a 3 to finish the story, saying, "There are 3 scissors on the table. How many things are on the table?" Then they use connecting cubes to represent the books and scissors as they tell the story and solve the problem, ending with, "Now there are 5 things on the table." They work together to draw a picture and write the story using numbers and words.

Kindergartners act out and write their own story problems using a playground story mat and picture cards of things found there.

Materials used by young children to tell story problems about school include picture cards (with matching words on the back), a numeral cube, and story mats.

Child-made story mats are used for telling and solving story problems. A different scene can be drawn on each side.

Teacher-created sentence frames include the use of stickers, coins, or crayons as manipulatives along with numeral cubes and a ten-frame for problem solving. Note the support for pronoun usage by the drawing of a boy or girl in the top left-hand corner of each frame. These may be used in small group before moving materials to math stations.

Sentence frames for addition and subtraction might also be included at this station to help students create story problems. Sentence frames can support children's math talk and move them beyond simple problems that just join two items. If you laminate the sentence frame pages, students can write directly on them with dry erase markers as they work. Or provide paper, pencils, and clipboards on which children can write and solve their problems.

Students enjoy using their names and those of their classmates in story problems they create, so you might provide name cards and matching student photos on a ring or a list of children in the class. An "I Can" list will help them remember what to do at this station.

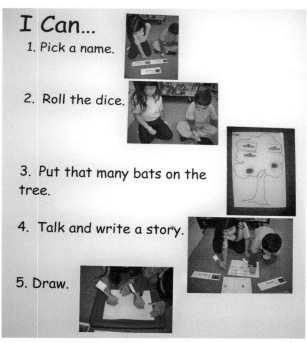

An "I Can" list helps kids remember what to do at this station.

First graders use a sentence frame as they act out and tell a subtraction story about bats in a tree.

Partners work with storytelling materials at a math station after the materials are introduced in small group to children ready to work with this language structure.

Over time, help students also move to working with "comparing" problems for subtraction. Be sure to include a variety of comparison word problems, as outlined in the "What the Teacher Needs to Model" section of this chapter. Provide opportunities for young children to make up these more advanced kinds of problems. Here is one example: Give kids two bags with a different kind of object in each. One bag might have red cubes, and the other black cubes. Player 1 grabs red cubes from a bag and counts out 6. Player 2 grabs 4 black cubes from the other bag. They compare how many they each grabbed and tell or write a story with it, such as the following: "Aiden got 6 red cubes. Maria got 4 black cubes. How many more cubes does Aiden have?"

To solve the problem, the partners line up the red and black cubes one to one to compare. Then, using an accompanying math talk card for support, they say, "Six compared to 4 is 2 more." (Over time, change the math talk card so they might say, "Six compared to 4 is a difference of 2.) It is quite a leap for many young children to describe and later record comparing subtraction number sentences, so model with this specific language many times before expecting students to do this independently. Over time, children also can write the number sentence 6 – 4 = 2.

Children pull cubes from bags and orally make up a story comparing their 6 red and 4 black cubes. They use the math talk card and also write a number sentence.

Make a class story problem book. Provide numeral cards with setting and character cards, as described in the opening of this chapter, for students to use to write their own story problems. Staple together plain white paper on which children can work together to write their own problems for their classmates to read and solve. Have a student create a cover for the book that other students can

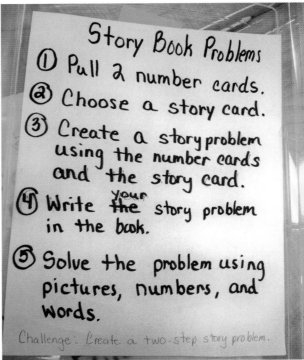

The class created these materials and directions for a story problem book station.

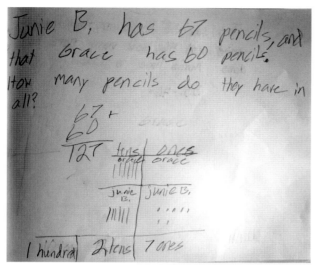

Second graders wrote this page about Junie B. Jones and Grace in "Our Class Story Book."

Two kids play Chutes and Ladders with addition and subtraction fact cards to determine how many spaces to move. Small toys may be provided for support if children need them to solve the facts.

add to as they come to this station. You might write directions with the class to help them remember exactly what to do here, and include these instructions with all the materials needed in a container for this portable station.

Learning Basic Facts

Play addition and subtraction fact board games. Use any blank game board you have available with spaces that go to 100, such as Chutes and Ladders. You'll also need basic math fact cards with missing answers, such as 3 + 4 or 12 – 6. Place these cards on a pile alongside the game board. Partners take turns choosing a fact card, reading it, and giving the answer. (Provide small manipulatives, such as plastic bugs or small toys, for children to use to find or to check the answer.) After giving the answer, they move the same number of spaces. For example, if a student got 2 + 2, he or she would move 4 spaces; if a student chooses 9 – 7, he or she would move just 2 spaces on the game board. Children take turns moving the number of spaces along the game board that match the answers to the facts they choose. The first child to reach the end wins.

For these board game stations, provide fact cards grouped by the strategies you'd like students to practice. For example, the doubles and doubles +1 facts could be one set of fact cards. The +8 and +9 cards (numbers that are used to make 10) could be another set, and +1, –1, +2, –2 could make up a third set of fact cards. An additional set could be comprised of 5+ facts.

Play Combos to 10. You'll need the following for a pair of students to play this game:

- two dot cubes (one with 0 to 5 dots on each face, and the other with 5 to 10 dots on it)
- five cards with 10 dots in a line (5 red dots and 5 black dots on each card)
- thirty clip clothespins with blue ends
- thirty clip clothespins with red ends
- dry erase board and a marker
- math talk card that says: *I have _____. I need _____ more to get to 10.*

First, students sort the clothespins into two piles, with blue in one pile and red in the other. The goal is for students to cover each dot card with some blue and some red clothespins to show a combination that makes 10. On each card, they start with blue clothespins and end with red to show the combos. Here is a scenario describing how to play: One child rolls a dotted cube and gets a 3, so he clips 3 blue clothespins to a dot card, matching a clothespin to each dot. Then, using the math talk card for support, he states how many dots he has matched and how many more are needed to make 10: "I have 3. I need 7 more to get to 10."

Then the other child rolls a numeral cube. She knows she needs 7 to get to 10 and complete the card, so she thinks aloud about which dot cube she needs to roll. "I'll use the dotted cube with bigger numbers of dots on it because I need a 7." If she rolls a 7, she clips 7 red clothespins to the remaining dots on the card, and records *3 + 7 = 10* on the dry erase board, placing her name or initials beside the fact to show she completed it. If she rolls a different number, such as 5, she clips 5 blue clothespins to another card to start a new combo and says, "I have 5. I need 5 more to get to 10."

Play continues in this way, as students try to fill cards with 10 clothespins of two colors to make a combo to 10. They must fill each card with two rolls, no more. For example, if they roll a 3, they can only use a 7 to fill that card (not a 4, then a 3). This rule keeps the focus on the 10 fact. Partners take turns rolling until they have completed filling all the cards with a different fact that's a combo to 10. Whoever has completed and initialed the most facts

is the winner. Note: This game can be adapted and played to practice any set of combinations by modifying the dots on the cards.

Use flash cards for basic fact work. Students can do sorts with basic fact cards. You might provide fact strategy sort cards with categories brainstormed by the class for children to use for support. For example, over time, addition sort cards might include these categories:

Facts That Make 5	Doubles Facts	1 More Than Facts	2 More Than Facts	I Know This Fact Fast
Facts That Make 10	Near Doubles Facts	0 More Than Facts	Facts with Ten and More	Turn- around Facts

Children work together telling the answers to the fact cards and placing the fact cards into categories. Many teachers I work with get their fact cards at a dollar store. As an additional visual support for students who need it, you might add tiny colored dot stickers to show the matching dot pattern on the cards.

Partners take turns choosing a fact card, solving it, and placing it in the category to tell how they got the answer. The categories are Make a 5, Make a 10, Doubles, and Near Doubles.

In Combos to 10, students roll dot cubes, use colored clothespins to mark that many dots on a card, and tell how many more they need to get to 10, using a math talk card for language support.

Colored dot stickers are placed on an addition fact card to provide a visual reference for children learning their facts.

Use playing cards to play addition and subtraction games. Only use playing cards with numerals from 2 to 10 on them for these games. (Remove the face cards from the deck, because they don't picture the number on them. Don't tell children the king or queen stands for 10, because there are not 10 things pictured on the card and this can cause confusion for young children.) Here are a few games you can teach with playing cards:

- *Sums of 10.* Show children how to place nine cards face up in three rows with three in each. The rest of the cards go in a pile facedown. The first child tries to find two cards that are face up that equal 10 when added. For example, the child might take a 2 and an 8 and say,

"Two plus 8 equals 10." He then draws two cards from the deck and places those face up in the empty spaces to replace the cards he took. Then the next student takes a turn to make a sum to 10. Play continues until all cards are used. The player with the most cards wins.

- *Differences and Dice.* This game is played in a similar fashion to Sums of 10, but a dotted cube is added. Students roll the cube and choose two cards whose difference equals the number of dots on the cube. For example, if they roll a 2, they choose two cards that, when the two quantities are compared, show a difference of 2, such as 9 and 7 or 10 and 8. Provide a math talk card to support children's language as they play this game. The card might say: *I can take _____ and _____ because their difference is _____.* For example, a child might say, "I can take 9 and 7 because their difference is 2."

This game is much more challenging than Sums of 10. To make the easiest version, provide a dotted cube with three sets of 1 and 2 dots. Later, give children a dotted cube with two sets of just 1, 2, or 3 dots. To add challenge over time, use a standard die numbered 1 to 6.

Partners take turns finding pairs of playing cards that make sums of 10.

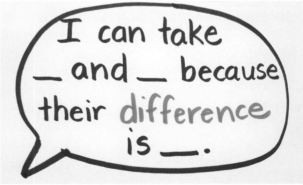

Students use this math talk card made from a 3-by-5-inch index card while playing Differences and Dice.

■ *Addition or Subtraction Action.* For this game, you'll need a deck of playing cards (with the face cards removed), a laminated facts sheet, and a dry erase board and marker. The goal is to make as many facts as possible and check the facts off the list as you play. Put the playing cards facedown on one pile. One player turns over the first two cards and writes down a fact using those numbers on a dry erase board. For example, if the first player turns over a 6 and a 3, he might write *6 + 3 = 9* or *6 − 3 = 3*. Then he searches the facts sheet and draws a line through the fact he made. The facts sheet can be set up by categories, so children can think about what kind of fact it is as they search for it: facts less than 10, +1 facts, +2 facts, doubles above 10 facts, and so on. You can designate if you'd like children to work with addition or subtraction facts or both. You might add a timer for students to use to try to beat the clock as they play.

Another variation is to provide cards that represent numbers in the facts your students need to practice. For example, if children need to work with addends from 1 to 6, remove the 7 to 10 cards. For children who need practice with addends from 5 to 9, take out the 1 to 4 cards. This can provide practice with decomposing and recombining more difficult facts.

Play How Many Are Hiding? with objects (adapted from "Bowl Game" in *Mathematics Their Way* [Baratta-Lorton 1975]). Provide a plastic bowl and small objects, such as Unifix cubes or small toys, for students to hide under the overturned bowl. Partners take turns rolling two numeral cubes (one with bigger numbers and the other with smaller numbers) and recording as they work together, using a sentence frame (found on page 248 of the appendix) for support that says:

We have _____.
We took out _____.
Now we have _____.

For example, one child takes the numeral cube with bigger numbers and rolls a 6; she then places 6 Unifix cubes under the bowl, saying and recording, "We have 6." Then her partner rolls the smaller numeral cube and gets a 2. Now he removes 2 cubes without showing how many are left and records and says, "We took out 2." Together the partners tell how many they think are still hidden and record their answer: "Now we have 4." Then they lift up the bowl and count to check their answer. When they are done with this problem, they remove all the cubes and roll the numeral cubes again to create a new problem.

To vary the work students do, change the numeral cubes to match numbers they need to work with. You might also suggest a designated number for them to continually subtract from (such as 12) and have them roll the numeral cube to tell how many to take away. They can record their thinking and look for patterns, which will aid their computational fluency. For novelty and to keep student interest high, change the container and objects, using items such as an empty Chinese food container and wrapped fortune cookies as the objects to hide.

Two boys play the subtraction game How Many Are Hiding? using simple materials: a bowl, cubes for hiding, and two different colored numeral cubes (one has larger numbers and the other smaller numbers). They record their work on paper using a sentence frame for support.

Explore subtraction facts with cubes and ten-frames to examine whole-part-part relationships for 10. Provide a ten-frame, ten small objects, a numeral cube, and a sentence frame.

Children begin by placing an object in each space on the ten-frame and saying, "I have 10." Then they roll the numeral cube, which tells how many they get to keep. If they roll a 6, they say, "I

get to keep 6." Then they figure out how many they'd have to take out to have 6 remain. They say, "How many do I take out?" and remove 4 objects. They count to see that they have 6 left.

Finally, they write the fact: *10 – 4 = 6* and say, "Ten take away 4 leaves 6." You might provide a facts sheet (found on page 249 of the appendix) so they can cross off and initial each fact they create. The game ends when they've found all the facts. The winner is the person with the most facts initialed. (If they roll a repeat, they act it out, record it again, and initial it on the facts sheet.)

Play Go Fish for Facts. There are several ways to play this popular game with facts. One way is to have students play Go Fish for Doubles. You'll need a set of cards that includes cards showing pairs of dots representing a doubles fact (like two pairs of 6 dots on a card) and matching numeral cards (a card with 12 on it would match the card with two pairs of 6 dots). Provide math talk cards to help students play the game.

Children roll a numeral cube and use a math talk card to make subtraction facts focused around the friendly number 10.

Materials for Go Fish include doubles cards and math talk cards for language support.

Students shuffle the dot and numeral cards together and place them facedown on one pile. Then each student takes 5 cards from the top of the deck and holds these in his or her hand. Partners take turns asking the questions on the math talk card to help them make matches. For example, if Player 1 holds the dot card with two pairs of 7 dots he might ask, "Do you have the number card 14?" If Player 2 has the requested matching numeral card, she must hand it over to the player who requested it. Player 1 then lays down his match and uses the other math talk card for support, saying, "The double of 7 is 14. Seven plus 7 equals 14." If Player 2 doesn't have the matching dot card, she says, "Go fish!" and Player 1 takes a card from the deck.

Then Player 2 asks Player 1 for a card she needs. Play continues until one child is no longer holding any cards. The player with the most matches wins.

To help children think about pulling out fives to make ten when adding 6 + 6, 7 + 7, 8 + 8, and 9 + 9, you might use picture cards that show "5+" domino combinations, such as 5 + 1, 5 + 2 , 5 + 3, and 5 + 4. You might also make a set of paired cards that let students play Go Fish to make a match for the near doubles (the +10 or +9 facts).

Students can also play Go Fish to make a match for any set of facts you'd like them to work with. You can tailor the game to the specific number cards you'd like children to use. For example, if you have children who need to work with addends from 6 to 9, use only cards with those dot combinations and numbers on them.

Play Battle games with facts. To play Battle with facts, students can simply use playing cards (with face cards removed), or they might use Ten Grid cards. The first player chooses two cards from the deck and adds them to create a fact. The second player chooses two cards from the deck and adds those. Players compare their sums to see who has the bigger number. That player wins all four cards. You might include a spinner labeled with *play for more* and *play for less*. One child spins the spinner to see if the winner of each hand (and the game) is the one who gets the bigger number (more) or smaller number (less) in the game. To give students practice with adding three addends, have children choose three cards at a time instead of two.

Another Battle variation you might want your students to play is 10+ Teen Battle. (This is good for students who need to become fluent with 10+ facts.) Ten Grid cards are great because of the visual for 10 they provide. Remove all the 10 cards and only use 0 to 9 cards in the facedown deck. Each student will need a dry erase board and marker. Children put one 10 card between them while they play, and they each turn over a card from the deck. They each add 10 to the card they picked. If one student gets a 7, he says, "Ten plus 7 equals 17." If his partner gets 3, she says, "Ten plus 3 equals 13." The player with the biggest number

Domino dot cards representing 5+ can be made with 3-by-5-inch index cards and large colored dot stickers to help students pull out fives to make ten when adding.

Two children play 10+ Teen Battle using Ten Grid cards from Great Source.

(or the smallest, depending on the game's rules) is the winner and records the winning fact on his or her dry erase board. Play continues until one child has five facts.

A final variation is to play Fast 10 Battle using Ten Grid cards. This game is adapted from *Every Day Counts Partner Games, Grade 2* by Janet Gillespie and Patsy Kanter (2005c). The goal is to make a "fast 10" through decomposing and recombining. Before students play this game, be sure they know their 10+ facts fluently. (You might use the 10+ Teen Battle game.) Again, children choose two cards and add them, but this time they try to make a 10 while finding the sum. For example, if a player turns over a 5 and a 7, he says, "I can make a fast 10 by moving 5 over to make 10. That leaves 2 dots on the other card, and 10 and 2 is 12."

His partner also turns over two cards and gets 3 and 4. That child says, "I can't make a fast 10. Three and 4 is 7. There's not enough to make a 10." The child who made a fast 10 gets all four cards from that turn. If both players make a sum under 10, the cards get inserted back into the deck. If both players can make a fast ten, whoever has the larger sum wins that hand. Play continues until the cards are all used.

Read or write addition and subtraction facts books.

There are many variations for the kinds of facts books kids can read and write. You might make a class book about doubles, using pictures of real objects to represent each fact. See the list that follows for ideas for each double:

- 1 + 1 = 2 (two arms)
- 2 + 2 = 4 (two sets of twins)
- 3 + 3 = 6 (two triangles with arrows pointing to each side)
- 4 + 4 = 8 (two dogs with arrows pointing to each leg)
- 5 + 5 = 10 (two feet with five toes on each)
- 6 + 6 = 12 (an egg carton)
- 7 + 7 = 14 (a two-week calendar)

Children make illustrated pages for a book called "Ways to Make 10."

- 8 + 8 = 16 (two spiders with eight legs each)
- 9 + 9 = 18 (two tic-tac-toe boards)
- 10 + 10 = 20 (two pairs of hands with 10 fingers on each)

Children can make their own book about doubles, too. Or they can read books about doubles. (See the "Literature Links" section in this chapter for ideas.)

Likewise, children can make books about ways to make 5 or ways to make 10. On each page they can draw and write about a way to make 5, such as 1 apple and 4 oranges or 2 cats and 3 dogs.

Make a fact family book.

Students can work together to make a book focused on all the sums of a number, such as sums of 6 (or 7 or 8 or 9). Children work together to make the pages needed for their book. They might each make separate pages and staple them together to make a book. Model how to draw a picture for the fact and how to write all the ways to put together and take apart a combination. For example, a page from the "Sums of 6" book might have a picture showing two dogs and four cats with the following facts:

2 + 4 = 6

4 + 2 = 6

6 – 4 = 2

6 – 2 = 4

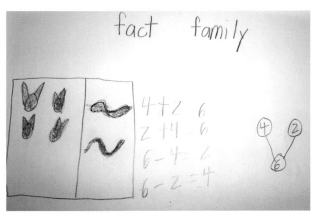

A child made this page for a "Sums of 6" fact family book.

Bigger Number Addition Sums is played with two-digit cards.

Students can also draw the number bond showing the part-part-whole representation to bridge the picture and the abstract. Place the finished books in your classroom library in a container labeled *Fact Books* for other children to read.

Adding and Subtracting Bigger Numbers

Play Bigger Number Addition Sums (or Bigger Number Subtraction Differences) Battle. You'll need 40 two-digit numeral cards and dry erase boards and markers to play this adaptation of Battle. Note: Don't use playing cards, since the picture won't match the actual number. Students can make the cards by writing two-digit numerals on 3-by-5-inch index cards. Or purchase two sets of numbers 1 to 100 flash cards from a discount store.

To play, one child chooses two cards from the deck, adds the numbers mentally, and records his or her thinking on the dry erase board to show his or her sum for Battle. The other child checks to be sure the computation is correct. (You might provide a calculator for checking.)

Then the other child chooses two cards and does the same. Again, his or her partner checks the work. They compare their sums. Whoever has the biggest sum wins and keeps all four cards. Play continues until all the cards have been used. The player with the most cards wins.

To play Bigger Numbers Subtraction Differences Battle, adapt the game by having each student subtract the smaller number from the bigger one of the 2 two-digit cards he or she pulls from the deck. Students compare differences, and whoever has the bigger number wins the hand and keeps those four cards.

Do sorts with story problems using bigger numbers. Use your core program or core curriculum materials to find sample story problems with bigger numbers. Start with addition problems only. Later, include subtraction problems. Then add a mixture so students sort and think about which operation to use before solving. Glue each problem on a 3-by-5-inch index card and write the answer on the back so students can self-check. Also include 1½-by-5-inch cards with a facts strategy listed on each, such as *doubles, doubles plus one, make a ten,* or *turnaround fact.*

Show students how to think about the bigger numbers and the imbedded facts (for example, in 38 + 27, the difficult fact is 8 + 7). Have partners work together to sort the story problem cards according to the fact strategy they can use to most efficiently add the ones instead of counting. This allows children to think about strategies that will most efficiently solve a problem rather than just use an algorithm procedure to solve it.

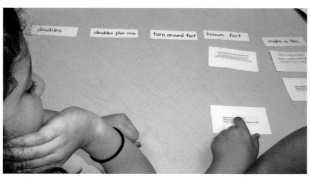

Partners work together to read story problems with bigger numbers and sort these by the fact strategy they'd use to solve each mentally.

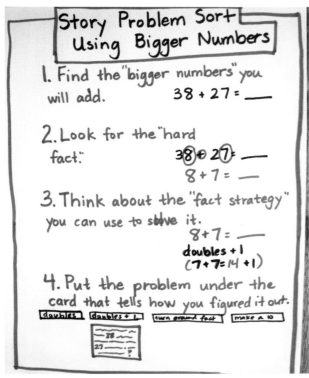

It's helpful to write directions with the class for Story Problem Sort Using Bigger Numbers. This will help them remember what to do for this activity.

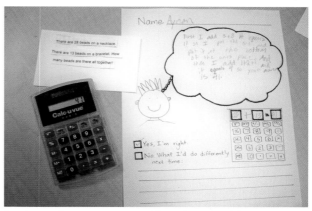

Students choose a story problem that uses bigger numbers and record their thinking about how they'd mentally solve the problem. Then they fill in the equation they'd type into the calculator to check their mental math. Finally, they check their math using the actual calculator.

Use mental math strategies to solve two-digit addition and subtraction problems. Use the preceding activity. Then, over time, have partners choose one of the problems to solve using mental math strategies, such as adding tens and then ones. Or they might add ones and regroup when possible in their heads. Or they could start with the greater two-digit number and add on tens from the second number, and then add the ones. Have each child use a copy of the think sheet found on page 250 of the appendix to record how he or she would solve the problem using mental math strategies, as well as a calculator for a fast check. Have each child write his or her thinking about how to solve the problem in the speech bubble, write the number sentence in the calculator space, and check off *Yes, I'm right* or *No*. If the student checks off *No*, he or she also needs to respond to the prompt *What I'd do differently next time*. When finished, partners compare their thinking with each other.

Start with just one operation, such as all addition problems. Be sure to have children explain their thinking just orally at first. When they are adept at doing this, add the think sheet. Move to subtraction or a combination of addition and subtraction problems over time.

Connecting number patterns to bigger numbers. (This activity is best for students late in second grade or above.) Have students put fact cards in a pile. They should then sort facts based upon the strategy they'd use to solve them, using the fact

Second-grade partners choose the fact card 5 + 2 and generate problems with bigger numbers that use this fact. They compare their thinking with each other. One child noticed, "Look! They all have sevens in the ones place when you do this pattern."

strategy sorting cards from earlier activities in this chapter. They take turns choosing a fact card from one of the categories and generating addition or subtraction problems they could easily solve using that fact. They show how they'd solve that problem with bigger numbers using the fact. For example, if they choose the fact 6 + 7 = 13, they could list problems such as these:

- 16 + 27 = 43 (10 + 20 = 30 and 6 + 7 =13, so the answer is 30 + 13 or 43)
- 26 + 37 = 63 (20 + 30 = 50 and 6 + 7= 13, so the answer is 50 + 13 or 63)

Play Trade or No Trade. For this activity you will need a set of cards with numerals from 10 to 100 on them. Students could make these cards using 3-by-5-inch index cards with a numeral on each. Or purchase two sets of numbers 1 to 100 flash cards from a discount store. These cards generally have numer-

als on both sides. To prepare the commercial cards, sort them into two piles, with 1 to 50 in one and 51 to 100 in the other. Mark each with a small colored dot so students know to use that side.

To play the game, partners take turns removing two cards at a time from the deck. If a player picks 26 and 45, she must say "trade," because she'll need to trade ones for a ten when adding these numbers together. She says "no trade" if she doesn't have enough ones to trade for a ten, like when she picks 33 and 64 (see the sample recording sheet that follows). To check their thinking and solve their problems, partners work together using a place value mat and manipulatives. (You might start with popsicle sticks that can be bundled and unbundled in groups of ten. From there, move to base ten blocks. Over time, have students use pennies and dimes.)

Each child uses a recording sheet (page 251 in the appendix) to keep track of his or her "trade" or "no trade" actions. The first to make five trades is the winner.

Students play Trade or No Trade using numeral cards, a place value mat, and popsicle sticks bundled in groups of ten.

Trade There are enough ones to make a group of ten.	26 + 45 = 71	34 + 29 = 63	18 + 55 = 73		
No Trade There are NOT enough ones to make a ten.	33 + 64 = 97				

This game can be changed to a subtraction game over time. For the subtraction version, children pick two cards and subtract the smaller number from the larger one. They must say "trade" if they need to "ungroup," or trade in a ten for ten ones in order to take away the smaller amount. Partners can check their answers by finding the difference using mental math or a hundreds chart to count up from the smaller number to the greater number by tens and ones.

Materials

You will want to organize materials children use while working at addition and subtraction stations to make the materials easily accessible. Place each kind of material in a labeled container on a shelf students can reach. Many of the things you used for beginning number concepts can be used at addition and subtraction stations, too. Familiar materials give children a sense of security that they can build upon to explore new ideas.

In addition to the materials listed here, many are available in a format that can be used on the overhead or other projection device for modeling. Although you may no longer be using an overhead for instruction, some teachers keep an old overhead to use as a station (kids love using it).

Here are suggested materials to have on hand throughout the year when teaching about addition and subtraction:

- connecting cubes (sorted into just one or two colors)
- counters
- small toys for acting out stories and facts (plastic zoo animals, little firefighters, plastic bugs, etc.; often found in dollar stores)
- dice and numeral cubes
- wooden cubes (used for custom-made numeral cubes)
- story mats (commercial or student-made)
- board games for addition and subtraction

- five-frames
- ten-frames
- dot cards
- dominoes
- clip-on clothespins
- playing cards
- Ten Grid cards
- basic fact flash cards
- numeral cards
- plastic bowl
- story problem cards
- hundreds charts
- bookmaking supplies (paper, stapler, markers, optional digital camera)

What the Teacher Needs to Model

I have observed that when teacher modeling is of high quality, the work children do at math stations is more effective. Here are some things to model well so your children can maximize their time spent at addition and subtraction stations:

How to tell, act out, and solve story problems. Begin by telling stories about your students in scenarios related to your classroom. For example, kindergarten teacher Mrs. Thrash tells a story about a few students while these students act it out for the rest of the class: "Kevin and Andre were going to the library. They met Suzanna and Rachel at the library. How many friends were together at the library?" While she tells the story, the two boys, Kevin and Andre, stand on one side of her and the two girls, Suzanna and Rachel, stand on the other side of her to show the two *parts* being joined into a *whole*. She tells the children they are *adding*, or joining parts, but she doesn't introduce the fact 2 + 2 = 4 yet. These abstract symbols will only be added when children have more understanding of the concepts of addition and subtraction. Instead, they orally tell the story in numbers, saying, "Two and 2 is the same amount as 4 children."

Later, the teacher reads aloud *The Crayon Counting Book* by Pam Muñoz Ryan and Jerry Pallotta (1996). She then has children help tell and act out stories joining groups of crayons. Using physical objects helps students understand what it means to join and separate sets. Over time, this teacher will also model stories where parts are separated from the whole to show subtraction. For example: "There were 10 crayons in a box. Miguel wanted 2 red crayons from the box. How many other crayons were in the box?" She won't wait until students understand addition to model subtraction, because these two operations are closely related. She wants her children to think flexibly about joining and separating and comparing groups of objects.

Young children act out a story about two boys and two girls going to the library.

A teacher models addition as she shows how to join sets of crayons.

How to record and solve addition and subtraction stories using objects or pictures and story mats. It is useful for children to use manipulatives to solve problems (rather than just memorize facts), as it helps them develop conceptual understandings of addition and subtraction. You'll want to model how to use objects or pictures to represent numbers. Use a dry erase board or interactive whiteboard to show how to record your thinking as you work. Use explicit language as you think aloud with the class and use pictures, words, and numbers to show how to solve a problem.

For example, a second-grade class helps make up the following story problem after reading several versions of "The Three Bears" in a study of folktales: "Three bears have 77 jars of honey. They ate 60. How many jars of honey do they have left?" They then work together to solve the problem, as the teacher records their ideas on the board. Different students volunteer their thinking:

One child says, "Seventy minus 60 is 10. And we still have the 7 from 77, so 10 and 7 is 17."

Another student shares how he's thinking about the problem: "I'm thinking that if they ate 60 out of the 77 jars, there will be 10 and 7 more left to get to 77, and that's 17."

Yet another second grader, who has written 77 – 60 in vertical form on the dry erase board, says,

A second-grade teacher records children's thinking about a story problem on her interactive whiteboard.

"Seventy minus 60 is 10, and 7 minus 0 is 7, so 17 is the answer."

Their teacher also shows how they might record their thinking by showing a representation of sticks for tens and dots for ones.

Start with simple problems, but be sure to model with a variety of word problems over time, including more challenging problems like the following:

■ Join problems. For example: *Brandon had 5 stickers. His teacher gave him some more. Now Brandon has 8 stickers. How many did his teacher give him?* Or: *Melissa is starting a rock collection. Her grandma gives her 10 rocks. Now Melissa has 25 rocks in her collection. How many did she have to start with?*

Give children counters and a work mat divided in half. Ask them how they might act out this type of problem. Some may put counters on the left side of the mat to show the part they know (i.e., 10 rocks), and use the other side to count out enough (the missing part) to reach the given total (25 rocks). Other students may start with the total amount in counters (25 rocks) on one side and move the starting amount known (10 rocks) to the other side, which leaves the missing amount on the first side.

A 12-by-18-inch piece of paper divided in half makes a work mat for "find the missing part" subtraction problems.

■ Separate problems. For example: *Levi had 10 cookies. He gave some to Sam. Now Levi has 8 cookies. How many did cookies did Levi give to Sam?* Or: *Kari had some Junie B. Jones books. She let Sarita borrow 4 of her books. Now Kari has 8 Junie B. Jones books left. How many Junie B. Jones books did Kari have to start with?*

Again, invite children to use counters on a divided work mat to act out and tell about their strategies for solving these types of problems. They might also draw pictures to show their thinking about how to solve these kinds of problems.

Cubes can be used on a divided work mat to solve "separate problems" in subtraction.

■ Compare problems. For example: *William has 6 more toys than Cayla. Cayla has 10 toys. How many toys does William have?* Or: *Brittany has 7 fewer crayons than Louis. Brittany has 10 crayons. How many crayons does Louis have?*

To solve this kind of problem, it's helpful for children to line up counters one to one, matching the two amounts. Don't give them a divided work mat in this type of situation; it will only confuse them.

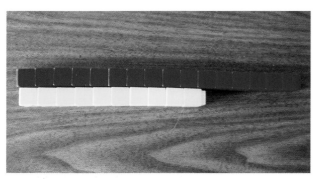

Have students line up counters one to one when solving "compare problems."

- Part-part-whole problems. For example: *Austin has 10 pencils. Some are sharp, 3 are broken. How many pencils are sharp?* The two-part mat can be very helpful when acting out missing part problems.

- Problems using zero. Students should be exposed to the idea that when zero is added or subtracted, they still have the number they began with. Again, the divided work mat can help children easily see the result of adding zero counters.

- Problems with the same addends, but in different orders. Have children compare these kinds of problems to see that it doesn't matter what order the numbers are added in. Have them examine two problems with similar scenarios and discuss how they are alike. For example, compare these two problems: (1) *Maria has 3 apple slices at morning snack. She ate 4 more in the afternoon. How many apple slices did she eat?* and (2) *The same day Marcus ate 4 apple slices at morning snack. He ate 3 more in the afternoon. How many apple slices did he eat?*

As children are learning to make up their own story problems, model how to use sentence frames, especially when you work with English language learners. Have students model for the rest of the class how to make up new problems using the sentence frames you provide as a scaffold. Eventually,

have students use open-number sentences to represent their thinking, such as 3 + 4 = _____ + 3.

You may also want to use larger numbers over time in these problems, to help children understand that the commutative property of addition applies to bigger numbers as well as basic addition facts. Expand to open-number sentences, such as 35 + 43 = _____ + 35. Observe to see if students are really able to apply this property.

If you'd like more information on different kinds of problems and ways to introduce them to your students, see *Teaching Student-Centered Mathematics: Grades K–3* by John Van de Walle and Lou Ann Lovin (2006) and *Children's Mathematics: Cognitively Guided Instruction* by Thomas Carpenter, et al. (1999).

How to use a variety of fact strategies. Fact mastery involves efficient, or quick, response, but has little to do with flashing addition and subtraction cards or rote repetition. Children's understanding of number relationships, especially anchored around the "friendly" numbers 5 and 10, builds the foundation upon which facts are learned. Help students determine and use fact strategies to help them internalize basic facts, first to 10 and then to 18.

Don't just tell the class a strategy. Have children use visual models, such as dominoes, Ten Grid cards, or counters, on divided mats to examine a group of related facts and tell how they are alike. Help them develop strategies to move them away from having to count to solve problems.

For example, show children several 0+ dominoes, and have them find the pattern. Ask: *What do you notice? What is the same?* Then record the addition for each domino pattern on the board. Ask students to think about how these are the same:

$$1 + 0 = 1$$
$$2 + 0 = 2$$
$$3 + 0 = 3$$
$$4 + 0 = 4$$

Ask the class to look for patterns, and help them discover that when 0 is added to any number, they still have the number they began with. If children have opportunities to work with counters or visual models that show a related group of facts *before* they look for patterns in facts written in vertical form, it is easier for them to see and construct that generalization. Have students add other facts to the generated list, and name the strategy, such as "zero more." Make a chart with this strategy and a few examples for students to use as reference.

Start with addition facts and then help children connect these to subtraction. As they examine numbers and their relationships, guide children to use and name some of the following fact strategies:

- Zero more
- One more
- Two more
- Doubles
- Near doubles
- Make a ten
- Ten plus
- How much to ten and more

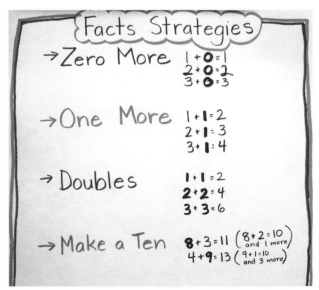

A first-grade class uses this chart as a reference for fact strategies.

Once students have mastered addition facts, be sure to include "think how many more" as one strategy for subtraction facts, especially for facts with sums of 10 or less. This will lead many children to use addition facts they know to figure out subtraction problems. In this way, they learn to connect addition to subtraction, which will make learning subtraction facts easier. For example, when computing 8 – 5, encourage students to think, "Five and what makes 8?" as well as "What does it take to get from 5 to 8?" and "How far apart is 5 from 8?"

You might want to consult *Zeroing in on Number and Operation: Key Ideas and Common Misconceptions, Grades 1–2* by Linda Dacey and Anne Collins (2010) for more ideas on teaching addition and subtraction strategies to your class.

How to play addition and subtraction games. Teach children how to play the games in this chapter (or games from your core curriculum) before asking them to work independently with the games at math stations. Model with one student being your partner and show the class explicitly what you expect. Show how to use the math talk cards (where included) as well as how to think about the math they are doing as they play. Allow children to use counters, even their fingers, as needed while they develop number concepts for addition and subtraction while playing these games. Whenever possible, use visual models and materials that help students see number relationships around the numbers 5 and 10, such as five-frames, ten-frames, cards with dots in patterns that show groups of 5, and Ten Grid cards.

After modeling a game with the whole group several times and if you have enough materials, you might have all students play with a partner while you walk around the room checking on their understanding. You might want to introduce some of the games to a small group, if only some children in your classroom need the kind of work provided. I've found it useful sometimes to write simple directions with the class on how to play a game. They seem to

A pair of students models for the rest of the class how to play the game Close to 100 from their core program, *Investigations*, after their teacher has modeled. The class has written directions for the game, which are posted nearby for reference.

better understand these instructions than the ones I have written or that may have come with a commercial set.

How to do sorts. Teach students how to sort cards by categories. You might use addition fact cards, subtraction fact cards, problem-solving cards, or even playing cards, as described in the section "What the Children Do at Addition and Subtraction Stations," earlier in this chapter. Include category cards, as suggested. Limit the number of cards and categories for sorting so students can spend more time thinking than hunting for cards. At first, you might start with just one category card and an "other" category to simplify sorting. For example, if students are doing an addition facts sort, provide *only* cards that are doubles and cards that are not doubles. Make a spot for each category, and label the spots with *Doubles* and *Other*. Students place doubles fact cards under the *Doubles* label (and solve and check them on back); they place cards that are not doubles under the *Other* label.

Model how children should sit beside each other so that they can both see the numerals right-side up, and model how to work *together*, talking about how cards are alike or different and why they go in each category.

How to use a variety of methods and tools to compute bigger numbers, including base ten models, mental computation, estimation, traditional algorithms, and calculators. Be sure to expose your students to many different ways to solve addition and subtraction problems. Help them move beyond counting by ones as they move to two-digit numbers. Suggest that they arrange counters in groups of ten and leftovers. They might make ten-sticks with connecting cubes or use cups with 10 counters in each.

Over time, encourage children to use mental computation to solve a problem in their heads. For example, to solve 34 + 57, they might use what they know about base ten concepts and think, "Thirty plus 50 is 80, 4 plus 7 is 11, and 80 plus 11 is 91." Or "Thirty-four plus 60 is 94, 57 is 3 less than 60, and 3 less than 94 is 91."

Likewise, for 65 – 37, they might think, "Sixty-five minus 35 is 30, take away 2 more and get 28." As they use larger numbers, they may need to write down what they did to keep track of it, but most of their thinking is done mentally. These flexible strategies help students apply what they know about number without formally being taught algorithms for addition and subtraction (with or without regrouping). You'll notice that students usually work from left to right, thinking about hundreds, then tens, then ones, rather than right to left as in traditional algorithms.

Many teachers still teach the traditional ways to add and subtract two- and three-digit numbers, because it is what was done when they were in school or it may be required in their curriculum. You might view these traditional algorithms as another strategy for solving problems. If children are expected to understand and use traditional regrouping algorithms for addition and subtraction, it is only fair to provide them with lots of hands-on experiences where they act out problems using materials to regroup ones into tens when adding, and to ungroup tens into ones when subtracting. Prior experience with addition trading games,

A first-grade teacher records students' thinking as they solve a story problem using a picture and numerals.

where 10 ones are grouped or exchanged for a ten (and 10 tens are traded for a hundred) provide a foundation for traditional algorithms. Likewise for subtraction. See Chapter 6, "Place Value Work Stations," for ideas for trading games.

Calculators are fun for children to use, and they can be used for checking problems they've solved using their own methods. Provide modeling in how to use a calculator, so students will be able to use them independently. Observe children working with calculators to solve various types of subtraction story problems to gain insight into their operation sense and ability to judge reasonableness of answers. For example, given the problem *The Celtics have 16 points, and the Rockets have 23 points. How many points are the Celtics behind?*, a child can use the number sentence 16 + _____ = 23 to solve the problem mentally, but the calculator can't. Follow the lead of your students to provide explicit modeling in calculator use.

Connections to Problem Solving

Teaching children about addition and subtraction should be imbedded in story problems to provide a rich context for learning, as described throughout this chapter. It is important to expose students to a wide variety of problems over time. Be sure to use the list on pages 121–122 for examples. You will also want to have available other kinds of problem-solving station work related to addition and subtraction. You might include this problem-solving work in your classroom math corner. Here are a few ideas:

- Prepare cards or sentence strips that list numbers representing counting by twos, fives, and/or tens. For example, 5, 10, 15, 20, 25, . . . or 2, 7, 12, 17, 22, 27, . . . or 11, 21, 31, 41, 51, ... Have children look at the numbers and answer the following questions on a recording sheet, as found on page 252 of the appendix: *What numbers do you think will come next? How do you know? Tell about the patterns you see.*

  Teach children how to bridge from one number to the next, recording the action each time. For example, students draw the bridge from the 5 to the 10 and record +5 on the bridge, reminding them that 5 is being added each time. Have them continue this action throughout the entire pattern. If students get used to doing this, they can access almost any number pattern.

- You might give students problems with combinations to solve with a partner. Write one problem per card for them to choose from. Here are a few to get you started: (These are also found on page 253 of the appendix.)
  - ☐ Jonathan spent $20 at a toy store. He had only $10, $5, and $1 bills in his wallet. What are the combinations he might have used to spend his $20?
  - ☐ Some friends were at the playground. Six played basketball, 5 played tag, and some played both. How many kids were playing in all?
  - ☐ Katherine bought 10 plants. She planted them in 2 containers. She put at least 1 plant in each container. What are the different ways she could put the plants into the containers?

☐ Jessica is sorting seashells. She has 4 more white than pink. She has 3 more gray than striped. She has just one that is spotted. How many seashells does she have?

■ Provide students with number puzzles where all lines must add up to a particular amount. You can find a game like this online at http://resources.oswego.org/games/Powerlines/powerlines1.html. Or try simple Kenken games for addition or subtraction. A sample can be found at http://www.hicolor.jp/puzzle/en/trial/index.html.

Literature Links to Addition and Subtraction

Picture books provide meaning for students learning to add and subtract. Kids can often use stories they have read to create problems. Here is a list of recommended picture books to read aloud to your students and place at math stations:

Addition

Adding Arctic Animals by David Bauer. Redbrick Learning, 2003.

Adding It Up at the Zoo by Judy Nayer. Yellow Umbrella Books, 2002.

Addition Annie by David Gisler. Children's Press, 2002.

Animals on Board by Stuart J. Murphy. HarperCollins, 1998.

Cats Add Up! by Dianne Ochiltree. Scholastic, 2006.

Domino Addition by Lynette Long. Charlesbridge, 1997.

Double the Ducks (MathStart series) by Stuart J. Murphy. HarperCollins, 2002.

Little 1 by Ann Rand. Chronicle Books, 2006.

Mall Mania (MathStart series) by Stuart J. Murphy. HarperCollins, 2006.

Mission: Addition by Loreen Leedy. Holiday House, 1999.

Baskets of addition and subtraction books may be used along with addition and subtraction stations. Or a book or two may be added to an existing addition or subtraction station.

Quack and Count by Keith Baker. Sandpiper, 2004.

12 Ways to Get to 11 by Eve Merriam. Aladdin, 1996.

Subtraction

Elevator Magic by Stuart J. Murphy. HarperCollins, 1997.

A Fair Bear Share by Stuart J. Murphy. HarperCollins, 1997.

Five Little Monkeys Jumping on the Bed by Eileen Christelow. Sandpiper, 2006.

Five Little Monkeys Sitting in a Tree by Eileen Christelow. Sandpiper, 1993.

Monster Musical Chairs (MathStart series) by Stuart Murphy. HarperCollins, 2000.

Pet Store Subtraction (Rookie Read-About Math series) by Simone T. Ribke. Children's Press, 2007.

Roll Over: A Counting Song by Merle Peek. Sandpiper, 1991.

Shark Swimathon by Stuart J. Murphy. HarperCollins, 2000.

Subtracting by Rozanne Lanzcak Williams. Gareth Stevens, 2004.

Subtraction Action by Loreen Leedy. Holiday House, 2002.

Take Away (Yellow Umbrella Book series) by Lisa Trumbauer. Redbrick Learning, 2003.

Ten Terrible Dinosaurs by Paul Stickland. Puffin, 2000.

(Another source you might want to use is *Teaching Math with Favorite Picture Books* by Judi Hechtman, Deborah Ellermeyer, and Sandy Ford Grove, 1998.)

Technology Connections

Young children love working on the computer. Technology is engaging and often provides automatic feedback. You might set up several computer math stations for your students to use. Bookmark appropriate sites, and teach students how to access these sites on their own. Likewise, today many teachers use interactive whiteboards in their math instruction. You might use materials from whole-group instruction to set up an interactive whiteboard station.

When looking for computer games for children to play, try them yourself before teaching them to your students. Some are just glorified worksheets with limited or no mathematical thinking needed. Also, think about the purpose of each computer game. If it is a drill for addition or subtraction facts, be sure the students using it have conceptual under-

standings for the facts before they spend time practicing them to develop fluency. Here are a few sites to check out that have some good addition and subtraction computer games:

www.aplusmath.com
www.arcademicskillbuilders.com
www.funbrain.com
http://www.abcya.com/math_bingo.htm
http://www.mathplayground.com/
    PartPartWhole.html

Also check out www.illuminations.nctm.org to find a five-frame, a ten-frame, and an abacus, which can all be used online by students to develop understandings about addition and subtraction.

Calculators are also fun and engaging. You might have children use calculators to check answers to word problems they have solved. Calculators can also be used to generate numbers that are "one more" or "five more" or "ten more." Simply have children enter a numeral + 1 =. They can continue pushing + 1 or + 5 or + 10 to watch the numerals that come up. When paired with a ten-frame or hundreds chart to plot out the numerals

A child uses a calculator to add "five more" to 6 and gets 11. She then adds 5 more and says, "Sixteen" before checking it as she pushes the equal sign.

generated, a calculator can be a fascinating pattern generator. This same kind of work can be done with subtraction as students find "one less" or "five less" or "ten less."

A subscription service for story problems in English and Spanish is available at www.mathstories.com. You can even submit original story problems to be considered for use in their database.

Troubleshooting at Addition and Subtraction Stations

Clearly modeling what is expected of students as they work independently will generally help students maximize the time they spend with partners at addition and subtraction stations. Here are some things to think about ahead of time:

Possible Problem	Troubleshooting Ideas
Children spend more time drawing pictures than thinking and solving when making up their own story problems.	■ Provide only pencils (no crayons) and teach kids how to make a quick sketch rather than a detailed drawing. Or give them a minute timer and let them spend two minutes drawing and the rest of the time working on the problem. ■ Teach children to draw a square or circle to represent an animal, such as a pig, that they are trying to draw in detail. They might also label these representations using known letters and sounds.
Students write the same kinds of simple story problems over and over again.	■ Include sample story problems in a variety of formats. (See pages 121–122 for samples.) You might put these samples on laminated cards with blanks for the numbers so they can be used in flexible ways.
Children don't know their facts. They cheat by flipping over the fact cards for the answers.	■ Realize that these students aren't "cheating." They're showing that they need extra support in figuring out basic facts. Work with these students in small group using visual models and explicit language to help them learn strategies for remembering their facts. Help them build upon what they already know to learn new facts. ■ Lay out fact cards and have kids show you which they know and which they don't.
Children are working problems at stations, but are getting the wrong answers.	■ Provide materials for self-checking. If students are working with facts, have a "facts sheet" for them to use for reference. Teach them how to use this to *check* rather than just to get the answer. ■ If they get the wrong answer, teach them how to rework a problem and think about another way to solve it. ■ See the "Differentiating at Addition and Subtraction Stations" section for ideas on providing different numbers for different groups of children.

continued

Students misuse materials. They pinch each other with clothespins, or put bowls on their heads.	■ Employ the "one strike and you're out" policy. Don't give warnings during math stations time. If students are playing around, remove them from stations immediately. Have them sit near you at your small-group table.
Children forget how to play a game using playing cards and make up their own rules.	■ You might write simple directions with the class on how to play a particular game and tape it to the lid of the station container. Also, be aware that sometimes students come up with great ideas for a new game. If their ideas provide opportunities for mathematical thinking in the game, have them show the rest of the class how to play.
Partners can't decide on who goes first in a game and get into an argument.	■ Teach ways to decide who goes first, such as Paper, Rock, Scissors or tossing a die. Or have one partner choose the activity, and the other go first.
You see students playing games but don't hear them having the math conversations you'd hoped for.	■ Include math talk cards with conversation stems on them, as pictured throughout this chapter. Also, you might place a tape recorder at the station so they can record their conversations.
Children work alone rather than with a partner when you have paired them.	■ Make clear the expectation for how to do an exploration or play a game *together*. Model explicitly how to sit beside a partner and work together.

Differentiating at Addition and Subtraction Stations

As you observe students in whole group, small group, and at math stations, take notes about what they can do well on their own and what they need additional support with. Use your notes to think about who needs practice with what.

One teacher's notes tell what she noticed about individual children's knowledge of basic addition and subtraction facts. She also compiled her thinking into a chart to denote who needs to work on what (see photos on next page).

This teacher sees that one group of students knows their facts fast and flexibly, so she won't assign them to stations with facts practice. She'll have them work at stations using ideas from the section "Adding and Subtracting Bigger Numbers" (on page 116) after she has introduced this kind of work in small group.

Since most of her students are familiar with strategies for facts but aren't fluent with them yet, the majority of them will benefit from working at stations listed under the section "Learning Basic Facts." However, several of her children need strategies for facts, so she will work with them in small group to develop these strategies. After these children have learned ways to more efficiently access basic facts, she will also move them into stations for learning basic facts.

All children in this class will also work at solving story problems types of stations. To meet the needs of individuals, this teacher will think about the numbers she provides at each story problem station. She will place different numeral cards in snack-size baggies at these stations with appropriate

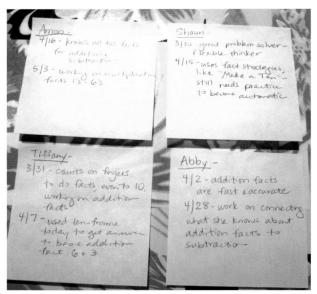

A teacher's anecdotal notes (left) help her make decisions about small groups for math (right).

numbers in each. A colored dot on the bag will indicate which group should work with these numbers. For example, children in the blue group will work with one-digit numeral cards or cubes. Most students will work with two-digit numbers, but three-digit numeral cards will be in a baggie marked with a yellow dot for the students who are ready to work with larger numbers.

Differentiated numeral cards are provided in ziplock bags labeled with colored dots at this addition station.

Ways to Keep Addition and Subtraction Stations Going Throughout the Year

Story problem stations are fairly easy to keep interesting throughout the year simply by changing out the scenario or settings students might work with. You might include some problems with bats and apples in the fall and switch to situations with flowers growing in a garden in the spring. But don't limit what students do here to the seasons. Many scenarios will be interesting to children all year long. Build these problems based on student interests, and ask them for their ideas. Whenever possible, have students help create problems to solve.

Basic facts stations can change as students' facility with these increases. As children learn basic addition facts, help them connect what they know to related subtraction facts. Likewise, some second graders will master addition and subtraction facts and be ready to learn multiplication facts. A wide variety of basic facts stations should be included, so you can change things periodically to keep student interest high. Novelty breeds student engagement, as long as the tasks provided offer just a bit of challenge.

As you observe your students throughout the year, you'll see when they are ready to work with bigger and bigger numbers. Build upon what they know and help them move to higher levels of problem solving as they show readiness. Keep notes, as shown in this section.

How to Assess/Keep Kids Accountable at Addition and Subtraction Stations

In order to meet students' needs, you'll want to watch how they're solving problems and have them tell you about their thinking. Don't just look at their answers. Ask them to tell you how they "know" a fact, just as you might ask them how they "know" a word when they're reading. When observing your students, consider and record notes about the following:

- When adding and subtracting with objects, which students count *all* the items, one at a time? Which students count on? Which students count by groups of ten?
- What strategies do children use for addition and subtraction facts? Which students count one at a time on their fingers? Who counts on? Who makes a ten or uses doubles? Who pulls out fives to make a ten? Who connects addition to subtraction facts known? Are children becoming more efficient when adding and subtracting?
- Which children are decomposing and recombining numbers easily? What strategies are students inventing when adding and subtracting two- and three- digit numbers? Do they compute from left to right or from right to left?
- What strategies do students use for mental computation? Which children make reasonable estimates?

During sharing time after math stations time, ask students to share story problems they told, acted out, and/or wrote. Invite them to show and tell the class about the strategies they used to solve their problems or figure out facts. Examine written work students do, too. Look at their drawings, representations, and written explanations about their thinking. You might refer to the book *Show and Tell: Representing and Communicating Mathematical Ideas in K–2 Classrooms* by Linda Dacey and Rebeka Eston (2002) for more ideas.

Have children share what is helping them learn the most at addition and subtraction stations. Ask them which stations they enjoy the most and why. Children learn best when there is a bit of challenge and they are experiencing success.

Kindergarten Considerations

Because of the distinct needs of young children, here are some things to think about if you are a kindergarten teacher:

- Provide your kindergartners with many opportunities for solving story problems that use their names and are related to things in their world. Young children love stories and will readily engage in this kind of work. Keep the numbers small enough for students to work with easily.
- Focus much of your work around the "friendly" numbers 5 and 10. Use five-frames to help children learn combinations to 5. They will enjoy station activities like Five-Frame Fun (see page 75). Build to ten-frames if children become fluent with five-frames, helping them think about 6, 7, 8, and 9; and 5 + 1, 5 + 2, 5 + 3, 5 + 4; and also 4, 3, 2, and 1 less than 10.
- Do lots of part-part-whole work with young children to develop thinking that will later lead to learning related addition and subtraction facts.

■ Focus on developing beginning number concepts in kindergarten before teaching addition and subtraction facts. Many times, parents might "teach" their children facts at home. But often these students have only memorized numbers such as 2 + 2 = 4 without really understanding what this means conceptually.

■ Do not teach children the simplistic idea that addition is put together and subtraction is take away. This is too narrow a focus for these operations.

■ Likewise, don't teach students to look for key words like *more* and tell them it means to subtract. This can be misleading. In the story problem that follows, students could use addition to solve it:

> *Rhea had 3 crayons. She wanted 2 more. How many crayons will Rhea have if she gets these from William?*

■ Use the language, _____ *and* _____ *is the same amount as* _____ for a long time with children to develop conceptual understanding before introducing the abstract symbols _____ + _____ = _____.

■ In a similar fashion, use *take away, take apart*, and comparing language to help young children develop conceptual understanding for different uses of subtraction. Later, _____ – _____ = _____ can be used to represent a variety of subtraction situations.

Reflection and Dialogue

1. What are you teaching your students to do in addition and subtraction? How does it match with the key math concepts in this chapter (see page 104) and your state standards? As you look across grade-level expectations, are there any prerequisite skills that some or all of your students need? Also, what foundations are you providing for the next grade level?

2. Which of your current math stations help students work with story problems? Basic facts? Adding and/or subtracting bigger numbers?

3. Which ideas from this chapter would you like to try? Why? What would benefit most of your class? What might you try with just a few students based upon their needs? Think about your more advanced children as well as those who need additional support.

4. What kinds of story problems have your students been working with (join, separate, compare, etc.)? Which types of problems do they solve easily? What other kinds of problems do they need exposure to? How will you provide these opportunities?

5. What strategies do your children use for addition facts? Subtraction facts? How can you help them become more efficient in solving and remembering basic facts?

6. How can you systematically focus on one category of facts at a time with children, building toward fluency with all facts over time? Take notes on your class, as pictured in this chapter. You might make a grouping chart as shown on page 130 to think about who needs what.

7. Who is ready to work with bigger numbers for addition and subtraction? What ideas from this chapter will you try in this area?

8. Listen to your students talk at math stations. What math language do you hear? How might you support students' conversations at stations using math talk cards like those highlighted in this chapter?

6

Place Value Work Stations

To connect math to the real world, second-grade students in one class I visited work with numbers on the calendar daily and talk about the number of days they have been in school. Starting on the first day of school, they gather in the whole-group teaching area near the calendar math bulletin board and work together to record on a large dry erase board the number of the day of school in tens and ones (and eventually hundreds), using words, numbers, and strips of ten and leftover ones to help them learn about place value.

Also as part of the daily calendar routine, the teacher in this second-grade class leads an engaging, thought-provoking discussion about the number of the day and then has volunteers take turns recording information about that number with input from the class. For example, while one child represents this number with paper coins, the teacher asks the rest of the class, "Are there other coins we could use to represent today's number? Talk with a partner about your ideas." Then she has two students share their thinking. Next, another student makes tally marks to show the number of the day. While this child is at the board, the rest of the class makes the tally marks in the air to keep them involved. Then the teacher asks, "How many more tally marks do we need to reach our next group of ten? To reach 100?"

Following this, a volunteer draws a square and writes the number of the day in the center. Then he adds a square to each side and, with suggestions from the class in unison, he records the numbers that represent one more, one less, ten more, and ten less in these squares, ending by outlining the corresponding configuration on a hundreds chart to check the answers. (See Figure 6.1 for a sample.) Finally, the teacher asks a more advanced student to create an addition pattern that increases by the number of the day (19, 38, 57, . . .). The class shows thumbs up or down to agree or disagree with each number as it is recorded, and the teacher calls on individuals to substantiate their thinking.

In years past, to summarize and review this information, the teacher in this classroom also had each student make a page daily for an individual "100 Day Book," but it consumed a great deal of instructional time.

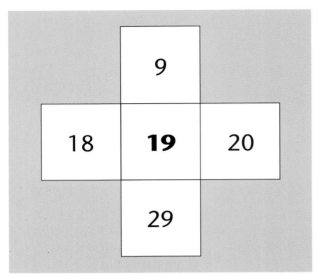

Figure 6.1 A student records the number of the day of school in the center and writes numbers that are one less, one more, ten less, and ten more in the surrounding squares, using a hundreds chart as a reference.

This year, she has decided to move the creation of "Our 100 Day Book" to a math station. Pairs of students work together on a page in a notebook, making a permanent record for the whole class to enjoy throughout the year. To be sure students can work independently and develop deeper understanding of place value and other mathematical concepts, the teacher models this activity daily at the start of the year and thinks aloud with the class as she models. In whole group, she and the class create an "I Can" list of what to do at this station, and then she tapes it inside the lid of one of the math station containers with all the supplies students will need (one spiral notebook, two pencils, a glue stick, paper copies of coins and paper copies of ten-trains, a hundreds chart, and connecting cubes for support as needed).

This second-grade teacher continues to teach about place value in many ways throughout the year and adds other math stations where students explore base ten concepts. Early in the year, she leads investigations with the whole class using pre-made ten-trains and individual connecting cubes. Children work with partners. Each chooses a two-digit number, builds it with cubes on a place value

A page from "Our Class 100 Day Book," which was created in a spiral notebook at a place value station on the nineteenth day of school.

Math (100 Day Book)

I Can......

- Find the next page to work on.
- Check the previous page to see if it is finished.
- Use the materials correctly.
  1. Glue the recording sheet on the page.
  2. Glue on the 10's and draw the 1's.
  3. Glue on the money.
  4. Create a number pattern.
  5. Write the tally marks.
  6. Put your names at the top of the page.
  7. Read the 100 Day Book.

An "I Can" list of what to do at the "100 Day Book" station. This was made *with* a second-grade class and is used to help them work independently.

Students count cubes as they work with groups of ten and leftover ones to play a place value game from their core program.

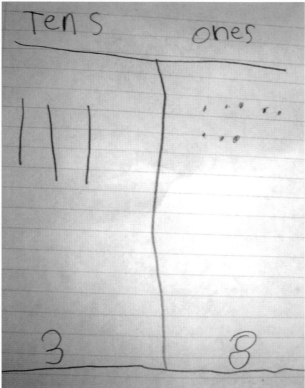

Second graders work in pairs investigating two-digit numbers. They use ten-trains and individual cubes to build, represent, and compare their numbers.

mat, and represents it with a picture. Then they compare their numbers, talking about groups of ten and leftovers. Ben says, "I have 38. That's 3 groups of ten and 8 leftover ones."

Jeremiah states, "And I have 26. That's 2 groups of ten and 6 leftovers. Your number is larger, because 3 groups of ten is more than 2 groups of ten."

Ben ends with, "Yeah, 38 is greater than 26."

This kind of work builds children's flexible, fluid understanding of groups of ten and leftover ones for regrouping and conservation, and creates a foundation for the work they will do with place value stations in the coming weeks. For example, at one station (which is duplicated so two pairs of students are doing the same activity in different parts of the room), there is a place value game from the math core program that the teacher modeled in whole group. Everyone played it together with partners in whole group before it was moved to stations.

At another station, two students are solving problems related to place value. They take turns choosing a card with a problem on it and work together to try strategies to solve it. For example, one card says *I have 5 tens and 14 ones. What number am I?* Their teacher observes for a few minutes as they work, so she can note what they understand about place value. The children use a place value mat for tens and ones, premade ten-trains using Unifix cubes and individual Unifix cubes. Alejandra places 5 ten-trains on the tens side of the place value mat, saying, "This is 5 tens." As she points to each stick, she counts, "Ten, 20, 30, 40, 50." Then Miles places 14 individual yellow cubes on the ones side, rather than using a ten-train and 4 more. Together, they touch each cube and count to see how many there are in all by saying, "Ten, 20, 30, 40, 50, 51, 52, 53, [and counting by ones] . . . 64."

As the teacher observes them at work, she notes that although they got the correct answer, they are not using the most efficient way to solve the problem. So she asks, "Can you think of another way to solve this problem?"

They shake their heads and say, "No." The teacher glances at the clock and realizes it is time to go to P.E. Using what she's just seen, combined with previous observations from whole-group instruction, she decides to work with these two students tomorrow in a small-group setting. Her goal will be to help them understand that they can group objects into sets of ten and leftovers instead of relying on just counting by ones. She will teach them a "trading game" or "collecting tens game" to give them the experience of putting together a ten-train of Unifix cubes (or placing ten beans in a paper cup, or trading ten pennies for a dime). Once they demonstrate understanding of this concept, she will set up the same kind of game for them to use independently during math work stations.

The children in this second-grade classroom have been working with place value concepts since kindergarten. Most know how to read, write, count, and build numbers to 100. But as the numbers get bigger, counting by ones (which many of them have done in previous grades) gets harder to keep track of. So they are now learning more efficient ways of counting by groups. With the aid of concrete and visual models, children who have a deep understanding of the *value* of each digit, rather than just naming what *place* it is in, will have an easier time grasping how to add and subtract two-digit numbers in first and second grade.

Key Math Concepts to Teach for Place Value

Undoubtedly, your school system or core curriculum will outline the place value concepts you should teach at your grade level. Use these guidelines when planning for place value stations. Talk with your teammates about ideas for teaching place value and stations that might grow out of your instruction. Share resources with each other for place value games or investigations students might use at math stations. Here are some key concepts to help you think about what you might be teaching (and what students might work with at place value stations):

In kindergarten, children will . . .

- Count by ones and be exposed to patterns in the numbers 1 to 100.
- Group and count by tens to 50 or more.
- Read, write, and understand numbers from 1 to 20, especially understanding teen numbers as one group of ten and 0 to 9 extra ones.

In first grade, children will also . . .

- Describe, compare, and order numbers to 100 using sets of concrete objects and pictures to represent those numbers in hundreds, tens, and ones.
- Count by ones to 100 fluently and accurately.
- Count by groups (twos, fives, tens) to 100.
- Use "broken counting," shifting from counting the groups to counting the leftovers (e.g., 5, 10, *15*, 16, 17 when counting the value of 3 nickels and 2 pennies or 17 minutes past the hour on an analog clock).
- Count by tens off the decade (14, 24, 34, 44, 54, . . .).

Basic Place Value Vocabulary (Kindergarten)

- more
- less
- greater
- fewer
- same as
- equal
- (number words from *one* to *ten*)
- groups of ten
- extra or leftover ones

Taking It Further (Grades 1–2)

- hundreds
- place value
- compare
- numeral
- least
- greatest
- more than
- less than
- between
- digit
- compose
- decompose
- value
- standard notation
- expanded notation
- (number words from *eleven* to *one hundred*)
- round

In second grade, children will also . . .

- Count by adding 10 or 100 to any three-digit number.
- Put together and take apart two-digit numbers (and by the end of the year, three-digit numbers) in a wide variety of ways, finding and using equivalent representations (such as 46 can be shown as 46 ones, as 4 tens and 6 ones, or as 3 tens and 16 ones; 325 can be shown as 3 hundreds + 2 tens + 5 ones or as 300 + 20 + 5).
- Develop understanding of place value as they solve addition and subtraction problems with two-digit numbers in flexible ways.
- Describe, compare, and order numbers to 999 using sets of concrete objects and pictures to represent those numbers in hundreds, tens, and ones.

What the Children Do at Place Value Stations

Let's first look at the kind of work students do at place value stations, so we can begin with the end

in mind. Your whole-group modeling and instruction about place value will lead to the math stations children will eventually use. Later in this chapter, you will find a materials list and suggestions of what you might model first in whole-group instruction.

When children are working at place value stations, they should be talking about their thinking and how they are representing numbers in a variety of ways. As you teach students about place value, be sure to model and support children in using *math talk* about hundreds, tens, ones, more than, less than, and so on. (See the preceding vocabulary list.) One reason to use manipulatives, such as ten-frames and counters or base ten blocks, is to give children something to talk about. The more we use the manipulatives to help kids use everyday language to describe the groupings of ten, to talk about adding ten and taking away ten, and counting up by groups of tens and then ones, the more children can gain ways to think about numbers flexibly and to develop deep understanding of the base ten system. Be sure to talk about *groups* of ten, *bundles* of ten, *cups* of ten, and *leftovers* or *extra ones*. These terms are more explicit for young children than simply using the words *tens and ones*.

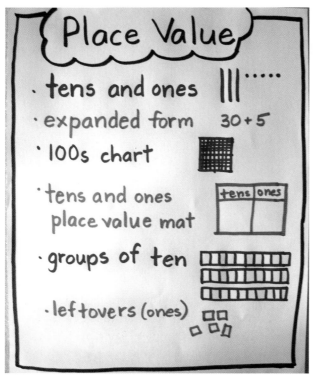

Place Value
- tens and ones |||•••••
- expanded form   30+5
- 100s chart
- tens and ones
  place value mat | tens | ones |
- groups of ten
- leftovers (ones)

This anchor chart with math vocabulary for place value was made with the class and is referred to during instruction as well as math work stations.

If your curriculum includes independent choice time activities for place value, use some of those activities in stations along with station ideas from this chapter. Most likely, some of them will be similar. You may also find place value lessons from your core program that can be moved into activities at place value stations. Look for partner games (especially collect and count, collect and regroup, and trading games) from your core curriculum or materials you received from trainings you've attended. Consult resources such as *Every Day Counts Partner Games, Grade K, Grade 1,* and *Grade 2* (Gillespie and Kanter 2005a, 2005b, 2005c) and *Developing Number Concepts Using Unifix Cubes* (Richardson 1984) for ideas that can be adapted to use at stations. The following are some independent stations ideas you may want your children to try. (Remember that you might duplicate any of these so that several pairs of students are working on the same activity in different parts of the classroom.) This is just a sampling of what students might do at place value math stations:

- **Teen Match Up.** Provide ten sandwich-size ziplock bags with ten to nineteen counters in each, paper cups for organizing groups of ten, and numeral cards from 10 to 19. Children put the numerals on the table in order. Then they group and count each collection, saying "One group of ten and _____ extra ones." Finally, they match the collection to the numeral card.

  A variation is to have children make their own teen counting books by writing numbers from 10 to 19, one number per page. Students draw the matching number of objects on each page, showing the group of ten and extra ones.

In Teen Match Up, partners work together to line up digit cards from 10 to 19. Then they count the small objects in each ziplock bag, placing a group of ten in a cup and leftovers outside the cup, as shown. They match each group of objects to a teen number.

- **Estimate and count collections.** Have available eight sandwich-size ziplock bags containing various collections of 10 to 40 counters (such as buttons, pennies, pebbles, paper clips, cotton balls, dried beans, pasta bowties, shells, or little plastic animals from a dollar store). Each bag is labeled with the name and picture of the collection. Partners take turns choosing a bag. Each

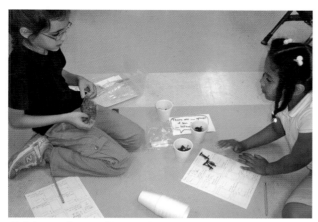

Children take a collection from a ziplock bag, estimate how many items (police) there are, and record their estimate. Then they work together to place the little objects in groups of 10 in cups. Leftovers are placed on the floor. They use a math talk card for support and record the actual number.

Each child takes a handful of what's in the plastic container (macaroni, in this picture). They each place their items in cups of ten and a leftovers pile on a place value mat and compare to see who has the most.

partner records the name of the bag and a guess of the total. Then they help each other organize the contents of the bag into ten-cups and left-overs. Finally, they use the sentence frame on a math talk card *(There are _____ groups of ten and _____ leftover ones.)* to describe and record the number of objects in the collection. You'll find a recording sheet on page 254 of the appendix. Children could also put the bags in order from least to greatest (or greatest to least) number of objects if time allows.

- **Have counting contests.** Each child takes one (or two) handful(s) from a container of small objects (use buttons, cotton balls, beans, beads, pennies, plastic counters, or pebbles in each lidded clear plastic container). Have several containers for students to choose from. You'll want children to work with numbers from 20 to 99 here.

Each child uses a place value mat to organize his or her handful of objects into groups of ten on the left side (using cups for each group of ten), places any leftovers on the right side, and records the total on the mat using a dry erase marker. Then the partners take turns stat-

ing their totals using the sentence frame written on a sentence strip or an index card to encourage use of this math language: *I have _____ groups of ten and _____ extra ones, which equals _____.* Children then compare to see who got more and state the comparison using a second sentence frame card: *_____ is greater than _____.* They record their results on a counting contest sheet, found on page 255 of the appendix.

Repeat to give practice with counting and grouping by tens and leftovers. To vary the activity, ask children to estimate before counting and compare their answers to their estimates.

- **Build a number (from 11 to 99).** Ask each child to write a favorite number from 11 to 99 on an index card and secure the cards together with a rubber band for use at this station. Have partners each choose a number card. Then have them work together with those two numbers using base ten blocks and place value mats to do any of the following (cards with these tasks and a recording sheet can be found on pages 256 and 257 in the appendix):

  □ Build each number using only groups of ten and leftover ones. Draw a picture showing your work. Record the number

Students use task cards on a ring for directions. Here, they choose a number, build it with base ten materials, and record their work with a drawing and expanded notation.

using expanded notation (e.g., *39 = 3 tens and 9 ones*).

☐ Build the largest number. Build the smallest number. Compare the numbers using the terms *greater than* and *less than*. Write a number sentence to go with your pictures using > and <.

☐ Build and record the number that is 10 larger than your number. Build and record a number that is 10 less.

☐ Find the difference between the two numbers. You might place the base ten blocks on top of each other and see what is left uncovered. Or use the class counting tape or hundreds chart to find the difference.

Use the same activity to have children build a number from 100 to 999. Provide cards with bigger numbers on them and adjust the task cards in the preceding list to accommodate hundreds, tens, and ones. Include numbers in the range your students need practice with. Limit the number of cards, so it doesn't overwhelm you or your students.

■ ***Compare numbers from 20 to 99.*** Students take two numbered dice (numerals 1 to 6 or 4 to 9) and roll them to create a two-digit number. For example, if they roll a 3 and a 4, they

could write *34* or *43*. Then students build both of those numbers with connecting cubes (using ten-trains and individual cubes) and a place value mat. Ask them to compare the two numbers and tell which is greater, how many more, and how they know that. They can put the models beside each other to compare. Have them record their thinking in a book you keep at this station and title "See How We Find the Difference." Simply make copies of the reproducible sheet on page 258 of the appendix and staple the copies together to make a book to keep at this station. Children can read the work that their classmates did as well.

Children can also play games like Who Has More? or "Who Has Less? similar to Battle, where each takes a number card (from 20 to 99) from a deck and tells how many groups of ten and leftover ones that card's number has. Whoever has more (or less) for that hand wins and takes both cards. The player with the most cards at the end wins.

■ ***Read commercial and class-made books about 100.*** Celebrating the 100th day of school has become a big part of K–2 math classroom teaching. You will most likely develop the concept of 100 as part of your calendar routine. You might also read aloud books about the 100th day of school that children can reread at a math station.

Often schools have students bring collections of 100 objects (not to be returned) from home. If you ask them to organize their collections in groups of 10, you might take photos of these collections and make them into a book for children to read.

Or you might give small groups of children a large sheet of paper and 100 small objects to organize by twos, fives, or tens. Have the class take a "guided tour" to see all the collections and check the totals. This experience could also be photographed and turned into a class-made book.

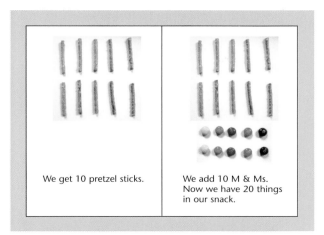

Pages from a class-made "100th Day Snack Book" show groups of ten.

These puzzles are made with cut-up hundreds charts.

As a class, you might also make a "100th Day Snack" big book for students to read over and over again. Create a simple recipe in this book, listing the ingredients on each page. Take pictures of the ingredients grouped by tens, showing what's been added to the snack, as pictured. For example:

Page 1: We will make a 100 Day Snack.

Page 2: We get 10 pretzel sticks.

Page 3: We add 10 M&Ms. Now we have 20 things in our snack.

Page 4: We add 10 Cheerios. Now we have 30 things in our snack.

Continue in this way to 100. Students will love to read and follow this recipe to make a 100th day snack as a class; likewise, they will like rereading this book and will practice looking at groups of 10 as they count to 100.

■ *Use hundreds chart puzzles* (adapted from *Math Every Day* [Gillespie and Kanter 1996]). You'll need a blank hundreds chart and one with the numbers on it for checking. Make copies of the chart with numbers on it. You might copy them onto different colored cardstock to create a variety of puzzles. Then, cut apart several copies of the hundreds chart in different ways. Start with easier puzzles (a hundreds chart cut into vertical or horizontal

strips). Make some with bigger chunks, too. Students put the numbered pieces on the blank hundreds chart to solve where numbers belong. You can also make puzzles using pieces from a two-hundreds chart to have children work with larger numbers.

■ *Play Collect and Count to 100 games* like those in *Every Day Counts Partner Games, Grade 2* (Gillespie and Kanter 2005c). To play, each of two students gets a place value mat and 100 connecting cubes of one color. (Each student can use a different color of cubes.) Students take turns rolling the dice (one or two dice, depending on the children's needs). One child rolls the dice and counts out that many cubes and places them on the place value mat. When the child reaches any quantity over ten, he or she must join ten cubes together and put this ten-train on the tens side.

At the end of each turn, have the child state how many groups of ten and extra ones have been collected in all. For example, on the first turn William says, "I got 6 and 6, or 12. That's 1 group of ten and 2 leftover ones." He joins together 10 connecting cubes and places them on the tens side of the mat, and then puts 2 individual cubes on the ones side. Next, Melinda tosses the dice and counts out her cubes in the same way.

In Collect and Count, each partner takes turns rolling a numeral cube and adding that many connecting cubes to her place value mat, showing how many groups of ten and leftover ones she has. They play until one child has collected 100 (or 50) cubes.

On his next turn, William rolls a 5 and a 4 and says, "I got 9 more." As he places 9 more cubes on the place value mat, he makes another ten-train out of his cubes and says, "That's 2 groups of ten and 1 more, or 21 all together." Play continues until someone has placed 100 (or 50) cubes on his or her place value mat.

If you don't have enough cubes, substitute 20 small paper cups and a bag of 200 counters for the children to share. Now whenever the child has collected 10 or more on the ones side, 10 counters are placed into a cup on the tens side of the place value mat.

■ *Play trading games, such as Race to 100 (or 50).* For a more advanced version of the preceding games, substitute bean sticks (popsicle sticks with 10 beans glued or drawn on) and beans, base ten blocks, or dimes and pennies, all of which can be used for exchanging or trading in 10 ones for one object worth ten.

These trading games are played much like the Collect and Count to 100 games described in the preceding section, except they require

exchanging or trading in 10 ones for 1 object worth 10. Students play in pairs using materials such as bean sticks (popsicle sticks with 10 beans glued or drawn on) and individual beans, base ten blocks, or dimes and pennies. They roll dice and place counting materials on their place value mats, trying to be the first to get 100 (or 50). But in this game, when they've collected 10 beans, they trade for a bean stick. When they have 10 pennies, they trade for a dime, and so on.

Again, be sure students are naming their actions by talking about the materials they traded, as in this example using bean sticks: "I had 6 bean sticks and 5 extra ones, or 65. I rolled 6. So that gave me 11 beans. I traded 10 beans for a bean stick. Now I have 7 bean sticks and 1 extra one, or 71." You might provide a large index card with the following sentence frames on it as a language scaffold:

I had _____ bean sticks and _____ extra ones, or _____.

I rolled _____. So that gave me _____.

I traded _____ for _____.

Now I have _____ bean sticks and _____ extra ones, or _____.

A variation of this game is Race to Zero (described in *Every Day Counts Partner Games, Grade 2* (Gillespie and Kanter 2005c). Children begin with 100 and try to get to 0 first. Both children start with 10 ten-trains on the tens side of their place value mats. This time, Melinda goes first. She rolls a 5 and a 3 and needs to take away 8 cubes. With no loose cubes available, she removes a ten-train and breaks it apart into 10 cubes on the ones side. Then she removes 8 cubes and says, "I took away 8 ones. That leaves 2 cubes on the ones side. So now that's 9 groups of ten and 2 leftover ones, or 92." On her next turn, she rolls a total of 10 and removes another ten-train from the tens side, saying, "I had 92 and took away a group of 10, so now I have 8 groups of ten

Students trade 10 pennies for a dime as they play Race to 100 with dimes and pennies.

Two boys play Rounding Bingo with a hundreds chart and math talk card for support. They take turns recording the number they rolled with two cubes (the boy on the left is rolling numeral cubes) and rounding to the nearest ten, which is marked on the Bingo board with a sticky note. The first player to get three in a row wins.

and 2 extra ones, or 82." The partners take turns until one of them has 0.

For greater challenge, substitute bean sticks and loose beans, base ten blocks, or dimes and pennies. These materials require children to take the additional step of actually exchanging one object worth 10 for 10 ones (as opposed to simply spilling out a ten-cup or breaking apart a ten-train) when loose ones are needed. For an easier game in kindergarten, children can each fill 2 to 3 ten-frames with counters, take turns tossing a numbered cube (with numbers 1 to 6 on it), remove this number of counters from the last ten-frame, and tell how many are left in tens and ones, until one player has none.

■ **Play Rounding Bingo.** Provide two laminated blank Bingo boards (found on page 259 of the appendix). Each student fills in a board with the numbers 10, 20, 30, 40, 50, 60, 70, 80, and 90 in random order. Also provide two numeral cubes with numbers from 1 to 9 on them. Children take turns rolling the numeral cubes and using those to make a number. For example, if they roll a 2 and then a 5, that number is 25. Then that student rounds the number to the nearest ten and marks that

space on his or her Bingo board. To support students, include a math talk card that says: *My number is between _____ and _____. It's halfway or more to the next ten, so I round up to _____. It's less than halfway to the next ten, so I stay with _____.* (Have a hundreds chart available for them to use as a reference.) The student then records his or her roll and what he or she rounded it to on the recording sheet provided on page 260 of the appendix. Next, the other student takes a turn, rolling the cubes to make another number and repeating the procedure. Children continue taking turns until one of them has gotten three in a row on his or her Bingo board.

■ **Compare numbers from 100 to 999.** Adapt the ideas from "Compare numbers from 20 to 99" on page 140 by using three numeral cubes to create three-digit numbers. For example, if students roll a 5, 1, and 2, partners work together to find and write down all the possible numbers: 512, 521, 125, 152, 215, and 251. They then pick three of these numbers and "build" each on a separate piece of paper with base ten blocks, labeling each with the number they have built. Finally, they put their buildings (and numeral labels) in order from smallest to greatest, or do the reverse. A sheet to record their work can be found on page 258 of the appendix.

■ ***Play $999 Monopoly Money Challenge.*** For this game you'll need Monopoly money in one, ten, and hundred dollar bills. Use 15 one-hundred-dollar bills, 25 ten-dollar bills, and 50 one-dollar bills. Put the money in a brown paper bag. Each student reaches in the bag and removes three bills at a time. Then they each add up the amount they grabbed, and whoever has the most gets to keep both players' money.

For example, if Daniel grabs 3 one-dollar bills to start, he says, "I only got $3." Maria counts the money she grabbed (a one-hundred dollar bill and 2 ten-dollar bills) and says, "I have 1 hundred and 2 tens, or $120, so I win." She gets to keep all the money from that turn and tells how much she has in all: "I have 1 hundred, 2 tens and 3 ones, or $123." Each student keeps track of how much money he or she has collected by placing his or her dollar bills on a hundreds, tens, and ones mat, making exchanges whenever possible. Play contin-

ues in this manner until someone gets $999 or they use up all the money. In that case, whoever has the most money wins the game. Once the game ends, all money is returned to the bag and they can play again.

■ ***Add or subtract two-digit numbers using place value materials.*** Set up situations where children generate two numbers, with at least one of those numbers having two digits, that can be added or subtracted. Mix experiences with and without regrouping, so students really need to think about the process. See Chapter 5, "Addition and Subtraction Work Stations," for more ideas.

Materials

Concrete materials are essential to helping young children develop their understanding of place value. The concept of tens and ones is very abstract. Children may be able to write 3 in the tens column and 2 in the ones column and tell you the number is 32, but they may not *really* understand what that means. There are quite a few kinds of manipulatives to use to develop thinking about our base ten system.

The best materials are proportional and show that a model for ten is ten times bigger than the model for one. I recommend beginning to teach place value with materials that children can put together to show tens and ones (such as connecting cubes joined together to make ten-trains along with individual cubes). From there, you might have chil-

These girls take turns picking three Monopoly money bills from the paper bag. Whoever gets the biggest amount per turn wins and keeps his or her money. They place their money on the place value mat to think about how many hundreds, tens, and ones they have. The first player to get $999 wins.

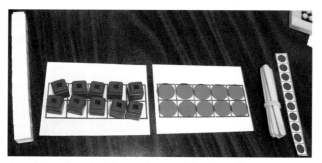

A variety of materials can be used to show ten.

dren work with bean sticks and individual beans and small paper cups into which children count groups of 10 beans. Popsicle sticks and rubber bands might also be used in making groups of ten and left-overs. Base ten blocks that involve an exchange are good for larger numbers once students really under-stand groups of ten. Listed below is a menu of options to use with your class:

- connecting cubes or Unifix cubes in one color
- counters (like beans) and cups
- popsicle sticks with 10 beans glued to each and individual beans
- popsicle sticks, coffee stirrers, or straws, and rubber bands to put them in groups of ten and leftovers
- base ten blocks (units, rods, and flats)
- ten-frames
- numeral cards from 1 to 100 (or 100 to 999)
- numeral cubes and dice
- bags of objects to count (beans, plastic coun-ters, cubes, teddy bear counters, etc.)
- chart of number words (to match the numbers your grade level needs to learn)
- place value mats (one kind showing tens and ones and another kind with hundreds, tens, and ones)
- hundreds charts
- pennies and dimes
- play paper money in denominations of one-, ten-, and hundred-dollar bills
- one-inch ceramic tiles (for measuring)
- bookmaking supplies (paper, stapler, markers, optional digital camera)

What the Teacher Needs to Model

Here are some things to model to help your stu-dents get the most from their time at place value stations:

How to read, write, count, and build numbers from 11 to 20. Some students have trouble with the teens, since these numbers have a different naming pattern from the twenties, thirties, and so on. Work with the teen numbers as part of calendar time. Teach children how to play games with numbers in the teens, including games from your core curricu-lum or from this book. Provide opportunities for students to find things in the teens during the day. For example, you might say: "Look on page 17—that's the same as one group of 10 and 7 leftovers—in your book" or "We'll need 13 boys to get in line. Count them with me. How many groups of ten [1 group of ten]? How many left over [3 left over]?"

One key to helping children better understand teen numbers is to emphasize that while we read the number 14 as "fourteen," when we write it we can say, "One group of ten and four more." This results in writing the 1 first and the 4 next, prevent-ing reversals, and reinforcing our base ten system. Then when they get to the twenties, they can use the same oral language pattern for writing the numeral. "I read 24 as 'twenty-four,' but when I write it, I say, 'Two groups of ten and 4 more.'"

How to read, write, build, represent, and compare numbers from 20 to 99 (and later, from 100 to 999). Begin to build this understand-ing during calendar time. Display a long piece of adding machine tape to create a counting tape in your calendar area (as used in the Every Day Counts series) and place a sticky note with the number of the day (how many days you've been in school) in the next space. Be sure to use sticky notes of one color for the first ten numbers and a different color for the second ten numbers to emphasize grouping and counting by tens and ones and place value. Also include a visual model of the days of school next to the counting tape to provide meaning. As you teach games like those mentioned in this section, remember to model the math lan-guage you want to hear while children are working independently at math stations. Your purpose is

The numeral 12 (to show how many days students have been in school) is added to the counting tape of the Every Day Counts bulletin board in a first-grade classroom.

twofold: teaching math games to reinforce place value concepts *and* building the math vocabulary you want your students to use on their own.

Play games with two-digit numbers, giving clues such as "I'm thinking of a number between 20 and 35. It is even. It is greater than 25. It is less than 30." Or remove several of the sticky notes from the counting tape and give them to individual children. Have them line up in front of the class and put themselves in numerical order. The class can help them as needed. Then have the students put the numbers back on the counting tape where they belong.

Another idea is for students to select numeral cards and then represent them by building models of those numbers. Children could use premade ten-trains and loose connecting cubes, bean sticks and beans, or bundles of straws or popsicle sticks and a place value mat with tens and ones. Demonstrate how to organize loose ones into groups of five on the *ones* side of the place value mat so students don't lose track of how many they have. Also teach them how to make picture representations of these numbers. Show them how to draw a stick to represent a group of ten and a dot to show a unit. Again, have them draw sticks and dots in groups of five.

After they successfully build two-digit numbers, you can move to having them compare two or more of these numeral cards. (Be sure each card has a different number of tens.) For example, you might choose the numbers 34 and 51. Have students work together in pairs to build each number on a different place value mat and compare their models using the words *greater than* and *less than*. Model and support children's talk about the numbers as they build and compare them, saying things like, "Thirty-four is 3 groups of ten and 4 extra

ones"; "Fifty-one is greater than 34 because there are more ten-sticks in 51. 51 has 5 ten-sticks and 34 only has 3 groups of ten." Over time, introduce the use of a recording sheet that says _____ *is greater than* _____ so students can keep track of their work and then share findings as a class. Eventually, they might determine the difference between the two numbers and record their findings in a class book called "See How We Find the Difference." (A reproducible for making this book can be found on page 261 of the appendix.)

Another adaptation of this activity would be to teach and then have all students play Who Has More? or Who Has Less? with partners using the numeral cards. In this adaptation, each student takes a numeral card and tells how many tens and ones he or she has. Whoever has the larger number (or smaller one, depending on the game) gets both cards. Again, model and encourage the use of math talk as they decide who has the greater or smaller number. To support math talk, include an index card that says _____ *has more groups of ten than* _____ on one side and _____ *has less groups of ten than* _____ on the other. Whoever has the most cards is the winner.

To teach about numbers from 100 to 999, adapt the preceding activities using these larger numbers. Teach students how to use base ten blocks, if you have them, for number building, along with place value mats with hundreds, tens, and ones spaces on them.

How to count large groups of objects (from 20 to 99, and, over time, from 100 to 999) in a variety of ways. Provide the students with opportunities to represent a quantity in a variety of ways without changing the value. For example, 28 could be represented with 28 ones, 2 tens and 8 ones, or 1 ten and 18 ones. We want children to develop flexibility with numbers; the purpose of having children work with the model of 1 ten and 18 ones is for them to experience the representation they will later see when regrouping. Help students use a variety of materials for counting, including connecting cubes, base ten blocks, and counters and counting cups. Provide place value mats for some activities to help children organize tens and ones. Also, make real-world connections to counting bigger numbers of objects and to using groups to make counting go faster.

After children understand 20 to 99, move to larger numbers from 100 to 999, having students show different ways to count—in ones, groups of ten and leftovers, and groups of hundreds, tens, and leftover ones.

You may also want to simply model and facilitate practice with rote counting from 20 to 99 or 100 to 999. Counting on and off the decade, forward and backward, such as 23, 33, 43, 53, 63, or 212, 222, 232, 242, or 94, 84, 74, 64, as well as recording and discussing the pattern, will add to students' place value foundation and provide background for later work with multidigit addition and subtraction.

How to estimate, measure (using nonstandard and standard units), inventory, and then collect data (related to counting larger numbers). As a class, think of things to measure or count. For example, how many cubes tall are the children in your classroom? Have students make estimates and discuss what it means to be *reasonable*. Then have children measure each other with connecting cubes, working in pairs or groups of four (depending on how many cubes you have). After they have joined cubes together to show height, have them break the cubes into groups of ten and leftovers. Then record their findings on a class graph and compare the numbers. Note: If students work in groups of four, assign a job to each student to make this activity more manageable: (1) child to be measured; (2) child who measures; (3) student who counts; (4) student who records.) Repeat this activity with several large things to measure in and around your classroom. In addition to cubes, inch tiles may be used to help children transition to the standard ruler, yardstick, or measuring tape.

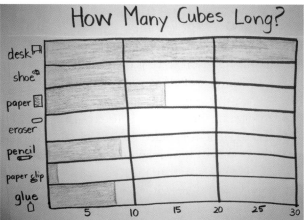

After learning to measure one another with connecting cubes in whole group, students at a math station measure objects around the room in the same way and record their results. Over time, they can graph their findings. This graph was made as a model with the class.

How to use a hundreds chart. Teach children how to count on a hundreds chart. This is often done as part of calendar routines in first and second grade. Teach children to skip-count by twos, fives, and especially tens to support place value understanding. Help children notice patterns using a

A student shares his thinking about number patterns using a hundreds chart displayed on an interactive whiteboard during whole-group instruction.

A teacher uses an interactive whiteboard to model for the whole class how to play a game.

hundreds chart. Also, teach the class to count by tens off the decade, such as 45, 55, 65, 75, 85, 95, using the hundreds chart.

How to play place value games, such as Race to 50, Race to 100, and Race to Zero. Be sure to model games that you want partners to play at stations. Start in whole group, modeling how to play the game with a projection device, such as an overhead projector or document camera, if you have one. Or have students sit in a circle while you show them how to play, with a student as your partner. If you model with a student partner, you each need a place value mat and counting cubes of one color. (You can each have your own color of cubes, if you'd like.)

Take turns rolling the dice and counting out that number of connecting cubes. Place your first cubes on the *ones* side of a place value mat. When you have ten cubes, make a show of connecting them to make a ten-train and tell children explicitly what you are doing. Then move that group of cubes to the *tens* side of the place value mat. Tell them, "I have 10 cubes. I'm putting them in a group of 10 by connecting them and moving them to the *tens* side to show a group of 10." Take turns rolling and placing that number of cubes on your mat, moving

groups of 10 to the *tens* side of the mat whenever you have a collection of 10 individual cubes on the *ones* side. The first player to get to 50 or more is the winner.

After you've shown students how to play the game with a partner, pair them up, place each pair in their own spot in the room, and hand out a place value mat and connecting cubes to each student. (If you don't have enough cubes, you might use popsicle sticks that you rubber-band together when you get ten, or counters and paper cups for organizing groups of ten. If you do so, be sure you model with those materials instead of the cubes. At a later date, you can play the same game with base ten blocks and use larger numbers.

Teach simple games like this that can be easily duplicated, and have the whole class play with partners while you observe their thinking. Then move the game to a station for additional practice.

How to trade a ten-train for 10 ones (or make groups of 10 popsicle sticks). Some children will have trouble with the concept of exchanging 10 objects for 1 object, as in the case of 10 pennies for a dime or 10 units for 1 ten-rod when using base ten blocks. Be patient. You might begin with connecting cubes that can be snapped together and used in a game like the one in the preceding description. Be explicit as you put 10 cubes together, saying, "Now I have 10 cubes, so I'll snap them together to show *1* group of 10 or *1* ten-train." Then ask, "How many groups of 10 are here?" (1) Next, unsnap the cubes and count them with the children, saying, "When I unsnap them, how many are there?" (10). Confirm their responses: "There are still 10 cubes."

Use a similar process and similar language with your students if you are using popsicle sticks. As you bundle 10 sticks together, say, "Now I have 10 sticks, so I can put them together in *1* group with this rubber band around them. I have *1* group of 10 sticks." Then remove the rubber band and ask students how many sticks you have in your hand. Count the sticks together and say, "There are still 10 sticks here." Over time, move to manipulatives like bean sticks made with popsicle sticks and beans or base ten blocks, and show them how to trade 10 loose ones for 1 bean stick or 1 ten-rod in a similar way. This is an essential understanding for being able to trade 10 pennies for a dime or a dime for 10 pennies when working with money, as well as for learning traditional addition and subtraction with regrouping algorithms later.

How to add and subtract two-digit numbers in flexible ways. Begin by having students build numbers with concrete objects, such as connecting cubes, bundled popsicle sticks, and, over time, base ten blocks. Choose two numbers to add together. (You might use numeral cards or cubes to generate the numbers.) Have children build the numbers on a place value mat, with spaces for hundreds, tens, and ones to show their thinking. Teach them how to record what they did using pictures, numbers, and words.

In first grade, start with numbers on the decade (e.g., 20, 30, or 40) combined with a number from 0 to 9. Then move to numbers off the decade, such as 26, 33, or 47, combined with a single-digit number. From there, combine 2 two-digit numbers, starting with two on-decade numbers, such as 30 + 50, so students can combine groups of 10 to solve these

problems. Then move to on-decade and off-decade combinations, like 30 + 27, followed by off-decade and on-decade numbers (27 + 30), so they can count by tens. For example, to solve 25 + 20, students will probably count *25, 35, 45,* if using a hundreds chart. In contrast, you'll find that when they put 25 cubes and 20 more cubes on place value mats, most children will add up all the tens first and then count the ones. This translates into a powerful mental math strategy that some call "front end addition." Acknowledge and validate the various strategies children have for putting together numbers and taking them apart.

Finally, teach children to add together two off-decade numbers and invite them to share their different strategies. Some may add the tens first and then add up all the ones to the total number of tens. Some may begin with one of the two numbers and count up by tens and then ones. Others may look first to see if they have enough ones to form a group of 10 and then add the tens, including the newly regrouped ten. This leads to a common U.S. textbook algorithm.

After children show these types of understandings, proceed in a similar way with subtraction. You may be surprised at the different ways first and second graders choose to find the difference between two numbers less than 99 when using the counting tape, hundreds chart, and base ten materials. Some counting up strategies will be more efficient than using the regrouping algorithm. (See Chapter 5, "Addition and Subtraction Work Stations," for more ideas.)

Connections to Problem Solving

Having children solve problems related to place value will help them understand how to apply these ideas in real-world situations. Place value is abstract, but children must understand it so addition and subtraction with larger numbers doesn't become overwhelming. Understanding place value will also build a foundation for working with decimals in upper grades.

Try solving problems as a whole class to engage everyone in the process and to have children learn from and with each other. Ask individuals to share different ways they solved a problem to encourage flexible thinking. You might make up problems with numbers from 20 to 99 and use students' names from the class, as in the following examples:

Together Karla and Jonathan have 35 presents. However, they do not have the same number. How many presents might each have?

There are 23 children in our class. Some children are absent and today's attendance is only 19. How many students are not here today?

Sharif lost 6 of his baseball cards and now has 47. How many did he have at first?

For solving problems like these, have children work with manipulatives and show what they tried in words, pictures, and numbers. The emphasis here is not on using the standard algorithm, but in having students use manipulatives or pictures to show how they solved the problem.

Students may be able to tell you there are 6 hundreds, 5 tens, and 3 ones in the number 653 by writing those numbers on a place value chart, but many don't understand what 6 hundreds and 5 tens and 3 ones really mean. Design problems to help their thinking go deeper than the surface level of naming hundreds, tens, and ones. Here are a few problems related to place value to use with your students at math stations (you might set up some of these in or near your classroom math corner):

- **Play What's My Number?** One child chooses a number from 20 to 99 and writes it on a slip of paper. The other child asks yes/no questions to figure out the number and crosses

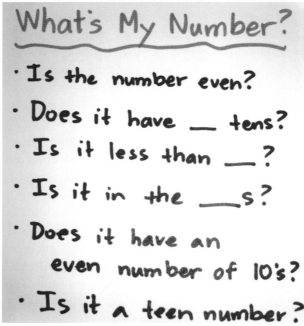

Using a clue card for What's My Number? partners work together. Child 1 asks, "Is it even?" Child 2 responds, "No." Child 1 then marks out all even numbers on the laminated hundreds chart with a dry erase marker.

out guesses on a laminated hundreds chart to keep track. Sample yes/no question stems could be written on a class-made chart for support. These question stems must be used prior to students making a guess and might include: *Is the number even? Is the number greater than _____? Is the number a teen number?* Limit the number of guesses for the number to keep students from just asking "Is it 28?" "Is it 17?" and so on.

If the number 16 has been picked, the game might go like this:

Is the number even? (Yes.)
Does it have 3 tens? (No.)
Is it less than 50? (Yes.)
Is it in the twenties? (No.)
Is it 46? (No.)
Does it have an even number of tens? (No.)
Is it a teen number? (Yes.)
Is it less than 15? (No.)
Is it greater than 17? (No.)
Is it 16? (Yes.)

To make the game easier, simply have children ask the questions *Is it greater than _____?* or *Is it less than _____?* As students show understanding of numbers from 20 to 99, expand to larger numbers, including those from 100 to 999.

■ *Create and solve word problems using bigger numbers.* With the class, brainstorm key words for problems, such as *stones*, *pencils*, *stickers*, *collected*, and *fewer*, and write each on an index card. Include a chart with students' names on it. Students work in pairs creating and solving their own word problems using numbers from 20 to 99. They record their work in pictures, words, and numbers. For example, a pair of students might develop this problem: *Johanna collected 36 stones at the park. Marcus looked for stones, too, but he found 13 fewer than Johanna. How many stones did Marcus find?*

To provide more support, you could brainstorm sample problems with color-coded blanks for children to fill in numbers and students' names:

_____ collected _____
_____. _____ found _____
fewer than _____. How
many did _____ find?

Teach students that the red and green blanks are for children's names, the short black lines

are for numbers, and the blue lines are for objects.

■ *Write a response.* In a math journal or on a recording sheet, have children answer questions like these:

☐ Which number is greater, 45 or 54? Explain how you know. Use objects, pictures, or words.

☐ What is a number that could come between 74 and 96? How does understanding place value help you solve this problem?

☐ Toss a numbered cube [from 0 to 9] three times and write down each number. Create as many numbers as possible from these digits and organize them.

■ *Use partner games like Should I Take Tens or Ones?* (adapted from *Every Day Counts Partner Games, Grade 2* [Gillespie and Kanter 2005c]). Each partner has exactly six tries to get as close to 100 as possible without going over. With each roll of a number cube (from 1 to 6), the partner determines whether to take the amount shown on the cube in tens or ones. For example, if a player rolls a 5, he or she would say, "Should I take 5 tens or 5 ones?" Each turn is recorded and the child keeps track of his or her total with tens and ones materials. The winner is the player closest to 100 after six turns.

To vary the game, students can use coins to get to $1 or paper money to try to get to $100. They could also play the game with the goal of getting as close as possible to 1,000.

■ *Solve problems with a hundreds chart.* Give students problems to solve using a hundreds chart. They might use crayons to color in paper charts. Or they could use clear plastic counters on a laminated chart. Here are some problems to get students started:

☐ Find numbers with 7 [or 3 or 9] in them. What pattern do you notice?

☐ Skip-count by twos (or fives or tens). What pattern do you notice?

A number pattern is colored in on this hundreds chart. This child said, pointing to the first column, "I see a pattern. All these have a 1 at the end, so I colored them green: 1, 11, 21, 31, et cetera." Pointing to another column, she said, "These all have a 5 at the end: 5, 15, 25, 35 . . . so I colored them purple."

☐ Think of a number pattern. Show your pattern by coloring in all the numbers that fit your pattern. Show your partner and have your partner figure out what is the same about all those numbers.

Hundred Number Board

1	2	3	4	5	6	7	8	9	10
11		13	14	15	16	17	18	19	20
21	22	23	24	25	26		28	29	30
31	32	33	34	35	36	37	38	39	40
41	42	43		45	46	47	48		50
51	52	53	54	55	56	57	58	59	60
61	62	63	64	65	66	67	68	69	70
71	72	73	74	75	76		78	79	80
81	82		84	85	86	87	88	89	90
91	92	93	94	95	96	97	98	99	100

One child covered up some numbers on this hundreds chart with small sticky notes, as shown. The other child writes the hidden numbers on a dry erase board. Then they lift up the sticky notes to check.

☐ Find the missing numbers. One partner covers several numbers on the hundreds chart with small sticky notes. The other student writes the hidden number on each sticky note. Then they check together, using the hundreds chart. Next, they put the sticky notes in order from least to greatest and/or from greatest to least and figure out the difference between two of the numbers.

☐ Add two-digit numbers using the hundreds chart. Have children choose 2 two-digit numeral cards. They work together to mark the first number with a clear plastic counter. Then they add the other number to it, thinking about how many groups of ten and leftovers are in that number. For example, if they choose 45, they mark that number with a counter on the hundreds chart. If the number they're adding is 26, they might count on from 45 by tens, saying, "Fifty-five, 65. That's two groups of 10. And 6 more would be 66, 67, 68, 79, 70, 71." Of course, this should be modeled in whole group before students do this kind of work at math stations.

Two students use a hundreds chart to add 2 two-digit numeral cards. They think about groups of 10 and leftovers as they work together.

Literature Links to Place Value

There are many children's books about counting, but not as many about place value. Since counting is foundational to understanding place value, several counting books have been included in the following list. After children read the books, they might want to deepen their understanding by choosing a number pictured on a page and building that number using manipulatives.

> *Can You Count to a Googol?* by Robert E. Wells. Albert Whitman, 2000.
>
> *The Cheerios Counting Book* by Barbara McGrath. Cartwheel, 1998.
>
> *Count and See* by Tana Hoban. Simon & Schuster, 1972.
>
> *The 500 Hats of Bartholomew Cubbins* by Dr. Seuss. Random House, 1989.
>
> *From One to One Hundred* by Teri Sloat. Dutton, 1991.
>
> *The King's Commissioners* by Aileen Friedman. Scholastic, 1995.
>
> *Millions of Cats* by Wanda Gag. Puffin, 2006.
>
> *More Than One* by Miriam Schlein. Greenwillow, 1996.
>
> *One Hundred Is a Family* by Pam Muñoz Ryan. Hyperion, 1992.
>
> *A Place for Zero: A Math Adventure* by Angeline LoPresti. Charlesbridge, 2003.
>
> *12 Ways to Get 11* by Eve Merriam. Aladdin, 1996.
>
> *Zero Is the Leaves on a Tree* by Betsy Franco. Tricycle Press, 2009.

There are also many books about the 100th day of school. One of my favorites is *Counting Our Way to the 100th Day: 100 Poems* by Betsy Franco (2004). Students can read the poems about 100 and then possibly write their own. Here are a few more suggestions of books about the 100th day of school for you to read aloud and place at stations for independent work with place value materials:

> *Jake's 100th Day of School* by Lester L. Laminack. Peachtree, 2008.
>
> *Miss Bindergarten's 100th Day of Kindergarten* by Joseph Slate. Puffin, 2002.
>
> *100 Days of Cool* by Stuart J. Murphy. HarperCollins, 2003.
>
> *100 School Days* by Anne Rockwell. HarperCollins, 2004.
>
> *100th Day Worries* by Margery Cuyler. Aladdin, 2005.

Technology Connections

There are several ways to use technology to help children learn about place value. If you have an interactive whiteboard, such as a SMART Board or Promethean Board, use the programs your district has purchased to use with this technology tool for teaching about place value. Your core math program might also have a DVD of place value games and activities to use on your classroom computers at computer math stations. Ask other teachers on your grade level about the computer resources they are using to teach place value, and share with each other.

Computer models of base ten blocks are available at the National Library of Virtual Manipulatives at http://nlvm.usu.edu/en/nav/category_g_1_t_3 .html. You will want your students to work with physical models before moving them to a more abstract version on the computer. But some children will find working on the computer motivational and it may be easier to help them keep track of what they have counted.

Computer games for place value are readily available. One source for these is http://www .gamequarium.com/placevalue.html. Choose games that promote thinking beyond just naming the place each number is in.

Troubleshooting at Place Value Stations

When teaching about place value, you will want to use manipulatives, such as counters, connecting cubes, or base ten blocks. The bigger the numbers you are working with, the more little pieces are involved. Here are a few ways to prevent problems at place value stations:

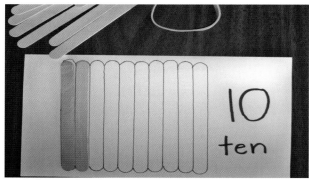

An index card with 10 sticks outlined on it can be used like a ten-frame to help children organize popsicle sticks into a bundle of ten.

Possible Problem	Troubleshooting Ideas
Children make patterns with connecting cubes instead of using them to make groups of tens and ones.	■ Give only one color of connecting cubes for making groups of tens and ones to each pair of students working together.
Students are confused about how to trade 10 ones for a ten-train (using Unifix or connecting cubes).	■ Use connecting cubes as described in the section titled "How to trade a ten-train for 10 ones" on page 148. Use explicit language as you model: "When I have 10 cubes, I snap them together to make one group of 10. How many groups of 10 are there?" Be sure to break the group apart to show there are still 10 cubes there.
Students have trouble using base ten blocks when a trade must take place.	■ Again, use explicit language as you model: "When I have 10 ten-rods, I can put them together to make a hundreds flat. Count with me while we match the rods to the hundreds flat." Lay each rod of 10 on top of the hundreds flat, one at a time, as students count with you, saying, "Ten, 20, 30, 40, . . . 100."
Students aren't bundling popsicle sticks correctly.	■ Teach them to count by twos or fives to get 10 in the bundle. Or make a strip with ten-sticks outlined on it (matching the popsicle sticks) to use like a ten-frame.
Students misuse rubber bands.	■ Teach children how to properly use rubber bands for bundling sticks. No snapping or shooting them. Have extras in case some break. Have a trash bag for those that do break at the station.
Children build numbers on the place value mat with numeral cubes or digit cards, but aren't understanding the value of digits.	■ Consider working with these students in small group. Have them work with smaller numbers and talk about what they are understanding and thinking.
Students mix up hundreds board puzzle pieces.	■ Color-code by scribbling on the back of the pieces with different colored crayons and store the color-coded pieces in separate snack or sandwich baggies.

Differentiating at Place Value Stations

If you have children who need practice with counting from 1 to 20, adapt stations activities to have children work with these numbers before moving into building larger numbers. Wherever hundreds charts are called for at math stations, give these students partial hundreds charts, with just 1 to 20 on them as a visual reference.

For students who are ready to work with numbers from 20 to 100, try using many of the place value stations in this book as they are written. When children show deep understanding of two-digit numbers, you can move to three-digit numbers from 100 to 999. Most of the activities in this chapter can easily be adapted to working with these larger numbers. At this point, base ten blocks may

Differentiated numeral cards are kept in a labeled ziplock bag for students who need to work with a different range of numbers than the rest of the class.

be easier for them to work with than counters or connecting cubes.

If you have just a few children in your classroom who need to work with numbers from 1 to 20, you might have a station or two just for them. Or you might put a baggie with materials just for them in a station container and put their name on the bag to show that only these students will use them. Do likewise if you have several children who need to work with larger numbers than the rest of the class.

Ways to Keep Place Value Stations Going Throughout the Year

Place value is not something you teach for a few weeks, and then have it understood by all students. Because of this, place value stations may be used all year long. Here are some ideas for keeping interest high at place value stations:

- Vary materials students work with for counting and building numbers. For example, use cups and counters at first or use connecting cubes (depending on what you have available). Then change materials to popsicle sticks and rubber bands. Later, put out base ten blocks. By changing materials periodically, students develop flexible thinking as they perform similar actions with new materials. Use the materials list in this chapter for other ideas.
- Money is another good model for place value, particularly in second grade or for advanced students in K–1. Instead of playing Race to 100, they can play Race to $1, using coins to trade.
- Stations that combine place value and measurement can be used throughout the year, too. Children enjoy measuring items around the room with nonstandard units of measurement. Later in the year, they can use standard

units of measurement (if these are part of your curriculum). Be sure to encourage students to estimate before measuring to give them opportunities to explore more deeply. Kathy Richardson's (1998b) *Developing Number Concepts, Book 3: Place Value, Multiplication, and Division* has many wonderful suggestions for integrating place value and measurement.

- After the 100th day of school, children will still enjoy reading books about this special celebration. You might have a station with several activities related to 100. See ideas from this chapter as well as ideas you might get from your colleagues.

- Another way to refresh a place value station is to have students make books about place value. You could make class books that they will enjoy reading over and over. Be sure to include place value materials for them to use to build the numbers in the books. Here are some ideas for these books:

  ☐ "Our Favorite Numbers." Have each child choose a number from 11 to 99 and tell why he or she likes that number. Then have the student illustrate that page using a "tens and ones" model. Put the pages in order from lowest to greatest number.

  ☐ "How Many (in Groups of Ten)?" Inventory things around the school to make this information book. Or students might look online for information. For example, pages might read: *There are 26 desks in our classroom. That's 2 groups of 10 and 6 more. There are 31 tables in the cafeteria. That's 3 groups of 10 and 1 more. There are 45 poetry books in the school library. That's 4 groups of 10 and 5 more.* Have children arrange the objects into groups of ten and leftovers; then take a digital photo to go with each page. Or have a child make an illustration for the page that shows the items in groups of ten and leftovers.

☐ "How Old Is . . . (in Groups of 10)?" Find out how old things are around your school or town. Each page in the book can have a different fact on it related to age. Add a photo or illustration to each page. For example, pages might read: *Our town is 156 years old. That's 1 group of 100, 5 groups of 10 and 6 more years! Our school was built in 1992. It is 18 years old. That's 1 group of 10 and 8 more. Our P.E. teacher is 25 years old. That's 2 groups of 10 and 5 more. Mandy's mom is 36 years old. That's 3 groups of 10 and 6 more.* They might add illustrations including the person or place along with birthday candles grouped in tens and leftovers to show the age.

This page was made by a child for a class book called "How Old Is . . . (in Groups of 10)?"

How to Assess/Keep Kids Accountable at Place Value Stations

It is important to walk around the place value stations in your classroom to observe what children are doing, saying, and understanding as they work. I recommend that you take notes about what you see and hear. During sharing time, ask several students who used place value stations to tell about numbers they worked with and show the class what they did or learned.

As you watch children working with place value, ask them to tell you about the digits and what each means. For example, for the number 210, ask: *What does the 2 mean? What about the 0?* Note if the student can tell you about the *value* of the digit using words, objects, or pictures. As children are working with bundles of sticks or base ten blocks, use prompts like these and have them build the numbers: *Show me [a number]. Show me 10 more. What number do you have? Show me 10 more. Add 20 more. Add 10 more. Show me 10 less. Now what number do you have?* If students are working with a hundreds chart, ask: *When we count by ones, how do we move on the hundreds chart? What about when we count by tens? Which direction do we go to count on by tens? To count back by tens?*

Or use a hundreds pocket chart for quick assessment. Pull out several numbers and have children tell where each belongs. For example, ask: *What's this number? Where would it go? How do you know?* Observe how students are counting (by tens, ones, etc.) to decide where to place the number on the chart. You might also ask: *When we count on the hundreds chart, what stays the same? What changes? How do the tens change?*

Kindergarten Considerations

Because of the distinct needs of young children, here are some things to think about if you are a kindergarten teacher:

- Children in kindergarten need to establish a strong understanding of numbers from 1 to 10. This is foundational to the development of understanding place value in first and second grade and beyond. Provide math stations from Chapter 4, "Beginning Number Concepts Work Stations," to build understanding for place value in kindergarten.
- Investigate the number of eyes or ears or hands or fingers in the classroom to begin to count by groups of twos and fives, and later by tens. You might graph this information with the class.
- Calendar time is a good time to expose kindergartners to the idea of place value as you talk about how many days we have been in school and the date. Instead of using bundles of popsicle sticks or straws to show tens and leftover ones representing the number of days you have been in school, consider using large paper clips hooked together to make a chain of ten (so children can see the individual ten objects that make the chain). The Every Day Counts series is a great resource to use for teaching place value concepts with the calendar. If you use this program, check out the Daily Depositor in K and 1, which has the class use different materials each month to represent the day's date in groups of tens and ones.
- A 100th Day Celebration is a big day in the life of a kindergartner. Use ideas from this chapter to help children picture what 100 means and how to count to 100 by ones and tens. Know that this work with 100 is a foundation for the place value work students will continue to do over the years.

Reflection and Dialogue

1. How do you use the calendar to build place value concepts? Is it enough? What else are you trying or might you use from this chapter (or from Chapter 4, "Beginning Number Concepts Work Stations")?

2. What place value concepts do your children really "own"? For example, when working with numbers 11 to 99, do they always organize around tens and ones? Are they able to look at two quantities being added or subtracted and know when they will need to regroup without using manipulatives? What do they need to understand more deeply? What activities from this chapter might you use to develop conceptual understandings of place value?

3. How will you manage the manipulatives needed to teach place value well? Share ideas with a colleague. Visit colleagues' classrooms to see how they store and utilize place value materials. Which materials will you begin with? What will you use over time?

4. What do your students enjoy doing at place value stations? What do they like the least? What could be done to improve the place value stations they aren't as engaged in?

5. What place value words do you hear your children using? Are they talking about ones, tens, and hundreds? Or are they just saying, "I have 31 sticks." Encourage them to use statements like these: *I have 3 bundles of ten* [or *3 groups of ten*] *and 1 leftover stick.* Or *I have 30 and 1 more.* Provide supports for math talk, and share with your colleagues what differences you notice.

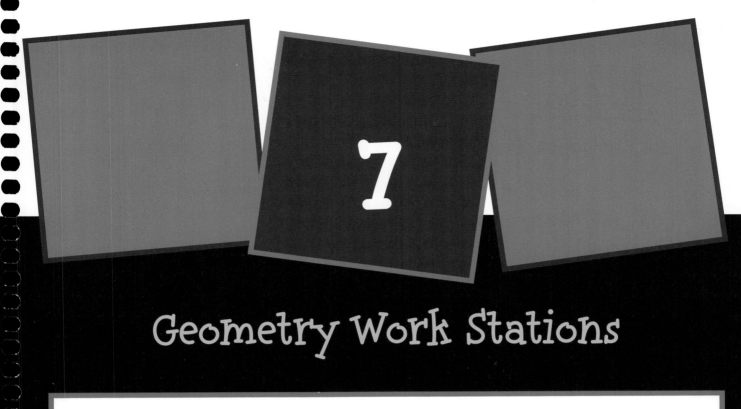

Geometry Work Stations

Two first graders are sitting on the floor sorting, comparing, and talking about attribute blocks. Working together, these students do an open sort (choosing how they want to classify the blocks), grouping blocks together that look alike to them and telling one another what they think is interesting about those shapes.

"Rudy, look at this shape. It has four sides. So does this one. Do you have any like this? Let's put them together."

"Here's one with four sides. It's big and yours is small. Should we put them in a group?"

"No, let's put all the big ones over there and the little ones here."

These students are creating their own categories and rules for sorting pattern blocks. The teacher didn't tell them how to sort, because she wants to see what they do on their own. As they explore shapes, they develop a deeper understanding of the relationships among objects than if the teacher had told them exactly what to look for.

Students also explore how shapes are alike and different at this geometry station, an activity that

has been taught in whole group. They each choose two shapes and place them side by side. Then they take turns talking about how the shapes are alike and how they are different. Finally, they draw a picture of their work and compare the shapes by writing what they noticed on an "Alike and Different" reproducible sheet (see page 262 in the appendix) and stored in a ziplock bag at that station.

If students tire of doing either of these two activities, there is also a book to read about shapes in this math station tub. Their teacher has shared a wordless book, *Shapes, Shapes, Shapes* by Tana Hoban (1996), with them in whole group, and it is one of their favorites. Reading the pictures and talking together about the book's shapes is part of their exploration at this station, too. An "I Can" list created with the class helps them remember what their choices are at this station.

In a different part of the classroom, another pair of students is seated at two desks, working at a similar math station. They are also sorting shapes, but they are using wooden blocks on a carpet square and are grouping objects in their own way. They

An "I Can" list for what kids can do at a geometry station provides choices.

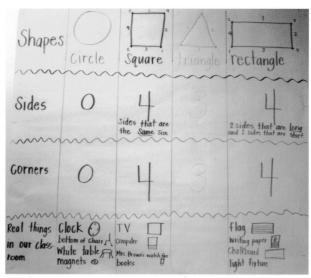

An anchor chart for shapes, made with the class, is often used by students at geometry stations to help them remember what they've been learning.

also are talking about how they are putting the shapes into groups. They have a different sorting game to play, which their teacher found in their core math program, and another shape book from read-aloud in their math station container.

At three other stations around the room, pairs of children are working with geoboards. This activity has been duplicated so more pairs of students can have this experience at the same time. Kids are stretching rubber bands over pegs on the geoboard and talking about the shape they are making and its attributes. (Ideas on how to use geoboards were also found in the teacher's guide that came with the district's core math program.) Some students use shape cards to copy shapes onto the geoboards; others make their own shapes. Everywhere students can be seen doing a variety of tasks to develop mathematical thinking.

During whole-group instruction, all students have done similar activities: they've sorted shapes in ways that made sense to them and talked about how these are alike and different; they've learned

how to work with geoboards to create shapes and compare how many sides and corners or vertices are on each (and how to use rubber bands appropriately); they've worked with partners and talked about their mathematical thinking (e.g., "This triangle has three sides. Look, I can change it into a square. Now it has four sides.") The teacher has created anchor charts of geometry words with corresponding shapes and pictures, and students glance at the charts often as they discuss what they are working with. Now they are getting additional practice working independently of the teacher during math stations time.

This is the kind of work that takes place in effective geometry work stations. Children are exploring relationships among shapes, just as their teacher modeled in whole group a week earlier. The students are beginning to talk about shapes using the anchor charts for help, because they have done this with teacher support during math instruction. Of course, the teacher will continue to reinforce this language as students describe what they did at stations during sharing time. Just exposing students to this new language does not guarantee its use.

Children know how to work with the math materials, because this has also been modeled previously. They are thinking like mathematicians, exploring and discussing shapes, space, lines, vertices, curved edges, and so on, because their teacher has shown them how to do this. Over time, they will develop shape and spatial sense and learn geometric content as their teacher provides them with rich independent opportunities to practice. Eventually, they will learn to apply their understandings about geometry to what they see and experience in art, nature, and architecture.

In this classroom there is still a math station focused on patterns, introduced earlier in the year. In a day or two, the teacher will replace the stamps and teddy bear counters currently in use there with pattern blocks. She thinks her students will enjoy the novelty of these new materials; plus, she wants her children's geometrical thinking to expand as they create repeating patterns with geometric shapes. She will model what she expects with these new materials before placing them in this station so kids don't build towers with the blocks.

This teacher has been careful not to put out too many new things at once, because it can be overwhelming and create confusion. Instead of changing all her stations to geometry stations at once, she layers on new ideas gradually. For example, after she introduces symmetry, she'll add a station or two where students explore symmetrical design using pattern blocks or art materials.

Over time, she will also add a problem-solving station in the classroom math corner so kids can create and solve story problems related to geometric thinking. Here, she'll provide pattern blocks and problem-solving cards that have geometry problems such as the following: *Suzanne built a design with 4 squares and 3 trapezoids. What might her design look like and how many blocks did she use?* The children will use pattern blocks to create designs and record their work to show during sharing time.

Key Math Concepts to Teach for Geometry

Use your state and district standards as your guide when planning for math stations for geometry. You may be implementing a standardized curriculum that already reflects the NCTM *Standards* and *Focal Points*, as well as the Common Core State Standards for Mathematics. Consult your district curriculum, core program, or planning documents to determine what you need to include while teaching geometry and deciding upon appropriate math stations for exploration and/or practice at your grade level. To get you started in thinking about what you'll be teaching and what students will work on at stations, here are some key concepts to consider:

In kindergarten, children will . . .

- Think and talk about geometry in the world around them, using ideas about shape, spatial relations, and the way objects are positioned as they explore a variety of shapes.
- Use positional words (such as *over, under, above, below*) to describe how one object is related to another.
- Identify, name, and describe a wide variety of 2–D shapes and 3–D solids. (See the related vocabulary list that follows).
- Sort shapes into groups and tell how the shapes are alike and different.
- Use basic shapes and spatial reasoning to build things and do puzzles.
- Combine what they are learning about geometry, pattern, and number to solve problems.

In first grade, children will also . . .

- Put together and take apart shapes (plane and solid figures) to make new geometric shapes and learn about part-whole relationships and the properties of shapes they are manipulating.

- Recognize shapes from a variety of perspectives and orientations and talk about attributes (color, shape, size, etc.) and properties (vertices, corners, sides, edges, faces, etc.) of the shapes.
- Describe how shapes are alike and different and group them according to attributes.
- Begin to explore congruence and symmetry as they explore shapes and their orientation in space.

In second grade, children will also . . .

- Build and take apart 2–D shapes, substituting smaller shapes for the larger ones or vice versa, to explore relationships.

- Use geometric knowledge and spatial reasoning to develop foundations for understanding area, fractions, and proportions.
- Solve problems involving movement of shapes and spatial relations.

What the Children Do at Geometry Stations

Before we look at the specific materials teachers need to gather for geometry stations, it's important to look at the big picture—what students will do at the stations. When children are working at geometry

Basic Geometry Vocabulary (Kindergarten)

- shape
- circle
- rectangle
- square
- triangle
- cube
- sphere
- cylinder
- curve
- round
- corners
- sides
- pointed
- edge
- straight
- flat
- line
- top
- bottom
- middle
- inside
- between
- right
- under
- over
- above
- below
- forward
- back
- outside

Taking It Further (Grades 1–2)

- two-dimensional
- polygon
- hexagon
- trapezoid
- parallelogram
- rhombus
- pentagon
- octagon
- quadrilateral
- three-dimensional
- cone
- rectangular prism
- rectangular pyramid
- triangular pyramid
- vertex, vertices
- point
- angle
- face
- base
- congruent
- symmetry
- slide, flip, turn

stations, they should be engaged in a variety of tasks, including those related to spatial sense, or being able to visualize objects and spatial relationships. For example, when building with blocks they begin to picture what they want the tower to look like and place blocks accordingly. They start to notice shapes in the world around them—in buildings, art, and nature. Students play with concepts of congruence and symmetry as they use mirrors and objects to build and make designs. They experiment with the vocabulary of geometry, naming shapes and comparing their attributes as they explore a variety of 2–D and 3–D shapes. By continually talking about what they see, students clarify their thinking, begin to own the mathematical concepts, and develop more confidence with the language of geometry.

If your curriculum includes independent choice time activities for geometry, consider supplementing them with the geometry stations that we will explore in this chapter. Many of you also will find geometry lessons from your core program that can later be reconfigured as math work stations and could work nicely alongside the geometry stations included here. You will want to make task cards or "I Can" lists to go with some of the stations to help students work independently. Make your own by inserting ideas from this section and/or your core curriculum that match the needs of your class.

This "I Can" list from a kindergarten class uses digital pictures of students working to help children remember what to do at a 3–D station. "I Can" lists are taped to the inside of the stations container lids, so the children know exactly where to find them.

This sample "I Can" list was made early in the year in a first-grade class. Students read and name shapes in a familiar book or go on a Shape Hunt around the room and list where they find each shape.

Following are samples of geometry station activities from which to choose, rather like a menu. This list includes a variety of geometry stations, some requiring more preparation time and materials than others. Choose the stations that will work best for you and your students. As you plan, keep in mind the importance of a balanced geometry experience for all children. Here are some ideas of what students might do at geometry stations:

■ **Play Guess My Shape in a variety of ways.** Young children love to play this game. Start by placing several shapes (pattern blocks or 3–D

These materials are used at a geometry station incorporating the Guess My Shape game with 3–D shapes.

solids) in a paper bag and having a student reach in to describe a shape by feeling it. For example, the student might say: "My shape has 3 sides and 3 vertices. Guess my shape." (Answer: triangle.) Another way to play is to have a child choose a shape from a bag and "draw" that shape with his or her index finger on a partner's back. The partner guesses the shape and tells why he or she thinks it's that shape. The partner might say: "I feel a shape that curves. I think it's a circle." Or have students use (or even create their own) clue cards and match the cards to pattern blocks. See page 263 of the appendix for Guess My Shape clue cards to get started. You could make some of these with the class (using pictures and words) in whole group, too. Start with 2–D shapes and expand to include 3–D shapes over time.

After students have taken turns guessing several shapes from the bag, they might look for those same shapes in picture books. See the "Literature Links" section in this chapter for suggested books.

■ ***Do shape sorts.*** Provide a variety of 2–D or 3–D shapes for students to sort. I recommend making cards for sorting *with* your class as you talk with them about different ways to sort. (Label index cards as follows: *color, shape, size,*

number of sides, number of faces, number of vertices, etc.). The cards help students label how they will sort the shapes.

Children might also play Guess My Sort. One child puts in a group several objects (such as attribute or pattern blocks) that go together in some way. The other student must "guess the sort" and tell why he or she thinks the items go together. The partner can use one of the sorting cards, if desired, to name the sort. Then he or she must find another item that goes with the group and tell why he or she chose it. Over time, students might record their sort by drawing (or tracing) shapes that go together and labeling them in a math journal or on a Guess My Sort recording sheet (as found on page 264 of the appendix).

Young children engage in 3–D and 2–D shape sorts using concrete materials.

■ **Compare two shapes.** Have students choose two shapes and tell how they are alike and different using geometry vocabulary, as suggested at the opening of this chapter on pages 159–160. More advanced students could use a Venn diagram to compare and contrast the two shapes or solids.

A student draws a Venn diagram to compare and contrast two rectangles.

■ **Go on a Shape Hunt.** Children look for real objects in the environment that match pattern blocks they pull from a bag, one at a time. They might record examples of each shape on a recording sheet, such as the one on page 265 of the appendix. Or they can look in magazines and newspapers for shapes, cut them out, and glue them on pages to match the shape they were hunting for.

A first grader uses a digital camera to take pictures of objects around the room shaped like a rectangle for a Shape Hunt book.

You can also give children a digital camera (after teaching them how to use one; you might find an old one at a garage sale or on eBay) and have them take photos of objects around the classroom that match particular shapes. (Limit the number of pictures they may take, though, or the battery might run down too quickly.) These photos can be printed and made into shape books for the classroom library.

■ **Create or duplicate geometric designs.** Children love to build shapes with elastic bands on geoboards. (Be sure to teach students how to use the rubber bands appropriately.) Children can use pattern blocks as models, or they can use geoboard dot cards and copy designs. You might have them make a permanent record of their designs on geoboard dot paper (as found in *Mathematics Their Way* by Mary Baratta-Lorton [1975]) by recording the names and number of shapes they see within the design. They might also hunt for a specific shape within the design or make a picture using only a certain number of rubber bands. (Have them roll a numeral cube and use that many rubber bands). Encourage children to use geometry vocabulary to talk with each other about the shapes they made.

Two students use pattern blocks to make a new shape and then create it on their geoboards. Then they look through a picture book and name the shapes they find.

This "I Can" list and materials are for a first-grade geometry station.

Children also can use pattern blocks or tangrams to make pictures or designs. They can copy or match shapes to cards or create their own designs. Pattern block stickers can be used to copy or make quilt designs. They can use picture books like Ann Jonas's *The Quilt* (1984) or Ann Tompert's *Grandfather Tang's Story* (1997) for inspiration. Encourage them to talk about the kind and number of shapes they used.

- ■ ***Build 3–D shapes with toothpicks, playdough, and other materials.*** Building shapes lets children experience three-dimensional geometry. Provide materials that are easy for them to build with, such as toothpicks or coffee stirrers and playdough or modeling clay. You might also use newspaper rolled tightly to create long narrow pieces, secured with masking tape. Or students may use plastic drinking straws and masking tape to connect the straws and build 3–D shapes. Cards that show pictures of 3–D shapes can be included, or you can let children build on their own. See page 266 in the appendix for some cards.

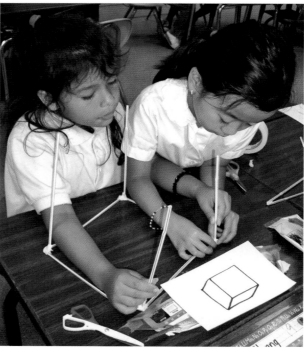

Partners work together to build 3–D shapes using picture cards as models, straws, scissors, and masking tape at a geometry station.

- ■ ***Use Ed Emberley books to draw things using shapes.*** This author/artist has created a series of books, including *Ed Emberley's Drawing Book of Animals* (1994), to help young children draw simple pictures using shapes. His books are great for helping students learn to follow picture directions from left to right,

Children use a task card and an Ed Emberley book as a guide to drawing animals using shapes. They follow picture directions and talk about the shapes they used.

too. Encourage students to talk about the shapes as they draw pictures using these resources. You might include task cards, such as those on page 267 of the appendix, that give directions such as, "Find and copy a picture that uses rectangles. How many rectangles did you use in your drawing?"

■ *Combine shapes to make new shapes.* Provide a wide variety of pattern blocks and have students combine shapes to make new

A student combines shapes to make a new shape and records his work.

ones. Have them record their work in pictures and words. Magnetic pattern blocks work really well for this activity.

Students might also make all possible triangles using only triangles, or all possible squares using only squares. This could be applied to any shape. Again, have children record their work.

■ *Make shape books.* You might make a class big book about shapes to introduce children to the idea that they can use geometry every day. Take the class on a walk around the school and its grounds. As you walk, ask children to look for shapes around them. Take a digital camera along and snap photos of what they notice. Then glue the best of those pictures onto 12-by-18-inch white paper and write sentences with the class to match the photos. A class-made big book titled "Our Class Shape Walk" might have pages that say something like this:

☐ There are circles on the floor.
☐ There are rectangles on the stairs of the slide.
☐ There are squares on the bulletin board.
☐ Our desks are rectangles. So are the backs of the chairs.
☐ There are lots of books shaped like rectangles.
☐ We found circles on clocks and watches.

Students combine squares to make more squares.

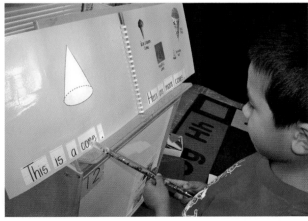

A student at a math work station reads pages from a class-made big book about 3–D shapes.

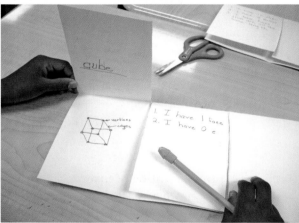

Students make flipbooks about shapes they are studying.

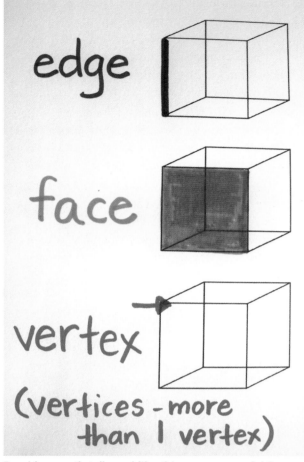

Provide a math talk card like this one as a model for new 3–D geometry vocabulary. Encourage children to use these words in their oral language and writing.

Students could read this big book as part of their work at a geometry station, identifying shapes in the photos and matching pattern blocks to the shapes.

During writing workshop, you might also teach students how to make their own shape books, such as the flipbooks pictured.

Read aloud shape books as models. (See the "Literature Links" section in this chapter for book suggestions.) At a geometry station for shape books, you might provide die-cut construction paper shapes, glue sticks, and white paper stapled together to make books. Have students glue shapes onto the pages and write text to go with each page.

They might also make their own books titled "Everything I Know about _____" (insert the name of a shape or solid in the blank). Each page in the book could include something they know about that shape. They could use photos, drawings, tracings, or crayon rubbings of the shape or solid on each page. Include a math talk card to give children models of geometry vocabulary to use in their writing.

■ ***Look for shapes in art, nature, and architecture.*** Ask the art teacher at your school (or a local art or children's museum) to borrow art prints with strong geometric shapes for children to examine. Have students look for and name shapes in art. The picture book *Museum Shapes* (NY Metropolitan Museum of Art 2005) is a good resource for this too. Some artists you might have children study include Mondrian, Picasso, Kandinski, Klee, Escher, and Thiebaud, as well as ancient Egyptian art, ancient Islamic art, ancient African art, ancient Native American art, and art deco styles. Look online for pictures of geometric art for children to examine. After children look at works by artists like these, let them experiment with similar styles as they create their own art using geometric designs with cut paper shapes, markers, crayons, or colored pencils. You might also provide shape templates for them to use.

Likewise, students might look at architecture books and use them to discuss and make buildings using pattern blocks, wooden blocks, Legos, Lincoln Logs, or Tinkertoys. Have students describe the shapes and patterns they are noticing. For example, a student might say: "The door of my building is shaped like a rectangle" or "Look at all the triangles we made."

To help students find examples of shapes in nature, make available photos from old calendars, nature magazines, or the Internet. Or have children look out a window and search for shapes in nature. Students can cut and paste (or draw) pictures to match pages labeled with the name of each shape they are looking for.

■ ***Play Find the Hidden Treasure to practice positional words.*** Write directions for students to follow on cards to find hidden treasures. For example, directions might say: *Start* under *the clock facing the wall. Take 10 steps to the* left. *Then look* inside *the top drawer.* (Have the next set of clues in the drawer.) *Walk* outside *the classroom into the hall and look to the* right. (Post the next clue there.) *Go back* inside *the classroom and look* under *the teacher's chair in the whole-group area.* Place a small treasure chest (or a picture of one, as

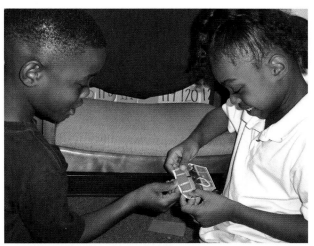

Two children find the treasure chest hidden under the teacher's chair after finding and following clues around the room while playing Find the Hidden Treasure.

found on page 268 of the appendix) at the final location.

Create several of these treasure hunts to go on as a class over a period of a few days until children understand the process. Then as a class, do a shared writing of treasure hunt directions for another class to take. Finally, provide a list of direction words, blank paper, a pencil, masking tape, and a small treasure chest (or a picture of one) so students can write their own directions for their classmates to use for a game of Find the Hidden Treasure. Children can either create or follow directions to find a hidden treasure at this station.

■ ***Make puzzles with a partner and use positional words to tell about where pieces go.*** Let children work with puzzles at a geometry station and remind them to use positional words when putting the puzzle together. You might include a copy of the positional words (and matching pictures) for them to use at this station. You should hear conversation such as, "Let's make the *outside* of the puzzle first. Then we'll find the pieces that go *inside*." "That piece goes *above* this one. That goes *below*." "This one belongs to the *right*," and so on.

Kids use a vocabulary card with positional words and pictures to talk with each other as they put together a puzzle at a math station.

Another possibility is for Partner A to build a design hidden from Partner B with only 5 to 7 pattern blocks. Partner A then gives positional directions to Partner B to replicate the design.

■ ***Explore symmetry by drawing, painting, and building.*** Have children investigate symmetry by placing a mirror alongside a pattern block or picture and then drawing and/or describing what they see. For example, they might say, "When we put the mirror beside a triangle, we saw a rhombus," or "When we put the mirror beside the picture of a tree and a flower, the flower was to the right of the tree on one side but to the left of the tree on the other side." Encourage students to look for examples of symmetry in art, architecture, and nature.

Another way kids can experiment with symmetry is by folding paper in half, unfolding it, and painting just one half with a design. While it is wet, they fold the dry side over the wet one and rub gently. Then they open the paper carefully and let it dry. Have them tell about what they notice about the symmetry of their picture.

Two girls use pattern blocks and a mirror to create and draw a symmetrical design.

Children can also build symmetrical designs with pattern blocks and then check to see if one side matches the other by placing a piece of yarn down the middle. Or for advanced children, have one child build a design with three, four, or five blocks and the other student add blocks to make it symmetrical.

Materials

There are many materials to use to develop geometric thinking (see the Picture Glossary of Math Materials in the back of this book). Listed here are suggested materials for your students to explore over time. Introduce one kind of manipulative at a time, so you and the class aren't overwhelmed. See the section titled "Troubleshooting at Geometry Stations" for some tips on using these materials with young children. Model the use of these materials in whole group using a projection device, such as a document camera. You may use plastic geometric materials designed for use on an overhead projector, too.

Look in your math materials to see what you already have that may have come with your math program. You might want to have on hand the following materials throughout the year when teaching about geometry:

■ pattern blocks (I prefer foam blocks to minimize noise. They come in six colors and six shapes and are used to teach geometric shapes and their relationships.)

■ magnetic pattern blocks (great for demonstrations)

■ pattern block cards (These can include pattern block picture cards or pattern block puzzle cards.)

■ pattern block paper shapes or stickers

■ attribute blocks (Attribute blocks are *different* from pattern blocks. Attribute blocks come in five shapes, three colors, and two thicknesses. They are used to teach shapes, sorting, congruent versus similar, fractions, proportions, patterns, etc.)

■ tangrams (These are geometric puzzles that include two large triangles, one medium triangle, two small triangles, one square, and one parallelogram. Together these shapes form a large square. These are best for students with advancing spatial skills. For students who need something easier, begin with pattern blocks.)

■ tangram puzzle cards

■ geoboards, rubber bands, and geoboard dot paper

■ geoblocks (These might be provided with your core program.)

■ attribute cards (with pictures for beginning readers)

■ assortment of 2–D shapes

■ assortment of 3–D shapes (include cylinders, cones, cubes, pyramids, prisms)

■ real objects to describe and compare (balls, boxes, cans, cones; collect as needed)

■ polygons for sorting

■ paper shapes (and a paper bag for Guess My Shape)

■ picture shape cards and materials for building shapes (playdough, toothpicks, straws, masking tape, newspaper rolled tightly)

■ pentominoes (These are sold as a set of twelve shapes, with each shape made by joining five squares. They are used for exploring symmetry, congruence, area, perimeter, etc. These can also be made by the students.)

■ unbreakable mirrors (for symmetry)

■ origami paper and project books (for symmetry)

■ Escher prints and other fine art prints that use strong geometric designs

■ magazines, old calendar photos of nature, scissors, paper, and glue (for cutting out shapes and making books)

■ bookmaking supplies (paper, stapler, markers, optional digital camera)

■ die-cut construction paper shapes

■ construction materials, such as Lincoln Logs, Legos, K'Nex, Tinkertoys, and wooden building blocks

■ small treasure chest (or picture of one) for positional word game

■ puzzles of varying degrees of difficulty

What the Teacher Needs to Model

Here are some things to model to help your students get the most from their time at geometry stations:

How to think about attributes. Seat students on the floor in a circle. Show a few pattern blocks and list on the board several attributes that describe them, such as *red*, *three-sided*, and *flat*. Give each child a pattern block to examine. Children should then take turns sharing one attribute of their block while others look to see if their shape possesses that same attribute. Add their observations to the list on the board and have the class summarize what they noticed. After doing this a time or two, you might begin to create attribute cards with the class for use at stations.

How to do shape sorts. In whole group, show students how to sort shapes and real objects into categories. Use a graphic organizer if you choose. Open sorts allow students to choose how they want to sort. Closed sorts have directions telling children how to sort.

Start with open sorts, allowing students to sort in any way they think of. This encourages them to think more deeply. Over time, introduce closed sorts, with directions such as these: *Sort all shapes that are triangles; Sort all shapes that are not triangles; Find other shapes that look like this; Sort by number of sides*; and *Sort all the triangles into groups.* You'll find sample sorting cards on page 269 of the appendix. Ask students why they put each object in that group. Have them justify their thinking. With young children, it is important to have them focus on what is the same about all of the shapes in a group, or how one group is different from the other. For an additional challenge, have students draw a picture of another item that would belong in the group and tell why.

How to play Guess My Sort. Gather several objects that go together in some way. Have the students "guess the sort," or tell why these objects were put together. For example, put 5 squares and rectangles together. Explain that these were sorted into a group because they all have 4 sides and are closed figures. Let children take turns sorting objects into a group and having others guess how they sorted them. For a bit of a challenge, you might have them draw or find another object that goes in the group.

How to use the vocabulary of geometry. Remind children to use new geometry vocabulary by making a math talk card and placing copies of it at geometry stations. Be sure the card has picture clues to help students remember the words and what they mean. Model the use of these words at every possible opportunity to reinforce this vocabulary.

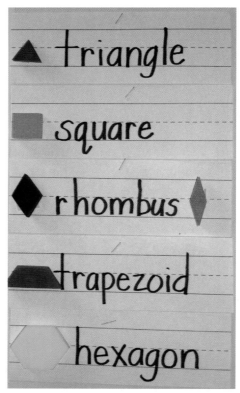

This math talk card names and pictures geometric shapes and is used as a reference by students at shape-related geometry stations.

Students use sorting circles to organize their shape sort after this has been modeled in whole group.

How to use a graphic organizer to show attributes of shapes. When modeling how to sort shapes, you might use a graphic organizer to help students think about which objects they are putting together and why. The organizer can be as simple as a piece of paper divided into 2, 4, or 6 sections with a shape at the top of each. You might want to make blank organizers and laminate them so you can use them in a variety of ways.

The whole class learns how to use rubber bands to make shapes on their geoboards *before* they ever use them independently at geometry stations. Here they are showing the teacher the triangles they made.

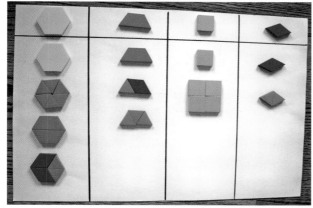

Students use this graphic organizer when sorting shapes.

How to build shapes from construction materials. Work together to learn how to make 2–D and 3–D shapes with all kinds of building materials. Students will enjoy using playdough and toothpicks to make shapes. Or they can use plastic drinking straws joined together with masking tape. Model how to use the materials before students use them, so they know what you expect. Be explicit about how to tear off and use small pieces of masking tape. You might want to provide pictures of shapes as models for building. Encourage children to use geometry vocabulary as they construct and build their shapes. (For example, you might model using words like this: "I am joining together these sides to build a cube. It has a square as a face. Here's another square face.")

How to use rubber bands on geoboards to make shapes. Be specific when teaching children how to use geoboards. If you don't, you may find rubber bands flying through the air! Show children

exactly what you expect and how to gently put a rubber band around the pins so it stays in place and doesn't snap or break.

How to get blocks (pattern, attribute, or wooden) out and return them to containers quietly. Taking the time to teach children how to get materials they need saves time in the long run and allows

A teacher models for the whole class how to quietly get one "scoop" of blocks from a larger container, so kids don't dump the blocks onto the floor or a desk.

more time for teaching and exploration. I have found that using a plastic cup and showing children how to quietly get one "scoop" of blocks from a larger container saves wear and tear on the teacher. If you don't do this, they may try to grab as many handfuls as possible or dump the blocks onto the floor or table, creating chaos. Ditto for returning the materials to the larger container when they have finished. Show kids how to gently push the blocks back into the cup and carefully (and quietly) pour its contents into the container. Model, model, model!

How to play games, such as Guess My Shape.

Show the class how to play Guess My Shape and then let them play it with a partner. (Note: this might take more than one day to do. You might model it one day and have them play it with a partner the next. Sometimes I even write directions *with* the class, so they can refer to them when working on their own and won't have to ask the teacher for help.)

To model playing the game, place a shape in a paper bag and reach in to feel and then describe it. You might say, "My shape has four sides. All the sides are the same length. Guess my shape." (Answer: square.) Another way to play is to have a child choose a shape from a bag and use his or her index finger to "draw" that shape on a partner's back. The partner guesses the shape and tells why he or she thinks it's that shape. If you'd like, use the clue cards from page 263 of the appendix. If you want students to make their own clue cards, make a few together. These can then be used at the station. Start with 2–D shapes and expand to include 3–D shapes over time.

How to make new shapes with pattern blocks.

Magnetic pattern blocks work well to model how to make shapes with pattern blocks. You might start with a hexagon and show how 6 triangles fit on top of it to make this shape. Likewise, put together 3 squares to make a rectangle. Then give students time to do this on their own and record what they find out. After they understand how to do this activity, it can be moved to a geometry station for independent exploration.

How to use shapes to retell stories from picture books.

After reading aloud a picture book (see the list in the "Literature Links" section) for enjoyment, show the class how to use pattern blocks to retell the story. For example, match up shapes in the illustrations of the book and talk about the shapes being used.

A teacher and a student model how to play Guess My Shape for the rest of the class.

These two students demonstrate for the whole class how to match 3–D shapes to the illustrations in a familiar book about shapes as they read it together.

How to look at art, nature, and architecture to identify shapes and symmetry. In whole group, examine art prints, such as those by Picasso. Discuss shapes and how they are used. Then create pictures with children using shapes. Likewise, take your class outdoors to look for examples of geometry. You might have them take paper on a clipboard and crayons and let them sketch outside. Show them how to label the shapes on their drawings. Encourage students to use math vocabulary as they talk about what they notice. Then move these materials to a geometry station for independent work time.

How to fold paper to do origami and explore lines of symmetry. This will work best with children with more developed fine motor skills. You might begin by reading aloud a story about origami (see the list of books in the "Literature Links" section) and then modeling how to follow directions to make simple origami projects. Again, encourage use of geometric vocabulary as you work.

How to use mirrors to explore symmetry. Show students how to place a mirror directly on the edge of a block or drawing. If you skip this step, students may not know where to place the mirror. Explain exactly how you want children to use the mirrors, or you may find them making silly faces in the mirrors instead.

How to use positional words in games, building, putting together puzzles, and giving directions. As you are modeling how to play a game or put together a puzzle, model the use of positional words. Make math talk cards that include the words you want students to use while working at a station. Plan for time to walk around and talk with children during math stations time so you can observe and support their use of this new vocabulary.

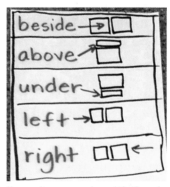

This math talk card was made *with* the class and then placed at stations where the teacher expects children to use positional words.

Connections to Problem Solving

You will want to give children opportunities to solve geometry problems. Begin by introducing geometry problems to the whole group and giving children time to solve them either alone or with partners. Be sure to allow students plenty of time to work out problems and share alternative ways of solving them. Then include at a station problem-solving cards (such as those found on pages 270–271 in the appendix) with scenarios similar to those you've practiced in whole group. You might also place these in the classroom math corner if you've set up this space in your room.

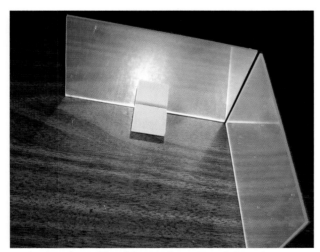

A plastic mirror, like this one from ETA Cuisenaire, can be used by children to explore symmetry with shapes and designs.

Geometry problems might be posed like this: "If you trace a face of a cube, what shape would you get? Find other shapes that have the same face." Have students make predictions and then have them test out their ideas with concrete materials. Repeat this idea with other 3–D shapes.

Another question you might pose is, "How many triangles could you build with 12 popsicle sticks?" Along with this question, give each student 12 popsicle sticks and let them have a go at solving this problem. Walk around and talk with individuals as they work. Take notes on what you see them trying. After they have had a chance to work the problem, have different students share the various ways they solved it. They might say things like, "I thought that a triangle has 3 sides, so I put the 12 sticks into 4 piles with 3 in each. Then I used each set of 3 sticks to make a triangle, and I made 4 triangles in all." Another child might share another approach: "I made a triangle with some of my sticks, and there were still a bunch left. So I made another triangle, and there were leftovers. I kept doing this until no more sticks were left. I made 4 triangles." Still another child says, "I made one big triangle. I put 4 sticks in a row, and then I joined 4 more sticks to it, like this. Then I put 4 more sticks together to make a big triangle."

As you plan for geometry stations, include activities that help children think more deeply about the concepts you are teaching. Help children discover what makes a triangle a triangle. *It has 3 sides, but the sides don't have to be equal. It has 3 corners and is a closed figure.* Instead of just finding one triangle, have them find all kinds of triangles and tell how these triangles are alike.

Here are a few math stations ideas for problem solving in geometry:

■ **Build 2–D shapes with popsicle sticks or yarn.** With these manipulatives, students can solve geometry problems, such as the following, written on cards:

☐ *How many hexagons could you build with 10 popsicle sticks?*
☐ *How many pieces of yarn would it take to make 2 squares?*
☐ *I drew 3 different triangles. What might they have looked like?*
☐ *How many different designs can you make using 5 red trapezoid pattern blocks? Try this with a different shape.*
☐ *How many different shapes can you make with 4 sides?*
☐ *Using the triangle pattern block shape, build other triangles.*

■ **Play Trace the Face.** Give students geometry problem-solving cards for them to solve. For example, cards might pose these problems: *If you trace the base of a rectangular prism, what shape would you get? Find any other shapes that have this same face* and *If you wanted to build a cube, what pattern blocks would you need? How many?* See pages 270–271 in the appendix for some sample problem-solving cards to use. You might also have more advanced students create their own problems for others to solve. Another idea is to have students match cards that show 2–D geometric shapes with the appropriate faces of 3–D geoblocks. Check to see if your core math program includes these.

■ **Play Mirror, Mirror to explore shapes and symmetry.** Have children take turns making up problems for each other to solve using pattern blocks and mirrors. They use the words "Mirror, mirror on the wall, what would I see if I put _____ by the mirror?" For example, if they put a triangle by the mirror, they might see a rhombus in the mirror. If they lined up a circle and then a square next to a mirror, they'd see the pattern of square, circle, circle, square. Have them name the solution and then check it in the mirror. They might write each problem on an index card with the answer on the back for checking.

■ ***Have advanced children use pentominoes to solve problems.*** Ask students to find all possible shapes made with 5 squares. (There are 12.) Compare what they make to the pentominoes. Have them try to use all 12 pentominoes to make a rectangle. (Note: This is very challenging.) One-inch tiles can also be used to explore all the possible pentominoes. One-inch grid paper representing the configurations of the pentominoes can be cut out and glued to a recording sheet to create a permanent record of all the arrangements children discover.

Literature Links to Geometry

There are many excellent books on shapes to read aloud to young children. Be sure to include books that give students opportunities to find shapes in the pictures, especially in art, nature, and architecture so they can see real-world applications of geometric concepts. These books can also be included at geometry stations along with pattern blocks. Encourage students to find and discuss shapes in the illustrations and photographs. They might match up the pattern block shapes to those used in the books they're reading. Also allow them to make their own shape books. You could put a basket of geometry books in your classroom library and include some of them as options for reading at some of your geometry stations:

Architects Make Zigzags: Looking at Architecture A to Z by Diane Maddex. Wiley, 1986.

Architecture Shapes by Michael J. Crosbie and Steve Rosenthal. Wiley, 1993.

Building a House by Byron Barton. Greenwillow, 1990.

Captain Invincible and the Space Shapes by Stuart J. Murphy. HarperCollins, 2001.

A Cloak for the Dreamer by Aileen Friedman. Scholastic, 1995.

Cubes, Cones, Cylinders, and Spheres by Tana Hoban. Greenwillow, 2000.

Ed Emberley's Book of Drawing Animals by Ed Emberley. LB Kids, 1994.

Fold Me a Poem by Christine O'Connell. Harcourt, 2005.

Grandfather Tang's Story by Ann Tompert. Dragonfly Books, 1997.

The Greedy Triangle by Marilyn Burns. Scholastic, 1995.

Houses and Homes by Ann Morris. HarperCollins, 1995.

How a House Is Built by Gail Gibbons. Holiday House, 1996.

Icky Bug Shapes by Jerry Pallotta. Scholastic, 2004.

Let's Fly a Kite by Stuart Murphy. HarperCollins, 2000.

Mouse Shapes by Ellen Stoll Walsh. Harcourt Children's Books, 2007.

Museum Shapes. The NY Metropolitan Museum of Art. Little, Brown Young Readers, 2005.

The Origami Master by Nathaniel Lachenmeyer. Albert Whitman, 2008.

The Paper Crane by Molly Bang. Greenwillow, 1987.

Pigs on the Ball: Fun with Math and Sports by Amy Axelrod. Aladdin, 2000.

Round Is a Mooncake: A Book of Shapes by Roseann Thong. Chronicle Books, 2000.

The Shape of Things by Dayle Ann Dodds. Candlewick, 1996.

Shapes, Shapes, Shapes by Tana Hoban. Greenwillow, 1996.

Snowflake Bentley by Jacqueline Briggs Martin. Houghton Mifflin, 1998.

So Many Circles, So Many Squares by Tana Hoban. Greenwillow, 1998.

What Shape Is It? by Bobbie Kalman. Crabtree, 2007.

When a Line Bends . . . a Shape Begins by Rhonda Gowler Greene. Sandpiper, 2001.

The Wing on a Flea: A Book About Shapes by Ed Emberley. Little, Brown Young Readers, 2001.

Technology Connections

Computer models that are used to build geometric thinking are engaging for kids at math stations. Check with your tech specialist to see what geometry software is available at your school. Programs are available that have electronic geoboards and pattern blocks. You can look for templates at the National Library of Virtual Manipulatives at http://nlvm.usu.edu/en/nav/category_g_1_t_3.html. It is probably best to have young children work with physical models before moving them to a more abstract version on the computer. But some children will enjoy working on the computer to manipulate and explore shapes and other geometric ideas.

    If you have an interactive whiteboard, use your school's geometry software programs on this technology tool to model concepts about geometry.

Your core math program probably also has technology-related geometry games and activities. Use what you've already got, rather than create more work for yourself.

Troubleshooting at Geometry Stations

Despite our best efforts, some children may still have trouble managing their behavior and/or materials while working at geometry work stations. The most effective way to prevent problems at these stations is to model explicitly. Of course, some children may require additional support or even need to be removed until their behavior shows they can work independently of the teacher. Here are some ideas for helping children work well at geometry work stations:

Possible Problem	Troubleshooting Ideas
Students make too much noise using pattern blocks.	■ Use soft math mats (cut from shelf liner) to minimize noise, especially on desks or tables. Or use foam pattern blocks.
Kids dump out blocks on the table or throw them back in containers noisily.	■ Teach children how to quietly scoop out pattern blocks using a strong plastic cup or one handful at a time.
	■ Show children how to quietly scoop up blocks when they're finished by sliding half of a file folder under their designs and gently pouring them back into the storage container.
Children break or shoot rubber bands.	■ Explicitly model expectations for rubber bands and geoboards. Show how to gently stretch them. If students misuse materials, remove children from the station immediately. No warnings!
	■ Include plenty of extra rubber bands in a snack-size ziplock bag in the station container with geoboards. Teach children to throw away broken rubber bands during cleanup time.
Children *play* with manipulatives, building towers and making pictures, rather than explore how shapes make new shapes.	■ Be sure you've allowed students to have enough exploration time with manipulatives before asking them to do a specific academic task like this.

Students don't clean up appropriately.

It's difficult to show students how a shape can be made of other shapes with pattern blocks. They slip out of your hands when you're trying to model.

- Include an "I Can" list or a task card at this station. Be sure to make the list *with* the children. Remind them that "make a picture" is not on this list.

- Model and practice how to clean up when introducing every geometry station. Show students what you expect and have peers demonstrate this for their classmates. Provide labeled baggies for materials to keep them organized in the station.

- Use magnetic pattern blocks for modeling. They can be displayed on your magnetic chalkboard or dry erase board.

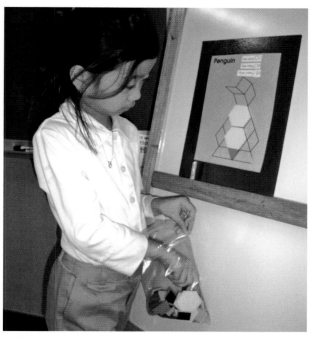

A child uses magnetic pattern blocks at a magnetic easel to match shapes and make designs. These magnetic blocks are great for the teacher to use for modeling in whole group, too.

Differentiating at Geometry Stations

Some children in your class will be able to identify shapes and their attributes easily. Others will need extra practice and support to do this. Be sure to pro-

vide math talk cards at as many geometry stations as needed to support the learning of this new vocabulary, and praise students for using these new words. Help children move beyond thinking about just naming a shape to talking about a *group of shapes and their properties*. Also encourage students to explore shapes by sliding, turning, and flipping them to see if and how they change.

When having students do activities like Shape Hunts, consider adding challenge by having them hunt for *properties* of shapes rather than just the shapes themselves. For example, ask students to find things that have *curves* or *lines* or *squares within squares*. They could also search for *two or more shapes that make another shape* or *three shapes that are alike in some way*.

Don't just include blocks and the study of shapes at geometry stations. Expand geometry ideas to help children understand positional concepts and how objects are located in space. Watch your students in whole-group instruction and see what they are taking on easily. Then provide opportunities for them to practice problem solving and spatial sense. Use computer models, too, for geometric exploration. Some of these will have built-in differentiation activities for your students.

If you use puzzles at a geometry station or two, be sure to provide a variety to meet the needs of children in your class. Students with more advanced spatial sense can complete more complex puzzles.

Likewise, as students work with tangrams, more advanced students can be given a puzzle to solve with certain pieces that fit together to make that shape. Beginners can simply match shapes to those drawn on the completed figure. Or students can make their own tangram puzzles for their classmates. Pattern block cards are often also differentiated.

Begin with simple materials, such as pattern blocks. Then move to more complex materials, such as pentominoes, for students who need a challenge. Be sure to allow all children to solve some kinds of puzzles, though. This thinking work should be done by every student in your class and not just limited to your advanced children.

Ways to Keep Geometry Stations Going Throughout the Year

Introduce geometric concepts, such as those related to shapes and their attributes, when determined by your core program or core curriculum. From there, you'll continue to build on that learning throughout the year. For this reason, you may have several geometry stations after you've begun to teach some basic understandings about geometry. As you progress through the curriculum and begin to teach about other mathematical topics, you will probably choose to keep at least one or two geometry stations open as you add new stations related to the new topics you are teaching. In this way, math stations provide ongoing practice with a spiraling curriculum.

Here are a few ways you might keep geometry stations going throughout the year:

■ If you have taught about patterns and shapes, have students use their new knowledge about shapes in making patterns. Encourage students to talk about the patterns they are creating using the geometry vocabulary you have taught. For example, a student might say, "My pattern is ABC using a hexagon, triangle, square, hexagon, triangle, square." Or, "My pattern only uses shapes with angles. It has an AB pattern . . . 3 angles, 4 angles, 3 angles, 4 angles."

■ Stations that combine geometry and measurement can be used throughout the year too. You might give students sheets of construction paper that can be laid out to cover a desk or table or small area rug. Have them estimate, then measure, how many rectangles will cover the area. Likewise, you might provide one-inch tiles to cover smaller areas, such as books, a work folder, or an "I Can" list. The big idea with young children is not to cover the space exactly with rectangles or squares, but to experiment with covering a surface with the same unit and to count those units.

■ An activity like Find the Hidden Treasure for exploring spatial concepts may become a favorite with the students—one that they will continue to explore and expand on their own. However, if their interest wanes, remove the station for a while. You might have it resurface later in the year when you sense the need for something new (but familiar), and it may feel like a brand-new activity for your students. Something old can be new again!

■ Another way to keep a geometry station fresh is to change the geometry-related book that's in the station container for students to read and reenact. Or change out the manipulatives that students work with at the station. If they were using pattern blocks, you might substitute 3–D figures later in the year.

■ To extend Shape Hunt later in the year, have students convert their findings into a table with tally marks and then convert their table into a graph. Do this after you've taught students how to create graphs and tally items.

■ If you use puzzles at geometry stations, be sure to increase the difficulty of the puzzles as the year progresses.

How to Assess/Keep Kids Accountable at Geometry Stations

Periodically observe your students working at geometry stations (rather than always meet with a small group during this time). On days that you observe, spend time with at least two children a day at math stations related to geometry. Jot down notes on a clipboard or a sticky note so you don't forget what you saw them doing. Note the geometric concepts the children are working with while you watch. Talk with the students about what they're doing, too. Of course, you can also observe students working with geometric ideas in small group.

Give children opportunities to share for a few minutes after math work stations time. If they were at a geometry station that day, have them tell briefly about what they did and have them tell what geometry words they used. For example, a student might share, "Today at station 3 we solved problems together. We did the one with *How many triangles could you build with 12 popsicle sticks?* We used the sticks and built 4 triangles. Here's a picture of what we did." This provides other children with a model of what they might do at this station.

When assessing how children are doing, here are some considerations:

1. Do children talk about a "class" of shapes, such as circles? Or do they just refer to one particular circle?
2. Do they understand that shapes do not change when they are moved, rotated, or flipped over?
3. Do they generalize what they are learning about one kind of shape to other shapes similar to it? Do they say, for example, "Oh, a rectangle has 4 square corners. So does a square. I think squares are a special kind of rectangle" or "This triangle has 3 sides but the sides are different lengths. It doesn't matter how long

the sides of the triangle are. It's still a triangle if it has 3 sides that connect."

4. As students are working with shapes, ask questions such as, *What is the name of this shape? What is a _____ [triangle or other shape]? How do you know this is a _____? How are these shapes alike? Different? What shapes do you/would you see in nature? In buildings? In art?*
5. When children are doing puzzles and building with construction materials, ask, *How did you make that? Tell me the directions for making that. What position is this object in? Put the object _____ [below, above, to the left, etc.]. Tell me about what you are building. Where does this piece go in the puzzle? How do you know?* Encourage use of positional words to build spatial concepts and geometry vocabulary.

Kindergarten Considerations

Because of the distinct needs of young children, here are some things to think about if you are a kindergarten teacher:

- Begin with 2–D shapes and then have children work with 3–D objects. Have students use playdough to create 2–D shapes. They might use playdough and plastic straws to build 3–D shapes.
- Use pattern blocks as an exploration station early in the year. Place attribute blocks at another exploration station.
- Be patient with young children as they learn about shapes and their properties. They may use simple terms to describe shapes, such as *pointy, fat,* or *big.*
- Teach students how to put puzzles together by building the border first and then filling in the rest. Some children haven't had experiences like this at home and will need some explicit modeling. Use positional words like *above, below, to the right, on top of, under,* and so on

while modeling how to do puzzles. Have a geometry station where students put together increasingly more complex puzzles throughout the year.

- Have children work primarily with foam, plastic, and wooden manipulatives (versus paper pieces) in kindergarten. These are easier for little fingers to handle and are more concrete.

Reflection and Dialogue

1. Do your geometry stations reflect a variety of geometry goals? Which stations develop geometric thinking about shapes and properties? What are students working on that builds spatial sense?

2. What opportunities have you included that allow students to draw, build, make, put together, and take apart two-dimensional shapes? Three-dimensional shapes over time?

3. What investigations and partner games can you use or adapt from your core program or trainings your district has provided to build geometric thinking? Work with your colleagues to share ideas and pool resources.

4. What is your students' favorite thing to do at geometry stations? What do they tend to ignore? What could be done to improve the geometry stations they aren't as engaged in?

5. Observe your students at geometry stations. How independently do they work there? What could you model or provide to help children work more effectively on their own?

6. What geometry vocabulary are your students taking on as they work at geometry stations? Which words are they using with ease and understanding? Which are they using, but confusing? What can you do to reinforce and support their learning of these new words?

7. What are students learning about geometry as they work at these stations? Share your anecdotal notes gathered on students across a week or two. What are you noticing? What might you add to one of your geometry stations to add a bit more challenge? Is there anything you might remove because it has become too easy? What will you put in its place? Why?

8

Measurement Work Stations

As mentioned in Chapter 1, even teachers who have been using literacy work stations and are transitioning to math work stations sometimes bump up against some trouble. *Planning* for stations in advance will head off many problems at the pass. Here's what happened with one group of first-grade teachers I met partway through the year. As you read about the work these teachers did, you may find the planning chart they implemented a useful tool for developing any concept.

These teachers had been using literacy work stations for several years, and I was invited to consult with their grade-level team to help them make math stations more effective.

In the following vignette, I recount how I worked with them to turn their math stations into a productive learning tool. Their initial comments gave me insight into what might be going awry:

Our first graders love to go to literacy work stations, but they just aren't engaged with math stations. They don't want to go to them. We bought a bunch of premade centers to make it

easier, but the students groan when it's time to use them.

When I first meet with these teachers, I ask them what they've been teaching children about measurement and how they've done that. Individual teachers share different ways they had introduced measurement to their children and how it went. One says, "I gave kids pieces of string. They went around the room finding objects that were longer, shorter, and the same length as the string. It was kind of crazy, but the children really enjoyed it."

Another says, "I tried to show them that they can measure length using different materials. I gave some links, some kids used cubes, and others had straws. They all measured their desks, and then we compared. Some got confused, because they didn't know which part of the desk to measure. Some used links and cubes together. Some lost count while measuring."

Still another teacher shares, "We used balance scales to weigh objects around the room. I showed them how to use cubes on one side of the scale and an object to measure on the other side. They had a lot of fun."

Next, I ask the teachers *what concepts* they are teaching children about measurement. Their responses vary:

"I want them to know how to use nonstandard units to measure. That's in our state and district standards."

"They need to compare and order two or more objects according to length, and we need to teach about weight, too."

"I'd like for them to know what capacity means."

This is a pretty tall order. As we talk further, teachers tell me that they introduced length, weight, and capacity over their two- to three-week unit on measurement. They admit that the children seem confused at times and are having trouble remembering what has been taught.

We talk about going deeper with teaching length and time, rather than simply touching the surface on *all* we've tried to teach young children about measurement in the past (often including length, weight, capacity, temperature, time, and area). Because length is easier for young children to understand than other types of measurement, we decide to slow down a bit and focus on teaching students more deeply about measuring, representing, and interpreting data related to length as we *plan* for measurement stations. Once their students have a better understanding of measuring and working with length, the teachers will revisit weight and capacity, examining one at a time. Late in the year, they'll teach how to tell time.

We use a three-column chart to record what the teachers need to teach children about measuring length and the materials they will use. (See page 272 in the appendix for a blank planning sheet.) As we talk about length and what we should be teaching, I jot down notes on the chart to help us remember what to focus on during instruction. By the end of our discussion, teachers have a more thorough understanding of the *concepts* their chil-

dren need to learn, in contrast to just knowing activities they might do. Here are some of their new understandings:

- We must teach kids to realize that the length of an object can be divided into a bunch of equally sized smaller lengths called units.
- Children must understand that when we measure, we must use *identical* units lined up side by side, with no gaps or overlaps, from one end to the other. We must be explicit in showing this.
- We should use specific and appropriate words, such as *8 cubes long*, to help kids understand what they are counting rather than just saying it is 8. This will later help them understand that numbers on a ruler mean units of length.
- Kids are used to counting discrete quantities. Now we are asking them to consider continuous quantities. That's a whole different task!
- Having kids make their own rulers can help them understand length units. Rather than having them just read the numbers on a ruler, we'll be teaching them what those numbers mean.

As we talk about what we need to teach and how to teach it, math stations ideas easily emerge. For example, as we talk about modeling how to esti-

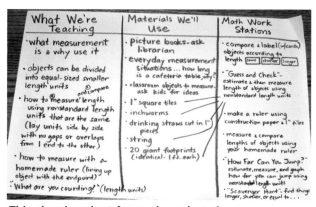

This planning chart for math work stations on measuring length was made with first-grade teachers midyear.

mate and measure classroom objects using nonstandard units, teachers realize that students can do this again at math stations. Children need lots of practice measuring objects, and this can be a station that is cloned so more students get this experience. Teachers will teach it in whole group first and then move it to stations. They will have to provide a recording sheet and a simple "I Can" list for stations that include several options. (See page 273 in the appendix for a sample recording sheet.)

As we discuss how to teach length measurement, I ask the teachers what they have noticed about children's use of measurement vocabulary. They share that some students say *bigger* rather than *longer* or *taller*. Nobody has heard students using the words *compare* or *estimate*. We decide to create an anchor chart for measurement words with each class and post it for reference when teaching students to measure. Our goal is for students to use this vocabulary on their own, too, especially when they work with partners at math stations.

We create a sample vocabulary anchor chart to give teachers a visual to build upon. They commit to creating a measurement anchor chart like this with their students during the next week, and they will share the charts during their next team meeting. I emphasize the importance of keeping the print on the charts to a minimum, using kid-friendly language, and using a picture for each term to help students remember it. They can take a digital photo of this chart and put a copy of it in each length measurement station to remind children to use the words while talking with their partner.

The teachers decide to go back and revisit measuring length with their students. They will begin by reading aloud a book, such as *Measuring at the Dog Show* by Amy Rauen (2008). Rauen's book introduces the concept of measuring using nonstandard units and tools—just where their first graders are. They will chart with children what they know about measuring length—why we measure, what we might measure, and who measures things in their job or at home. From there, they will explore meas-

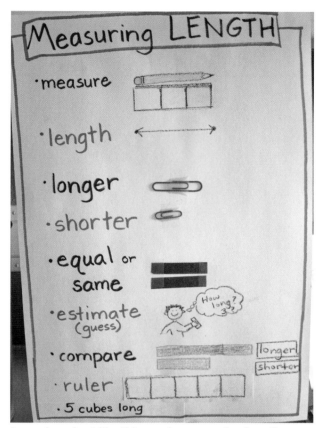

An anchor chart like this one for measuring length vocabulary should be made *with* the class. A photo of this chart is glued on a large index card and included at each measurement station related to length.

uring length in detail, using the chart we created for guidance.

Also, the teachers will consult professional resources available from their district. I suggest they read the measurement chapter on length from *Learning and Teaching Early Math: The Learning Trajectories Approach* by Douglas H. Clements and Julie Sarama (2009) and think about how children's understanding about measurement develops. Their principal says he will add this book to the school's professional library.

In a few weeks, their math stations will be updated. I ask them to send me photos of their new stations for measuring length. I can't wait to hear how much more engaged their students become at math stations!

Key Math Concepts to Teach for Measurement

As seen in the preceding scenario, even seasoned teachers are sometimes overwhelmed by thinking about all they must teach in math, especially in measurement. Likewise, it's overwhelming for children to remember all the measurement vocabulary we ask them to use, especially if we teach all the strands of measurement at once. This is a very important (and foundational) area of mathematics, so be sure to provide enough time to teach measurement concepts well. If possible, start by teaching students how to measure length over several weeks, since it is easier than other types of measurement but is still filled with challenging concepts for young children. A few weeks or even months later, teach about measuring weight or capacity. Instruction on measuring time should take place later in the year.

Use your district curriculum, state standards, core program, or planning documents to determine what (and when) you need to include while teaching measurement, and decide upon appropriate math stations for exploration and/or practice at your grade level. To get you started in thinking about what you'll be teaching throughout the year and what students will work on at stations, here are some key concepts to consider for measurement:

In kindergarten, children will . . .

- Understand what it means to measure objects (according to attributes such as length, weight, and capacity).
- Compare and order two objects by lining them up beside each other according to length (longer/taller, shorter, or the same).
- Compare two containers according to capacity (holds more, holds less, or holds the same) and then use nonstandard units (such as a scoop or small cup with rice or beans).
- Compare two objects according to weight/mass (heavier, lighter, or the same) and

then use balance scales and nonstandard units (such as connecting cubes).
- Compare events according to duration of time (takes more or less time).
- Develop understanding of concepts of time (morning, afternoon, evening, today, yesterday, tomorrow, week, month, year, etc.)

In first grade, children will also . . .

- Order objects according to length by measuring and comparing using nonstandard units, such as one-inch tiles, connecting cubes, or paper clips.
- Order objects according to weight by measuring and comparing using nonstandard units.
- Compare and order containers according to capacity using nonstandard units.
- Tell time to the hour, half-hour, and quarter-hour using analog and digital clocks and relate everyday events to those times.

In second grade, children will also . . .

- Estimate and measure the length of objects using standard units (inches, feet, centimeters, meters) and tools such as rulers, yardsticks, and measuring tapes.
- Understand that these standard measuring tools are used to find out how many standard length units span an object with no gaps or overlaps, when the 0 end of the tool is aligned with an end of the object.
- Understand relationships between measurements of length. (It takes more inches than feet to measure something, because inches are smaller units of measure than feet; 1 foot can be decomposed into 12 equal measures called inches).
- Tell time in increments of 5 minutes using analog and digital clocks.
- Understand relationships of time (the number of minutes in an hour; the number of days in a week).
- Determine how long something takes in hours (such as from 10 a.m. to 2 p.m.).

Basic Measurement Vocabulary (Kindergarten)

- measure
- compare
- equal to/same
- more/less

LENGTH
- length
- tall/taller
- long/longer
- short/shorter

WEIGHT
- weight
- scale
- heavy/heavier
- light/lighter

TIME
- time
- clock
- digital
- analog
- calendar
- day, week, month, year
- hour, minute, second

Taking It Further (Grades 1–2)

- estimate
- nonstandard unit
- standard unit
- tally

LENGTH
- *3 cubes* long or *5 feet* tall (rather than just "3" or "5")
- inch, feet
- centimeter, meter
- ruler
- yardstick
- measuring tape
- height

CAPACITY
- capacity
- cup, pint, quart, gallon
- metric
- measuring cup, scoop
- funnel

What the Children Do at Measurement Stations

Most of the following stations involve hands-on measurement with estimating and checking, then recording. These stations should be based on measurement investigations done in whole-group instruction before moving the activities to independence. You'll want to let everyone experience the act of measuring with partners as a whole class so you can guide and observe them. At measurement stations, students will estimate and measure a variety of objects with nonstandard units in K–1 (followed by standard units in grade 2) and then compare their findings and new learning with one another.

Add recording sheets *after* children have had a chance to try measuring for a few days. At first, they will need to pour beans into containers through a funnel or line up cubes end to end beside an object to learn what it means to measure. Add recording sheets only after they've had sufficient practice with the basics of measurement. You might want to use some of the recording sheets found on pages 273–280 of the appendix. Model with the recording sheets in whole group and then move them to stations for practice.

Measuring is fun, so students will not tire of estimating and measuring tasks at stations at a later time. Remember that math stations offer opportunities for review and practice, and learning about measurement over time makes more sense than trying to cram it all into a three-week unit. As students work together, support their use of *math talk*, encouraging them to use the vocabulary of length or capacity or time. You might also brainstorm an "I Can" list for each measurement station with the

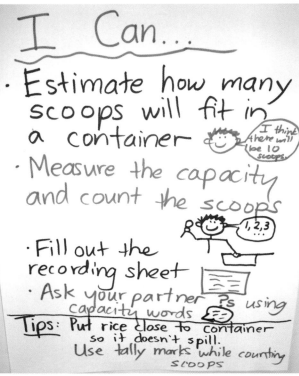

This "I Can" list was made *with* the class for a capacity station in grade 2.

students to help them remember what to do there. One of the students in a class I worked with suggested adding "Tips" at the bottom of an "I Can" list to make the station more productive. Be open to ideas like this from your students. Be sure to consult your core curriculum for key vocabulary and independent choice time activities for measurement to use along with station ideas from this chapter. They will probably be very similar.

Remember that our goal in K–1 is to help young children understand what it *means* to measure. In grade 2 you might introduce standard measurement units *if* (and *when*) children understand measurement concepts that precede this. If we introduce *inches* and *feet* too early, we might mask what it means to measure length. (See the "Materials" and "What the Teacher Needs to Model" sections of this chapter for more information.) The following station ideas are listed devel-

opmentally by measurement attribute to help you find what you need quickly.

Length

Longer, Shorter, Same As. Give students a non-standard unit, such as a 10-inch length of string, to use for measuring. Have them find objects around the room that are shorter, longer, and the same length as the string. They work together to draw and label what they found on one recording sheet and share with the class.

Partners measure objects around the room with popsicle sticks, a nonstandard unit of measurement. Then they use a recording sheet to show what they found.

You might vary the unit of measurement from time to time. For example they could use a different length of string, a popsicle stick, or a paper clip.

Second graders might find things that are longer, shorter, or the same as 1 inch, 1 foot, 1 centimeter, or 1 meter to help them gain familiarity with these standard units of measure. You'll find recording sheets for this activity on page 273 in the appendix.

Put Them in Order. Provide objects for children to order from shortest to longest or longest to shortest. You might include some crayons of different colors and sizes, a few decorated pencils of different lengths, a small paper clip, a large paper clip, and so on. Include cards that say *shortest* and *longest* with picture clues. Have students order the objects and represent their work by drawing and labeling. Items can be changed out to provide a different experience at this station.

These materials are used at a Guess and Check: Length station. Students use connecting cubes to measure objects here—a CD case, a playing card, a toy, a pencil, a glue stick, etc. The math talk card has length vocabulary for language support.

Kids compare crayon lengths, arranging them from shortest to longest, and then record their thinking with a picture.

Guess and Check: Length. Include some small items for students to measure, along with nonstandard measuring units (such as connecting cubes or paper clips). Be sure students estimate first and then measure. You'll want to address the challenge of measuring to the nearest unit when items are not an exact number of units long. Provide a math talk card to encourage students to use their new vocabulary about measuring length as they work. Over time, add a recording sheet (as found on page 274 in the appendix) and pencils for recording.

An adaptation of this station is to have students measure distances from one place in the room to another. They can estimate and then use big footprint cutouts (1 foot long) to measure how far it is from one end of the room to another, for example. As an extension, students might work together to create a bar graph representing length units of objects and/or distances measured.

Another variation at this station is to provide several 8½-by-11-inch sheets of cardstock with "paths" drawn or taped on them. Label each path with a letter. Students guess and check how long each path is. Begin with straight paths and cubes for students to use to measure them. Over time, add crooked and curved paths. (A few samples are on pages 275–276 of the appendix.) You could provide string for students to use to measure by matching string to the path, and then measuring the string using nonstandard units, like connecting cubes, or standard units, such as a ruler.

A student-made ruler (with numbers added over time) is used to measure a pencil that is 7 squares long.

Students measure crooked and curved paths with non-standard units of measurement (string). They create their own recording sheet.

Second graders might do Guess and Check using standard rulers if they have conceptualized how to measure. You might have them make their own rulers, as suggested in the following station description, before they move to using a standard one.

Make a Ruler and Measure (adapted from *Teaching Student-Centered Mathematics: Grades K–3*

by John Van de Walle and Lou Ann Lovin [2006]). Having students make their own ruler will help them better conceptualize length units. In this math station container, provide the following materials stored in ziplock plastic bags: precut 1-by-1-inch pieces of paper in two colors (six of each color per child); 2-by-12½-inch strips of white paper (one strip per child); two glue sticks. Children will glue the colored paper squares in an AB pattern, end to end, onto the white strip.

Students then use their new "ruler" to measure objects (crayon, pencil, book, block, small toy, etc.) at this station. Be sure each thing they measure is less than 12 inches long so the ruler will be easier for them to use. Have them guess and check as described in the preceding station activity.

After children have used their rulers without numbers for a week or two, have them add numbers to help them transition to using a standard ruler with inch markings.

How Far Can You Go? Children roll labeled toy cars, one at a time, down an incline to see how far they roll across the floor. They use a piece of cardboard and a short stack of books to create the incline. Then they take a small piece of masking tape to mark the end of the incline. Next, they release a car at the top of the incline and watch how far it rolls. When the car stops, they mark its location with another small piece of masking tape. (Have the tape precut and placed on a laminated index card with one end folded over to create a tab. This way it will be easy to peel off the floor and they can reuse it.) They measure the distance between

Students roll toy cars down an incline and measure distances using Unifix cubes in How Far Can You Go?

You might also ask students for ideas of what they else they could measure.

What Am I? Length Riddles. Students may enjoy making pages for a riddle book about length. On the front of the page, they give clues about an object that can be found in the room. Each clue should include a measurement. For example, a clue might read: *I am about the same length as a cube. You roll me to play a game. What am I?* (Answer: dice.) or *I am thinking of something that is about 3 feet or 1 yard wide. It opens and closes. What am I?* (Answer: classroom door.) They write the answer on the back of the riddle card and can draw a representation to show their thinking.

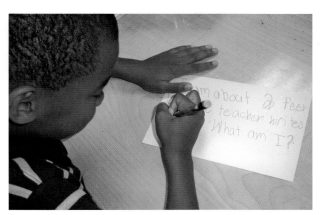

A second grader writes a measurement riddle: *I am about 2 feet tall. My teacher writes on me. What am I?* (Answer on back: dry erase board.)

Weight

Which Weighs More? To familiarize students with the attribute of weight, first have them compare the weight of two objects by placing one item in each hand to see which is heavier. Then have children place each item on a balance scale to see which weighs more (by noting the one on the side of the scale that's down).

Have students work together to make and record a guess before they weigh the two items. Then have them draw and write about what they

the two pieces of tape. Younger students can use giant footprint cutouts (1 foot long) to measure. More advanced children might use a ruler or yardstick for measuring.

For variety, students could take two giant steps from a line made with masking tape and measure, using yardsticks, to see how far they walked. Be sure they have space to walk in a straight path as they do this. (A giant step can serve as an approximate body benchmark for one yard. Measuring in giant steps and comparing the results to yards and feet can help children estimate lengths using these standard measurement units.)

Another adaptation (used for measuring shorter distances) is to have students blow through a straw to move a feather from a starting line. Or they could kick a pom-pom from the line. If you change from having students measure using big units (like footprints) to smaller ones (like cubes) with feathers or pom-poms, remove the original materials from the station so children don't mix up the units.

found. Provide a variety of objects that can be placed on a balance scale so children have plenty to compare by weight. Include objects of different sizes and weights, like a big sheet of paper, a shoe, a rock, a candle, and a book. Use the recording sheet found on page 277 in the appendix.

Guess and Check: Weight. Provide some small items for students to weigh, along with a nonstandard measuring unit (such as connecting cubes for light objects or large metal washers or 1-inch ceramic tiles for heavier items). Be sure they estimate first and then weigh. This time they will only measure one item at a time, and then they'll compare weights. Provide a math talk card to encourage students to use their new vocabulary about measuring weight as they work. Over time, include a recording sheet and pencils for recording. As an extension, students could work together to create a bar graph representing how many units each object weighed.

You might have them measure lighter objects and compare these using connecting cubes for a while. Then change out objects and have children use metal washers as nonstandard units of weight measurement so they don't get confused and try to mix measurement units.

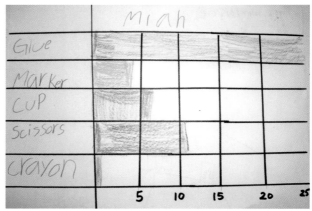
Over time, students might create a graph to show how much each object weighed.

Note: When the balance scale doesn't balance exactly, model and talk with children about how they will determine the weight to the nearest cube (or washer). This will require some reasoning to decide whether the balance scale is closer to balancing with the cube added that makes it go over the weight or without that cube.

Capacity

Which Holds More? Give students several containers of varying shapes and sizes, labeled with letters (*A, B, C, D, E*, etc.). Have them choose one container to be the "star" container. They place a star sticker on that container and set it aside. Then they choose a second container and estimate if it will hold *more than*, *less than*, or *the same as* the star container.

They first work together using a funnel to fill the star container with rice (or dried beans), leveling it at the top with their hands. Next they pour the contents of that container into the second one. They talk about if the second cup or box has extra room left over and therefore holds more, if it has beans spilling over and therefore holds less, or if it holds about the same as the star container.

Partners work together to transfer the contents of the star container to each of the other containers to see which holds more, less, or the same amount.

Kids weigh a bottle of glue with a balance scale and cubes as a nonstandard unit of measurement.

I Can...
- **Choose a ★ container.**
- **Choose another container.**
Estimate if it holds more,
less, or the same. Record.
- **Fill the ★ container** with beans.
- Pour the beans from the ★
container to the other container.
- Record what you found out.

An "I Can" list with picture support is made with the class to help children remember what to do when they come to the Which Holds More? station. The list is taped inside the lid of the math station container.

Name _____

I estimate: A holds more than N

I found out: A holds all of the Beans.
N holds almost the same as the A container
but A holds more.

I estimate: _____

I found out: _____

N and L holds the same.

This recording sheet shows children's estimates and what they found when measuring capacity: *I estimate A holds more than N. I found out A holds all of the beans. N holds almost the same as the A container, but A holds more.*

First graders compare which container holds more and then measure and record what they found.

(They will need to return the contents to the star container between tries to keep track of how much it holds.) Give children time to learn how to measure capacity before asking them to use a recording sheet (found on page 278 in the appendix).

Guess and Check Capacity. Partners will need a recording sheet (see page 279 in the appendix), pencils for recording, and a variety of different-sized and different-shaped containers (label each with a letter) to fill with little cupfuls of rice or beans. Children should first estimate how many units it will take to fill a container and then measure. (Small paper cups make a perfect *capacity unit* for measuring. Containers should be chosen so the measurement with paper cups is pretty close.) Provide a

First graders use a paper cup as a nonstandard *capacity unit* to fill a container with dried beans. They estimate how many cups they'll need to fill a labeled container, and then measure.

math talk card to encourage students to use their new vocabulary about measuring capacity as they work.

Again, be sure to model and discuss what to do if the last paper cup unit added spilled out too much to be counted. See the "What the Teacher Needs to Model" section for ideas about how to deal with rounding off to the next measurement unit.

Second graders might do Guess and Check using standard measurement tools, such as cup, pint, quart, and gallon containers. First they can predict how many scoops it will take to fill a cup or a pint. Later they might see how many cups it takes to fill a pint, and so on. Again, have them record and write about what they learned. Be sure to discuss how full a pint or quart container needs to be to equal a pint or quart exactly. You might draw a line with a permanent marker to show how high to fill the container, so equivalencies are correct.

Students could also make their own measuring cups before using standard capacity measuring tools, as described in the following activity.

Make a Measuring Cup (adapted from *Teaching Student-Centered Mathematics: Grades K–3* by John Van de Walle and Lou Ann Lovin, 2006). Have second graders make their own measuring cups to help them understand what it means to measure capacity using units. Each student will need one clear plastic cup, a small measuring unit, such as a medicine cup or a small coffee scoop, and a black permanent marker.

The child should fill the measuring unit cup or scoop with rice, dump it into the plastic cup, and then make a horizontal line with a permanent marker on the outside of the plastic cup to show how full it is. Then the child should fill the measuring unit again, pour this second scoop of rice into the plastic cup, and mark the new level of the rice. The child continues like this until the plastic cup is almost full. Now the child can use this homemade measuring cup to see how much other containers hold.

Time

What Takes Longer? Ask the class: *What are some things you could time at a station?* Write each viable idea on a card and add a sketch for support, if needed. Here are some things one class brainstormed: *write your name; tie your shoe; write numbers from 1 to 10; read a little book; count to 50; touch your toes 10 times.* Put the cards in a small ziplock bag along with a sand timer and a recording sheet.

Partner 1 is the actor; he takes two cards and reads them aloud. Partner 2 is the timer and recorder; she will record how long it takes for Partner 1 to perform each task. Both partners first predict which task will take longer and write down what they think. A sample recording sheet can be found on page 280 in the appendix.

After they record their predictions, Partner 1 does the task on the first card while Partner 2 times him. (She uses a sand timer, recording a tally mark for each time the sand empties out.) Be sure Partner 1 does both tasks and Partner 2 records how long each event took separately. Finally, partners switch jobs, and Partner 2 acts out two new tasks while Partner 1 is the timer/recorder. Students might also write about their experience and what they learned.

Once more, you'll have to model and discuss what to do when the sand timer is partly empty at the moment the actor finishes a task. See the "What the Teacher Needs to Model" section in this chapter for ideas.

A variation of this is to have students do a Time Picture Sort. You'll need pictures of events children might do during the day that take varying amounts of time (for example, brushing teeth, riding the bus to school, eating lunch, sleeping in bed, etc.). Colored workbook pages often provide these kinds of pictures on pages for telling time practice. Just cut out these pictures and glue them to individual 3-by-5-inch index cards. Also make cards that say *about one minute, about one hour*, and *a lot more than one hour*.

Students talk about the pictures and sort them in columns according to how long each event might take. They should order the columns from those activities that take the least amount of time to those that take the longest. Make the cards self-correcting by putting a small colored dot on the back of each picture and time card. All the *about one minute* cards would have a blue dot on back; the *about one hour* cards a red dot; and so on.

Clock Match. Have students match analog and digital times on clocks. Again, you might use a cut-up workbook page that depicts a variety of clocks showing different times. Glue each picture on a card. Put colored dots or stickers on the back to show matching times on the analog and digital clocks.

Clock picture cards can also be put in time order (such as 1:00, 2:00, 3:00, etc.). Or students could use little plastic Judy clocks with movable hands to show the time on the clocks pictured on the cards. Finally, students can choose a clock and tell/write about what they do at that time.

Students proudly show they know what to do at this time-related station by using their "I Can" list. Here they are sorting events by how long each might take. (The pictures at this station came from a cut-up workbook page.) They check their answers on the back by matching up colored dots. Children can also write about time at this station.

Children match analog and digital times using paper cutout clocks. Again, these pictures might come from workbook pages.

Clock Puzzle. As a class, have children help you assemble a class clock puzzle to help them understand how numbers on a clock work. You can use a commercial puzzle with removable numbers, such as the Tick Tock Clock puzzle made by Puzzibilities. Or you can make one from a white paper plate, Velcro, and cardstock. Build this clock together during whole-group instruction as you talk about each number on the clock representing the number of minutes counted by fives.

At this station, a pair of students works together to put together the clock. They put the numbers in order on the clock face, using a small Judy clock as a model. They match how many minutes each number shows, counting by groups of five. Remind them to be sure the numbers aren't upside down as they do this. Have them count by fives to review how many minutes each number represents. For example, have them use the language, "One group of 5 minutes is 5 minutes; 2 groups of 5 minutes is 10 minutes; 3 groups of 5 minutes is 15 minutes," and so on as they assemble the clock.

A student builds a clock puzzle made with a paper plate, cardstock, and Velcro to reinforce counting minutes by fives.

Make a class book called "What We Know About Telling Time." Each student makes an 8½-by-11-inch page for the book, telling something he or she knows about telling time. A page could be about any of the following (brainstorm ideas with your class):

- different kinds of clocks
- how to tell time
- how long something takes to do
- our daily schedule (with clocks showing what the class does at different times of day)
- facts about time (24 hours in one day, 7 days in a week, etc.)

Individual finished pages can be placed in clear plastic page protectors and gathered in a folder fastened with metal brads. This station could be used for a short time until everyone has had a chance to write at least one page for the book. Or you might choose to do this as a whole-class activity. When completed, this book could be added to the container at another math station related to telling time.

Materials

When planning for measurement stations, think about what you'll have students measure and the units they'll use to measure. Here's a suggested developmental sequence of how to introduce measurement of length and which materials to use (adapt it to teaching about measuring weight or capacity):

1. Students compare length of two or more objects. Which is longer? Shorter? How can you tell?
2. Students measure with nonstandard length units. It may be best to have them use units that approximate the size of standard units. For example, use 1-inch tiles for the smaller

unit of measure and 12-inch footprint cutouts for larger units of measure. This may give them familiarity with standard units of measurement later on. Some believe it's best to have students stick with one kind of equal-length unit rather than switching units constantly. For example, have all students use 1-inch tiles, rather than providing links, cubes, teddy bear counters, and so on, for measuring length.

3. Students measure with standard length units using rulers, tape measures, and yardsticks. Having them make rulers can help children understand these tools and how they are used to measure.

Here's a list of some of the materials you might want to have on hand to teach different aspects of measurement:

Length

- items to measure (small and large objects around the classroom; students might brainstorm lists with you)
- string and scissors
- nonstandard units, such as drinking straws (cut into 1-inch pieces and strung on yarn or string), paper clips, connecting cubes, 1-inch square tiles, or plastic inchworms, for measuring small items
- nonstandard units, such as 20 identical giant footprints each measuring 1 foot long, for measuring larger lengths
- nonstandard units, such as the little white unit cubes from Cuisenaire (these are one centimeter long), for measuring very small items
- materials for student-made rulers (pencils, paper, glue sticks)
- rulers, measuring tapes, and yardsticks

Weight

- small objects to weigh that will fit in a balance scale (small plastic farm or zoo animals from

dollar stores work well) and some heavier objects, too (like a shoe, hardback book, rock, stapler, and large magnet)
- balance scales
- nonstandard units for measuring weight (For lighter weights, connecting cubes or plastic 1-inch tiles work well; so do plastic milk jug lids if you have a large collection of them. For heavier weights, you might use large metal washers from a hardware store or 1-inch ceramic tiles from a tile store.)

Capacity

- variety of unbreakable containers (label each with a letter so children can refer to them by name), such as plastic cups, small plastic containers, cans, small boxes, and so on.
- adhesive gold stars (for labeling the "star" container when comparing capacities)
- plastic scoop or paper cup to use as a capacity unit for filling containers
- funnel (to make pouring easier)
- rice or dried beans (for filling containers)
- 12-by-18-inch construction paper to place under a container to catch spilled beans or rice (or use a larger container, such as a dishpan or box lid, to sit the smaller container inside while measuring)

Time

- picture cards of daily events that can be sorted by how long they take to do—from old workbook pages
- pictures of analog clocks, pictures of digital clocks, and cards with times written on them that match the clocks (8:00, 10:00, etc.)—from old workbook pages
- sand timers and digital timers
- Judy clocks
- digital and analog clocks (for comparing times)
- paper plate clock puzzle (paper plate, Velcro, index cards, and a metal brad to make a clock puzzle)

What the Teacher Needs to Model

Most of the work students do at measurement stations will grow out of whole-group instruction. Consult your core math curriculum for specific suggestions on how to teach measurement. Then integrate many of those same ideas into measurement work stations. Here are some of the things you'll want to model well before having children work independently at stations:

The importance of measurement in everyday life. Read aloud picture books, such as those listed in the "Literature Links" section of this chapter, to introduce your students to what it means to measure and why we do this. You might make a chart together as a class about why we measure and who measures things. When children understand *why*

A teacher makes a chart with the class telling *why* we measure and *who* measures to help them connect measurement to everyday life.

they are learning to measure, they may move beyond the fun of just pouring beans into a cup or making a block tower, and think more deeply about measurement as a part of daily life (such as measuring ingredients in a recipe or determining how much fruit weighs at the grocery store).

Also, throughout the day as opportunities arise, talk with your students about what it means to *compare* two or more items. For example, you might say, "Let's *compare* these towers. That means we'll check to see if they are the same height or if one is taller and the other is shorter." Or, "We'll see whose backpack is heavier—Jon's or Beth's. We will *compare* the backpacks by holding one in each hand and feeling which weighs more."

How to compare and order two or more objects. Depending on the measurement attribute being studied, demonstrate to your class how to directly compare two objects according to length, weight, or capacity. Show them how to line up two items end to end, and discuss which is longer, shorter, or the same and how you can tell. Then let them work with a partner using nonstandard units of measurement. Find opportunities throughout the school day to do this with everyday items. For example, ask children to choose the *longest* pencil in their box or to find two books that are the same size. When lining up for recess, have children get in order from *shortest* to *tallest* or vice versa.

Likewise, model how to decide which of two objects weighs more by holding one item in each hand and feeling which exerts more force to push your hand down. You might bring two hand weights (i.e., a 1-pound and a 3-pound weight) to school to demonstrate this. Tell the children, "This morning before school I was working out with weights. I brought two to show you. Which do you think weighs more? Why?" Then let students take turns comparing the weights by holding one in each hand. (If you don't have weights, you might bring in a 1-pound bag of beans and a 5-pound bag of sugar. Adjust your story accordingly.)

Students guess which is heavier, the hand weight or the medicine ball, in this whole-class introduction to measuring weight using everyday objects.

Have children think throughout the day about things that are heavier or lighter. For example, have them compare (estimate first and then hold the items) a book and a pencil, a globe and a playground ball, or a flashlight and a box. Try to use some items where the heavier thing is smaller in size than the one that weighs less (like a blown-up balloon and a marble).

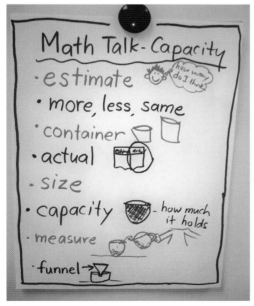

A math talk card for capacity is included for use at capacity stations.

Be sure to make math talk cards that show the language of measurement and encourage students to use these all day long, including during the time they work at math stations.

How to measure using nonstandard units. Give students opportunities as a whole class to measure length (or capacity or weight, depending on the type of measurement you're focusing on). Have students help you make a list of classroom objects they'd like to measure. Be sure to clearly model lining up the nonstandard units with no gaps. Then let them work with a partner using connecting cubes or plastic inchworms or paperclips (whatever you have a lot of) to measure those things. You might have them record what they found out on the class chart. Encourage them to use the language of measuring in your discussion, including language such as, "My pencil is *about 10 paper clips long*" rather than "My pencil is 10."

Boys line up inchworms end to end at a measuring station, just as it was modeled in whole-group instruction.

How to round to the nearest unit. Learning how to round to the nearest unit can be bewildering to children working at independent stations unless these situations have been dealt with in whole-group instruction when measuring length, capacity, and weight using nonstandard and/or standard units. Instead of starting off by defining the term *rounding*, let this exploration evolve naturally through class discussions.

For example, ask the class, "Is the pencil closer to 6 tiles long or do we need to add another tile to make it 7 tiles long since it is closer to 7?" Talk with young children about measurement being "about" that length, weight, capacity, or time: "The pencil is *about the same weight as 3 cubes*" or "It takes *about one second* to snap your fingers one time."

How to Guess and Check. It's important for students to work *together* as they measure so they will talk and use new math vocabulary (written on math talk cards) as well as learn from each other. Model how to do this during whole group by choosing a student to be your partner. Have that student choose an item to measure first. Both of you then estimate and, over time, record your individual guess for the measurement on separate recording sheets. After guessing, take turns measuring the same item (and recording) to the nearest unit. Finally, compare your work. When finished with that item, choose the next item for both of you to guess and check in the same way.

How to transition from nonstandard to standard measurement. It is fun and memorable for students to use "body benchmarks" as referents for standard measurement. For example, they might learn that a centimeter is about the width of a pinky finger or that an inch is about the width of two fingers (pointer and middle finger) beside each other. You might make a chart with the class of these body benchmarks.

How to use measurement tools, such as 1-inch tiles or a balance scale. Be explicit about your expectations for using measurement tools. Students will need to go through a brief period of exploration with these materials first, just as they did with pattern blocks in geometry or connecting cubes when learning about numbers. You might let children measure their desks with 1-inch tiles or practice fill-

This "Body Benchmarks" chart made with the class helps children transition from nonstandard to standard units of measurement.

ing cups with beans *before* you expect them to actually learn about measurement.

Tell students how to use the materials. For example, you might explain, "Use the tiles for measuring; don't build them into towers. Lay them beside each other, like this, as you work." Or, "When pouring rice into a container, place the container in a box lid on this big piece of paper first,

A teacher models how to use a balance scale to weigh plastic farm animals.

just in case some spills over. Pour very carefully and hold the rice near the container so it doesn't go all over the place. If any spills, pick up the paper like this (taco-style) and pour the contents into the ziplock bag with extra rice." See the "Troubleshooting" section in this chapter for more ideas on materials management.

How to estimate measurements. Work with children to increase the reasonableness of their guesses. Know that they will get better at estimating by estimating! For example, when students first estimate how many scoops a container will hold, they often guess way too high or way too low. Show them how to "eyeball" a unit of measurement or use a body benchmark to simulate it. For example, they might use the width of two fingers held together (pointer and middle finger) to estimate one inch. They will get better with practice. Often, they'll want to change their guess as they begin to measure. Tell them it's okay to change their mind as they better understand the units of measurement they're learning about.

How to keep track of measurement units counted. Ask students for their ideas about how to keep track of counting measurement units. Partner A might measure while Partner B records, and vice versa. They might use tally marks to keep track. Model how to use any recording sheets you expect children to use on their own. If the recording sheet seems too difficult for them to understand, use a simpler one.

How to write a riddle. Begin by reading aloud riddles to children. You might do this as a "sponge activity" when you have just a minute before class ends. Or have "Read a Riddle" time after coming in from recess. First and second graders love riddles! After students have been exposed to lots of riddles, teach them how to write a riddle in writing workshop. Model how to give clues, and end with the question, *What am I?* Make an anchor chart titled

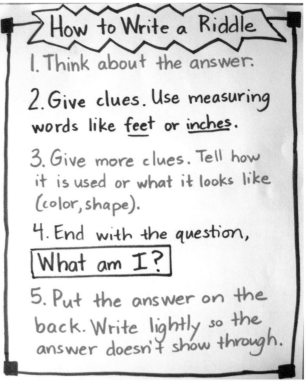

How to Write a Riddle
1. Think about the answer.
2. Give clues. Use measuring words like feet or inches.
3. Give more clues. Tell how it is used or what it looks like (color, shape).
4. End with the question, What am I?
5. Put the answer on the back. Write lightly so the answer doesn't show through.

This anchor chart on "How to Write a Riddle" is used at a measurement station.

"How to Write a Riddle" so students have something to refer to later.

How to think about duration of time. Make a game of comparing how long it takes to do certain tasks. Have two children model for the rest of the class. Tell the class what each child will do, and have students predict which will take the longest. For example, "Maya will clap 10 times, and Brady will tie his shoe. Which do you think will take longer? Why?" Then have each volunteer do his or her task. Discuss which took a longer or shorter time. Repeat with other students and new tasks, such as writing names (choose a name that has 3 letters and another name that has 7 letters) or reading a little book (use one with 8 pages that the child can read) versus touching your toes 5 times.

Introduce children to the idea of how much time things might take. Have them whisper *one*

In whole group, two students perform tasks to see which takes the longest. One claps 10 times while the other ties her shoe. The rest of the class predicts which will take longer.

potato, two potatoes, three potatoes . . . to estimate the passage of seconds. Use a timer to have them sit quietly for *about a minute*. Explain that watching two TV shows lasts *about an hour*. Make a class list of things that might take *about a second, about a minute, about an hour*, and *a lot longer than an hour*.

Use daily calendar routines to talk with the class about concepts about time, such as *today, tomorrow, yesterday, next week, 7 days in a week, 30 to 31 days in a month*, and so on.

How to tell time. Telling time is challenging for young children, and it will take a lot of exposure before they master this skill. Model by demonstrating how to read the clock in your classroom frequently each day. If you use the Every Day Counts series, you might use the 8½-by-11-inch clock that comes with this program to teach students how to count the minutes each day as you color in and count them. Also, use a large model, such as a Judy clock or an old battery-operated analog clock, to show how the hands on a clock work by moving them around and having students observe the motion. Help children understand that the long minute hand goes all the way around the clock once in an hour, tracking 60 minutes, while the shorter

hand moves from one numeral to the next, representing the hours.

Teach children how to *first* look at the long minute hand and count the minute spaces to determine the number of minutes past the hour. *Then* have them look at the shorter hour hand to see what hour the minutes come after. In first grade, as you teach students how to tell time to the hour and half-hour, model and encourage them to use math talk like this: *The long minute hand is pointing straight up to the 0, and the short hand is pointing to the 2. So it is exactly 2 o'clock.* And *The long minute hand is pointing straight down to the 30-minute mark, halfway around the clock, so it is half past 2, or 2:30.*

Also, help students understand that the numbers on the clock tell *two* things: (1) how many minutes have gone past the hour, with each number representing another group of five minutes, and (2) what the hour is. A first grader put it well when she told me, "I get confused because I see the numbers on the clock, and I think that's how many minutes."

To demonstrate that each number shows 5 minutes, point out and count the 5 spaces the minute hand passes through in order to reach each number on the clock. As the class counts the

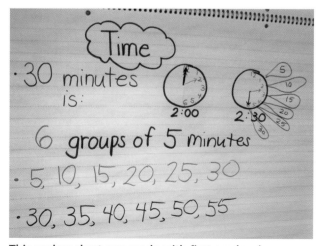

This anchor chart was made with first graders in response to a student's comment: "I get confused because I see the numbers on the clock and I think that's how many minutes."

Post a daily class schedule that uses either analog or digital clocks and use it to discuss telling time with your students. Use digital clocks with younger students and analog clocks when you are teaching about telling time to first and second graders.

minutes by ones, emphasizing the groups of fives, you might have a volunteer use tally marks to record each minute, accumulating a group of 5 each time the minute hand reaches the next numeral. Children can see that the numeral 1 is at the 5-minute mark and goes with 1 group of five, that the 2 goes with 2 groups of five, or 10 minutes, and that the 3 goes with 3 groups of five, or 15 minutes, and so on. Continue counting the minutes and emphasizing each new group of 5 to the 12.

This explicit demonstration is very different from teaching children simply to look at pictures of an analog clock showing time at the hour (reading just the short hand), as shown in many math books and on tests.

Make a class schedule using analog clocks to teach students how to put time shown on clocks in order. Children won't necessarily know that 2 o'clock follows 1 o'clock, so be sure to highlight this in your teaching of time as well. Also, knowing what comes next in their day can reduce anxiety for some children.

Connections to Problem Solving

Use ideas from your core math curriculum to create problem-solving opportunities at measurement stations. Look for open-ended problems related to everyday experiences. You might write one problem per card and include several cards, along with measuring tools, in your classroom math corner if you've set one up. Or place a laminated problem-solving card (samples are on pages 281–285 in the appendix) that corresponds with the attribute students are measuring at each station. For example, put problems related to length at a station that focuses on measuring length. Here a few samples of what the cards might say:

Length

- How many things can you find that are about an inch long? List them.
- How many things can you find that are about a foot long? List them.
- How many things can you find that are about a yard long? List them.
- Get a box. Estimate which ribbon is long enough to go around the box and tie it in a bow. Choose that ribbon and give it a try. What did you find out?
- We are getting a new table for our classroom. It must fit through the doorway. Which string shows how long the table could be?
- The teacher must measure the bulletin board to cover it with new paper. Which tool should she use to measure? Tell about your thinking. (Note to teacher: include a ruler, yardstick, tape measure, cup, and plastic inchworm)

Weight

- Which fruit do you think weighs more? Look at the pictures and put them in order from lightest to heaviest. Then weigh each and put the fruits in order from lightest to heaviest. Check your thinking. (Note to teacher: you might include an apple, orange, grape, banana, and pear.)

Capacity

- We have to fill up a fishbowl for a new class pet. Which would be the best tool to use for measuring the capacity of the bowl? Why do you think that? (Note to teacher: Include a teaspoon, large cup, ruler, string, and cube.)

Time

- During the summer I am trying to read for one hour each day. What time might I start and when might I finish? List some possible starting and stopping times.
- We have one minute before lunch. What could do we do in one minute? We have one second before lunch. What could we do? We have one hour before lunch. What could we do?
- It is _____ o'clock. What time will it be in 1 hour? 2 hours? 3 hours?

Literature Links to Measurement

There are many picture books that relate to measurement, so I've arranged them by measurement strands, starting with some books that introduce students to all kinds of measuring. Be sure to read aloud books that show children real-life applications of measurement. These books can also be used at measurement stations.

All Kinds of Measuring

Me and the Measure of Things by Joan Sweeney. Dragonfly Books, 2002.

Measuring Penny by Loreen Leedy. Henry Holt, 1997.

Length

Carrie Measures Up by Linda Williams Aber. Kane, 2001.

Inch by Inch (50th anniversary edition) by Leo Lionni. Knopf, 2010.

Keep Your Distance! by Gail Herman. Kane, 2005.

Length by Henry Arthur Pluckrose. Children's Press, 1995.

Measuring at the Dog Show by Amy Rauen. Gareth Stevens, 2008.

Super Sand Castle Saturday by Stuart J. Murphy. HarperCollins, 1999.

Too Tall Tina by D. M. Pitino. Kane, 2005.

Weight

How Heavy Is It? (Rookie Read-About-Math Series) by Brian Sargent. Children's Press, 2006.

Is It Heavier Than an Elephant? by Allyson Valentine Schrier. Perfection Learning, 2008.

Mighty Maddie by Stuart J. Murphy. Perfection Learning, 2004.

The 100-Pound Problem by Jennifer Dussling. Kane, 2000.

Weight by Henry Arthur Pluckrose. Children's Press, 1995.

You Can Use a Balance (Rookie Read-About-Science Series) by Linda Bullock. Children's Press, 2004.

Capacity

LuLu's Lemonade by Barbara deRubertis. Kane, 2000.

Pastry School in Paris by Cindy Neuschwander. Henry Holt, 2009.

Room for Ripley by Stuart J. Murphy. Perfection Learning, 1999.

Time

The Grouchy Ladybug by Eric Carle. HarperCollins, 1996.

It's About Time by Stuart J. Murphy. Perfection Learning, 2005.

It's About Time, Max! by Kitty Richards. Kane, 2000.

Me Counting Time: From Seconds to Centuries by Joan Sweeney. Dragonfly Books, 2001.

Telling Time by Jules Older. Charlesbridge, 2000.

Telling Time with Big Mama Cat by Dan Harper. Harcourt, 1998.

Tell Time with the Very Busy Spider by Eric Carle. Grosset & Dunlap, 2006.

Time by Penny Dowdy. Crabtree, 1998.

Technology Connections

Most measurement work should be done hands-on using real objects and measuring tools, such as connecting cubes, rulers, balance scales, and beans and cups. However, there are some fun computer games and other online resources available for students to use for telling time. Here are a few you might bookmark and integrate into use at a computer math station:

- www.apples4theteacher.com
  http://www.abcya.com/telling_time.htm
  (Games for telling time.)
- http://www.shodor.org/interactivate/activities/ClockWise/
  (Has an animated clock; students can type in a time and watch the minute and hour hands move to that time.)
- http://www.woodlands-junior.kent.sch.uk/maths/measures/measure.html
  (A site from the United Kingdom that includes a wide variety of computer measurement games.)
- http://www.online-stopwatch.com/online-alarm-clock/
  (Has a variety of digital timers. You might use these when timing how long things take to do in your classroom to give students a feel for duration of time.)

Troubleshooting at Measurement Stations

Young children love to measure, which increases student engagement at these stations. Hands-on measurement activities will generate excitement, which can produce noise, so you'll probably want to review expectations for voice levels and your signal for "It's too loud in here."

Organization will be important as you set up measurement work so that children can easily use a variety of materials as they estimate and check length, weight, capacity, and time. Labeled ziplock bags with materials stored inside might help children easily use measurement tools. Here are some specific ideas to help you think about solving problems at measurement stations before they ever arise:

Possible Problem	Troubleshooting Ideas
Students get too loud and/or run around the room as they work at measurement stations.	■ Review voice level expectations *before* students go to these stations. I often tell them, "If I can hear what you're saying from across the room or at my teacher table, you're too loud." Have a predetermined signal, like a bell or chime, to use if it gets noisy.
	■ Contain each measurement station to a place in the room. Don't let children go all around the room measuring anything they want. If you want them to measure a desk or doorway opening, teach them how to move to the place nearest them by *walking* there.
	■ If you have a station where students measure objects found all over the room, have only one pair of students use this station at a time to avoid distractions to the rest of the class and small-group instruction.
Students finish measuring too early. They need something else to do.	■ Be sure children understand that they should estimate, then measure, then (over time) record what they did and learned. You might also include a book related to that station's measurement attribute (such as length or time) and a problem-solving card.
Children mix up recording sheets and measurement activities.	■ Don't put too many different activities in each measurement station. Each station should focus on just one measurement attribute. You might color-code recording sheets that go with a particular task. Put a matching colored dot on the ziplock bag containing all the materials for that activity.
Strings start to unravel after being used by several children for measuring.	■ Use masking tape to bind each end of string used for measuring.
Students have trouble lining up things end to end when measuring length.	■ You might place a long piece of masking tape along a desk, table, or the floor as a guideline for young children to use at a measuring length station.

Kids mix and match different kinds of units when measuring length. For example, they use paper clips of different sizes. Or they run out of cubes, so they use links.

■ At first, you might provide only *one* kind of nonstandard length unit for students to use so they don't get confused.

■ Eventually (when they understand that units must be of equal size), you might give them several kinds of units to choose from so they can demonstrate understanding of measuring an object with the *same* unit. They can then compare measurements using a variety of units. For example, they might find that a pencil is 7 inchworms long or 10 paperclips long.

Children measure beginning at 1 on a ruler rather than 0. Or they measure from the wrong end of the ruler.

■ Have students make their own rulers before they ever use standard rulers. At first, have them count the squares without numbers on the ruler. Over time, help them label each length unit to help them transition to understanding the meaning of 0, 1, 2, 3, etc., on a standard ruler.

Students forget how many cubes they've used when measuring weight or capacity.

■ Show them how to record how many cubes they're using with tally marks. Or one child can be the counter/recorder while the other partner places the cubes in the container.

Kids overfill (or underfill) the container while measuring capacity.

■ Model how to fill a container and then level it off by running your hand across the top (much as you do when measuring a cup of flour and leveling it with the back of a knife).

Rice or dried beans go all over the place when children are measuring capacity.

■ Teach students to place a 12-by-18-inch piece of construction paper under the container when measuring rice or beans. If there is any spillage, they can simply pick up the paper, put the two long ends together to make a tube, and pour the leftovers back into the container.

■ Or they could place the container they are using for measurement inside a large box lid or dishpan to catch any beans or rice that might spill.

Students work at measurement stations without using math vocabulary you've been teaching. Or they're getting measurement terms confused (e.g., using weight words when measuring capacity).

■ Provide a math talk card at each measurement station with vocabulary and matching pictures to remind them to use this language. You might color-code each math talk card to match a measurement strand. For example, everything having to do with length could be on yellow paper, and things related to measuring weight could be on pink paper, etc.

■ Focus on just one measurement attribute at each station.

Differentiating at Measurement Stations

It will be important to observe your students closely to see what they understand about measurement as they work at stations. Most children in kindergarten and first grade should begin by working with direct matching to compare length, capacity, or weight. Then have them use nonstandard units to develop foundational understanding about what it means to measure. However, if you notice that some students are advanced in their understanding of measuring length (as illustrated by their drawings and talk about how they measure), they could begin to measure with simple rulers, especially the homemade ruler described in this chapter.

As you plan for measurement stations, pay attention to the developmental sequence described in the "Materials" section on page 196. Be careful not to push children too quickly into using standard units of measure.

Measurement stations are a great place for students to apply what they're learning about counting. Consider the numbers children can manage when planning for measurement work. If most students can only count with one-to-one matching to 10, then use units that will yield numbers within this range. Later in the year, when students can count higher, you might provide smaller units so students will be working with slightly higher numbers that match their counting levels.

Ways to Keep Measurement Stations Going Throughout the Year

Instead of trying to teach everything about measurement in one unit, break your measurement instruction into mini-studies throughout the year.

You might start with direct comparisons of length, and later move into measuring length with nonstandard units. Or you might study length in the fall, weight in the winter, capacity in early spring, and time at the end of the school year. Use your district guidelines for support. If your school system requires that all the measurement work is crammed into a short amount of time, talk to your curriculum leaders to possibly make adjustments in how long and when measurement is taught.

To provide spiral review, always have one or two stations focused on some measurement attribute after you've initially introduced it. Children love to measure and will be happy to return to these stations time and time again. But to keep interest high, change out the items they are measuring. Get their ideas on what they'd like to measure to increase student engagement.

Children can graph their findings at a measurement station. As they learn about different kinds of graphs, have them represent their findings with these. At one time in the year, they might make bar graphs; at another time they might make pictographs. This simple variation can provide novelty and keep measurement stations feeling fresh.

How to Assess/Keep Kids Accountable at Measurement Stations

Ongoing assessment of what children understand about measurement will help you plan for instruction and math work stations. It's helpful to create a checklist or observation sheet (using district guidelines) of what you're looking for and fill it out as you watch children work in small group or at stations. This can come in handy when you're doing report cards, too.

I recommend that you spend time talking with children while they work at stations doing measurement. Here are some of the questions you might ask them:

Length

- How can you find the length/height of this object?
- How can you tell which objects are the longest/tallest, or shortest?
- How would you put objects in order when measuring?
- What are you counting?
- Why do we use length units that are the same when measuring?
- What do you do with leftover space when measuring?

Weight

- How can you find the weight of an object?
- How can you tell which object is heavier, lighter, or the same?
- How can you make both sides of our scale balance to show the same weight on each side?
- What would happen if you put more blocks on this side of the balance scale?

Capacity

- How can you find the capacity of a container?
- How can you tell which container holds more, holds less, or the same amount?
- Which is larger, the bowl or the cup? How can you tell?
- Which would hold more rice? Why do you think that?
- How many cups of rice does it take to fill the bowl?
- When do we need to stop pouring beans into the bowl? How do we know when the cup or bowl is full?

Time

- What takes longer, eating breakfast or brushing your teeth?
- What's something you might do that takes about one minute? One second? One hour?
- What time is it? What time will it be in one hour? Two hours? How do you know?
- How do we measure time?

Have students record their estimates and measurements as they work at a variety of measurement stations over time. Be sure they *first* learn how to measure; add the recording sheet later. If you try to introduce the recording sheet while they are learning to measure, you will probably encounter confusion about how to fill out the sheet.

Students might place their recording sheets in a "Finished" folder or basket somewhere in your classroom. Or they could bring their recording sheets to sharing time to show one another (and you). Five minutes of sharing their work at the end of math workshop can be very helpful. It gives children a chance to tell about what they did that day; others can ask questions or compare their experiences with measurement. It's a great time to reflect and problem-solve. You'll find out what children enjoy doing with measurement as well as things that aren't going so well.

Kindergarten Considerations

Because of the distinct needs of young children, here are some things to think about if you are a kindergarten teacher:

- Explore measurement informally with children at traditional kindergarten centers, such as blocks and sand/water. For example, as they build with blocks, ask questions like *Which block is longer? Shorter? Whose tower is taller? How do you know? How long is your road? How do you know it is that long? Show me how you know that.* Also, kindergartners could build pens for zoo or farm animals with blocks and estimate how many blocks long and tall each pen would need to be. At the sand table, questions might sound like this: *How many scoops of sand will it take to fill this bucket? How can we find out? How will we know when it's full?*
- Use measurement in everyday classroom situations. Have students put themselves in order

according to height when they're going to have class pictures taken. They might sort crayons or pencils according to length and get rid of those that are too short to use comfortably. Blocks might be sorted according to shape and size. Use measurement vocabulary whenever possible: *This paper is too long to hang in this space. Which of our snack items do you think weighs less—a pretzel or an apple slice? Why do you think that?*

■ When children represent how many units long something is, let them use numbers, tally marks, or number stamps to record their information.

■ Let children practice measuring skills by making simple recipes together, such as homemade playdough, Jell-O, or smoothies.

■ It is challenging to teach kindergartners how to tell time using an analog clock. If possible, save that for introduction in first and second grade. Of course, if your district or state standards require that kindergartners learn to tell time to the hour, expose your children to this skill, knowing that it will be difficult for most students to master this in kindergarten.

Reflection and Dialogue

1. What are you teaching your students about measurement? Is it mostly procedural or conceptual knowledge? What do your students understand well? What is difficult for them?

2. Create a three-column planning chart like the one you read about at the opening of this chapter, pictured on page 184. Work with others at your grade level to plan for math stations that dovetail with your measurement instruction. Take one strand of measurement at a time, such as length or weight.

3. Measurement can be a bit overwhelming (for teachers and for children). What management tips will you try from this chapter?

4. How can you involve your students more in making decisions about measurement stations? What kind of input might they have—in what to measure, how to compare measurements, using their language in anchor charts, and so on?

5. What math talk are you hearing at measurement-related stations? With your class, make a math talk card like the ones described in this chapter. Put a copy of it at each related measurement station and teach children how to use it to support what they say while working there. You might videotape students talking together at a measurement station. (I love my tiny Flip video camera for doing this.) Bring samples of your math talk cards and your video or anecdotal notes about students' language use at measurement stations to a team meeting and discuss how these tools provide support for children.

6. Make an "I Can" list with your students related to one attribute of measurement (length, weight, capacity, or time) and bring it to a professional learning community meeting to share with your colleagues. What did you learn from making this chart with your class?

7. Based upon reading this chapter, what changes will you make in how you teach measurement? What changes to your measurement stations might you make?

Picture Glossary
of Math Materials

This picture glossary will help teachers new to teaching with math manipulatives avoid confusion.

When I first began teaching math in the 1970s, we made most of our own math materials or collected things kids could use for counting. Today, there is a plethora of manipulatives you might use for teaching math.

In this glossary you will find some of the things I find most useful for math work stations. This is not meant to be an exhaustive list. There are many items for teaching math that will be readily recognizable to you, such as money, clocks, rulers, scales, and calculators, that are not pictured here.

anchor chart

■ chart made with the class that you will refer to time and time again to help kids remember new content

attribute blocks

■ for sorting, patterns, and geometry

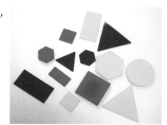

balance scale

■ for weighing objects
■ good to use with nonstandard measurement units, such as cubes

base ten blocks

■ for place value and addition/subtraction

bean sticks

■ for place value and counting and for addition/subtraction; 10 beans are glued onto a popsicle stick

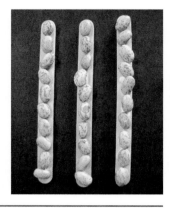

Bingo marker

■ for making patterns

connecting cubes

■ general name for cubes that can be joined together
■ Unifix cubes are a kind of connecting cube
■ for counting, patterns, addition/subtraction, part-whole relationships (including fractions), and nonstandard measurement

counting tape
- for place value, counting, and addition/subtraction

Cuisenaire rods
- for place value, patterns, counting, and nonstandard measurement

desktop sorting circles
- use with any kind of sorting

dot card
- for beginning number concepts, counting, part-part-whole relationships, and instant recognition

dotted cube
- can be made with tiny adhesive dots on small wooden cubes from a craft store

- you can put a different colored dot on each face to make a "color cube" or put a different number of dots on each face for a "dot cube"

five-frame
- for building number concepts to 5
- for counting and addition/subtraction

geoblocks
- for geometry

geoboard
- for geometry

100s chart or 100s board
- for place value and looking at number patterns and relationships for 1 to 100

1	2	3	4	5	6	7	8	9	10
11	12	13	14	15	16	17	18	19	20
21	22	23	24	25	26	27	28	29	30
31	32	33	34	35	36	37	38	39	40
41	42	43	44	45	46	47	48	49	50
51	52	53	54	55	56	57	58	59	60
61	62	63	64	65	66	67	68	69	70
71	72	73	74	75	76	77	78	79	80
81	82	83	84	85	86	87	88	89	90
91	92	93	94	95	96	97	98	99	100

"I Can" list

- list of choices at a math station; made *with* students to help them remember what to do here

I Can play...

- Chutes and Ladders with addition facts
- Combos to 10
- Read and act out facts in an addition book

inchworms

- for measuring length

Judy clock

- for telling time (a gear on the back allows hands to travel together)

links

- for patterns, counting, and nonstandard measurement

management board

- pocket chart for showing kids which math stations they go to with whom (available from Really Good Stuff)

math mat

- provides a soft work surface; foam shelf liner works well

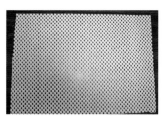

math talk card

- card with specific language you'd like to hear kids use at math stations as they work (make *with* students)

I have ___.
I need ___ more to get to 10.

numeral cards (or digit cards)

- for counting, place value, and addition/ subtraction

numeral cube (or numbered cube)

- I like to make my own with small wooden cubes from a craft store

1-inch ceramic tiles

- for measuring (especially on balance scales)

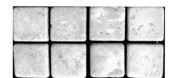

partial hundreds charts

■ a cut-up hundreds chart to show smaller number range for students who aren't ready to work with 100

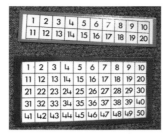

pattern blocks

■ for patterns, geometry, and fractions

place value mat

■ for place value and addition/ subtraction
■ kids use them for counting Unifix cubes, bundled popsicle sticks, bean sticks, or cups of ten beans in them

plastic counters

■ for counting, patterns, and addition/ subtraction

rekenrek

■ for counting, place value, and addition /subtraction

sorting mat

■ for sorting by color, shape, size, etc.
■ might have 2, 3, 4, or more columns

story board or story mat

■ used as a setting for story problems students might make up and/or solve

tangrams

■ for geometry

teddy bear counters

■ for patterns, counting, and addition/ subtraction

ten-frame

■ for counting, place value, and addition /subtraction
■ for numbers to 10
■ for modeling, can be made out of a cookie sheet with round magnets that have a large colored dot sticker on each

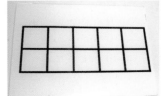

Ten Grid cards

■ for beginning numbers concepts and addition/ subtraction (available from Great Source)

ten-train

■ 10 connecting cubes joined together for counting, place value, and addition/subtraction

3–D shapes

■ for geometry (foam shapes are quietest)

Unifix cubes

■ smooth cubes that connect
■ for counting, patterns, addition /subtraction, part-whole relationships (including fractions), and nonstandard measurement

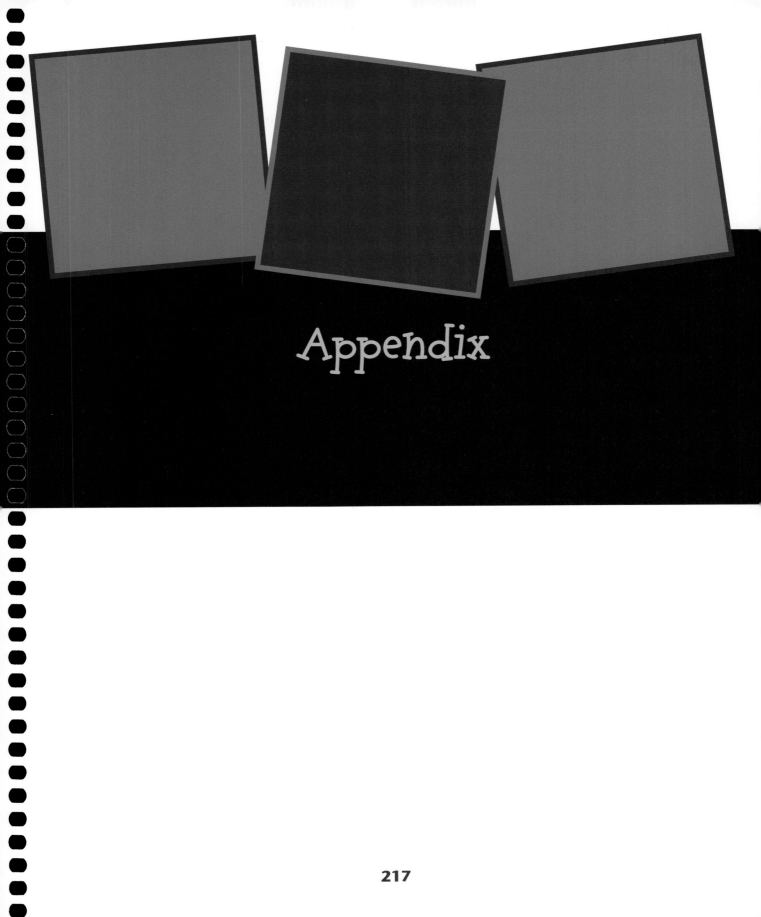

Appendix

Appendix Contents

English and Spanish versions of these forms are available online at
www.stenhouse.com/mathworkstations.

Parent Letter

Dear Parents,

   We are collecting small items to use for counting work at school. If you could donate any of the following, please send it to school in a ziplock bag. Please be sure that items are clean, since children will be handling them while counting.

Things You Might Send to School:

- Milk jug lids
- Old keys
- Loose buttons
- Lids from markers
- Little toys from the dollar store (that your child no longer wants)
- Seashells or small stones

Thank you,

Adapted from *Mathematics Their Way* by M. Baratta-Lorton (Addison Wesley, 1975).

Numeral Icons for Management Board

1	2
3	4

Numeral Icons for Management Board *(continued)*

5	6
7	8

Numeral Icons for Management Board *(continued)*

9	10
11	12

Math Work Stations Sharing Time Cards

What did I do at math stations today? And what did I learn?

What didn't I like doing at math stations today? Why?

Math Work Stations Sharing Time Cards *(continued)*

How did I help someone else solve a problem today?

What else would I like to do at math work stations?

Math Work Stations Sharing Time Cards *(continued)*

How did I collect and use data today?

What math talk did I hear or use today?

Math Work Stations Sharing Time Cards *(continued)*

What did I enjoy doing at math stations today? Why?

How did I solve a problem today?

Math Work Stations Sharing Time Cards *(continued)*

How did I represent or record what I learned?

What do I think we should change at math work stations?

Math Work Stations Sharing Time Cards *(continued)*

What math connections did I make today?

What did I do to become a better thinker/ problem solver today?

Numeral Cards

1	2	3
4	5	6
7	8	9
10	11	12

Five-Frames

Ten-Frames

Survey

Name _____

Do you like _____?

Yes	No

Totals: _____   _____

Odd and Even Ladybug

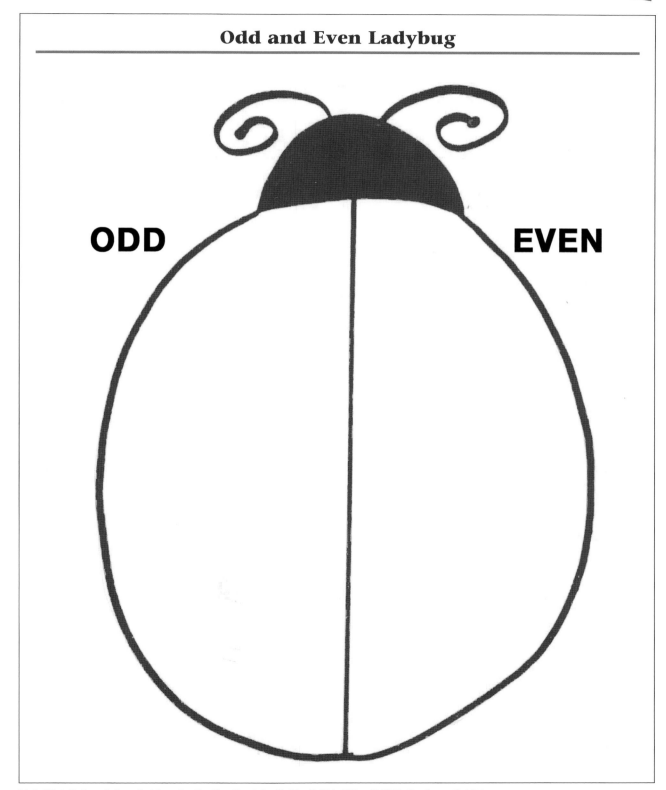

ODD

EVEN

Caterpillar Counting Mat

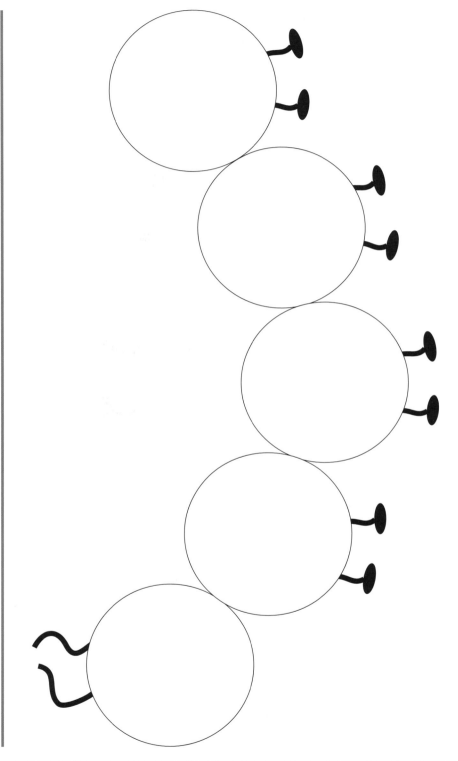

Directions to teacher: Cut and glue this and the next page onto 9-by-24-inch black construction paper to make a long caterpillar counting mat. Laminate and provide dry erase markers to children so they can write a numeral in each circle at they count.

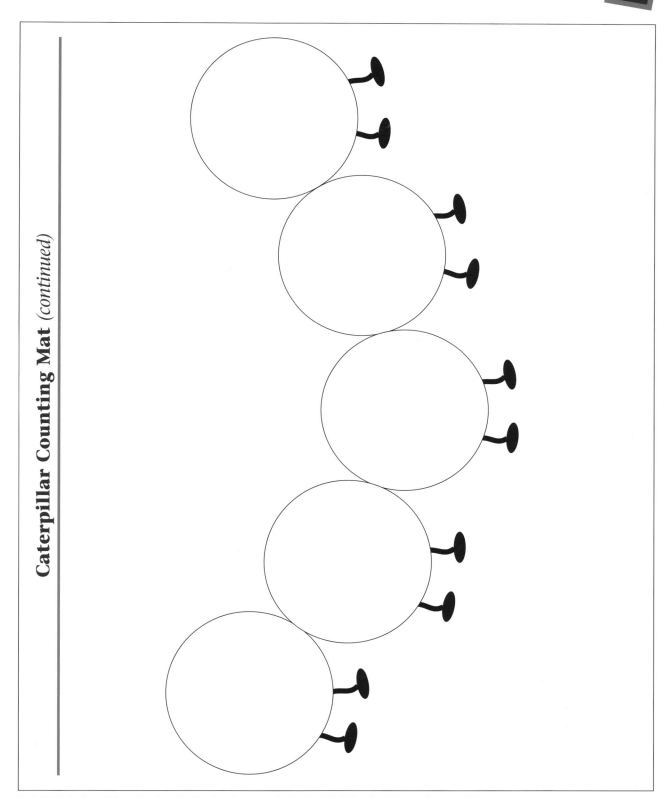

Caterpillar Counting Mat (continued)

Caterpillar Counting Cards

→ count forward	count by 5s
← count backward	count by 10s
count by 2s	count by 100s
count by even numbers	count by odd numbers

Numeral Dice Toss 1–5

Name _____

1	2	3	4	5

Numeral Dice Toss 6–10

Name _____

6	7	8	9	10

Numeral Dice Toss 11–15

Name _____

11	12	13	14	15

Numeral Writing Practice

Name _____

Direction: Listen to the tape and follow the directions for writing your numerals. Be careful! Start at the dot and check your work to make sure the number is going the right way.

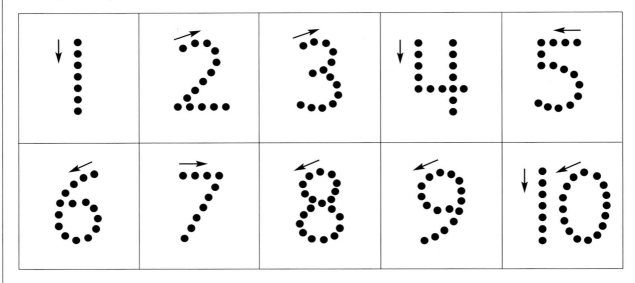

Try again!

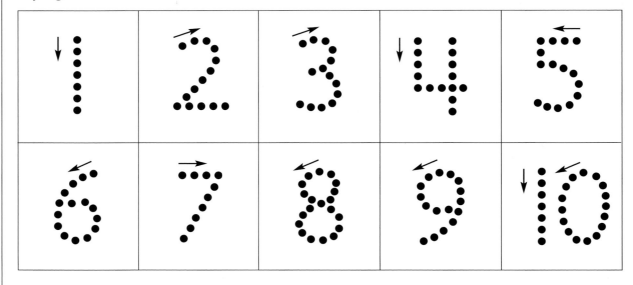

Estimation Station

Name _____

Jar	
A	My estimate is _____. There were _____.
B	My estimate is _____. There were _____.
C	My estimate is _____. There were _____.

Shopping at the Store

Name _____

Item	Coins	_____ ¢	$ _____

Piggy Penny Game Board

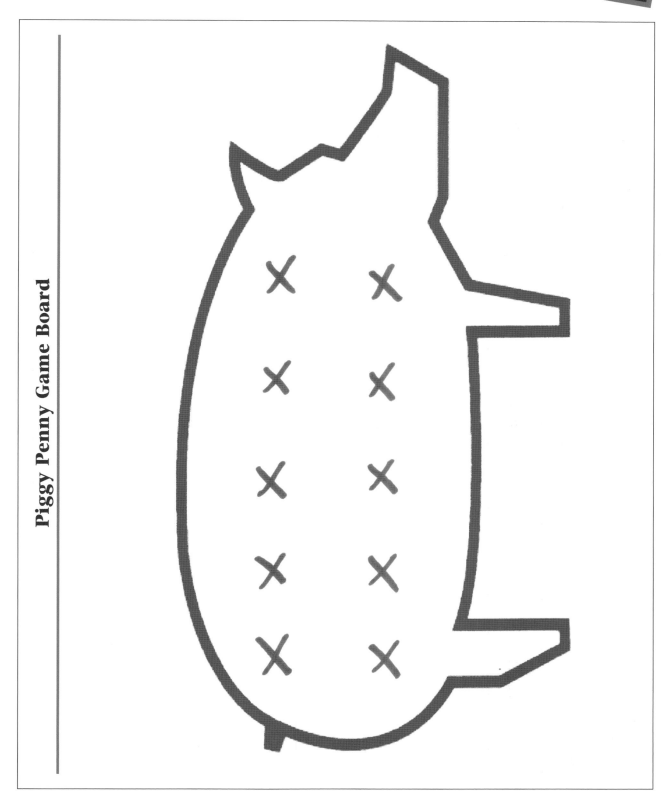

Coin Combinations

Name _____

Quarters	Dimes	Nickels	Pennies	Total Amount

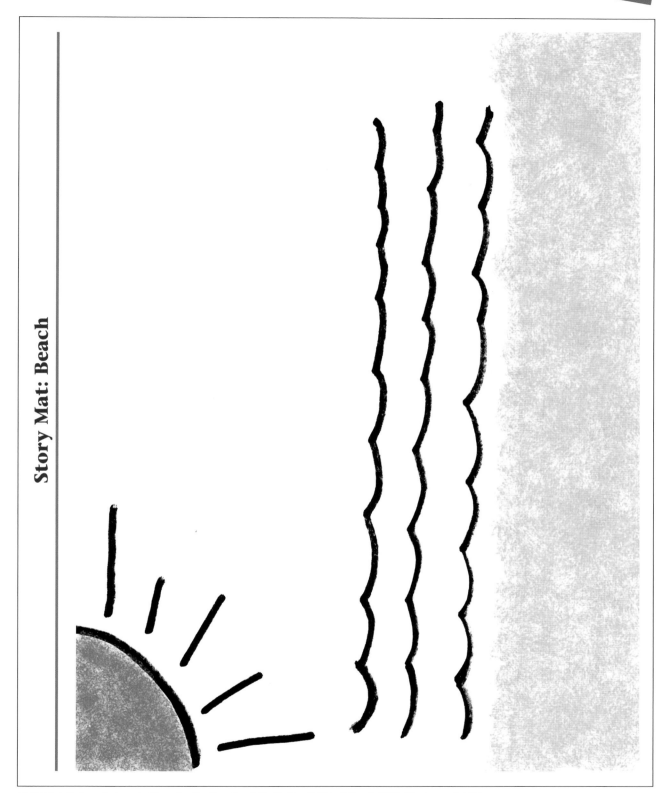

Story Mat: Beach

Story Mat: Classroom

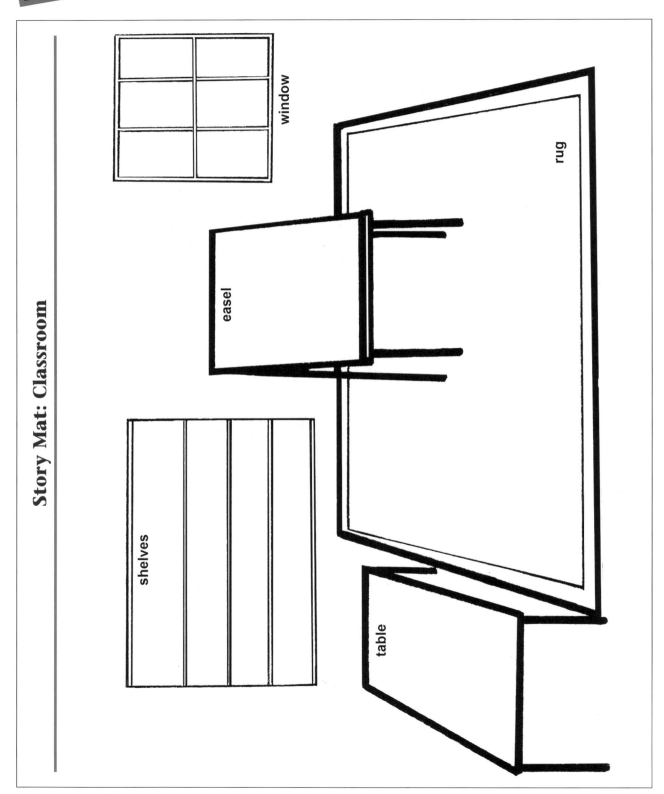

window

easel

shelves

rug

table

Math Work Stations: Independent Learning You Can Count On, K–2 by Debbie Diller. © 2011. Stenhouse Publishers.

Story Mat: Playground

How Many Are Hiding?

Name_____

We have _____. We took out _____. Now we have_____.	We have _____. We took out _____. Now we have_____.
We have _____. We took out _____. Now we have_____.	We have _____. We took out _____. Now we have_____.

Subtraction Facts for 10

$$10 - 0 = 10$$

$$10 - 1 = 9$$

$$10 - 2 = 8$$

$$10 - 3 = 7$$

$$10 - 4 = 6$$

$$10 - 5 = 5$$

$$10 - 6 = 4$$

$$10 - 7 = 3$$

$$10 - 8 = 2$$

$$10 - 9 = 1$$

Think Sheet

Name _____

☐ Yes, I'm right
☐ No. What I'd do differently next time:

_____

_____

_____

_____

Name _____

Trade or No Trade

Trade There are enough ones to make a group of ten.	**No Trade** There are NOT enough ones to make a ten.

Problem Solving and Patterns

Name _____

What numbers do you think will come next?

How do you know?

Tell about the patterns you see.

What numbers do you think will come next?

How do you know?

Tell about the patterns you see.

Math Work Stations: Independent Learning You Can Count On, K–2 by Debbie Diller. © 2011. Stenhouse Publishers.

Problem-Solving Cards

Jonathan spent $20 at a toy store. He had only $10, $5, and $1 bills in his wallet. What are the combinations he might have used to spend his $20?

Some friends were at the playground. Six played basketball, 5 played tag, and some played both. How many kids were playing in all?

Katherine bought 10 plants. She planted them in 2 containers. She put at least 1 plant in each container. What are the different ways she could put the plants into the containers?

Jessica is sorting seashells. She has 2 striped shells. She has 4 more white than pink. She has 3 more gray than striped. She has an equal number of gray and pink shells. How many seashells does she have?

Estimate and Count Collections

Name_____ E = estimation A = actual

E _____

A _____

There are _____
groups of ten
and _____
leftover ones.

E _____

A _____

There are _____
groups of ten
and _____
leftover ones.

E _____

A _____

There are _____
groups of ten
and _____
leftover ones.

E _____

A _____

There are _____
groups of ten
and _____
leftover ones.

E _____

A _____

There are _____
groups of ten
and _____
leftover ones.

E _____

A _____

There are _____
groups of ten
and _____
leftover ones.

E _____

A _____

There are _____
groups of ten
and _____
leftover ones.

E _____

A _____

There are _____
groups of ten
and _____
leftover ones.

Math Work Stations: Independent Learning You Can Count On, K–2 by Debbie Diller. © 2011. Stenhouse Publishers.

Counting Contest

Grab a handful. Estimate and record. Count and record. Who got more? That person scores a point.

Names _____ _____

Estimate: _____	I have _____ groups of ten and _____ extra ones, which equals _____ .	_____ is greater than _____ .
Estimate: _____	I have _____ groups of ten and _____ extra ones, which equals _____ .	
Estimate: _____	I have _____ groups of ten and _____ extra ones, which equals _____ .	_____ is greater than _____ .
Estimate: _____	I have _____ groups of ten and _____ extra ones, which equals _____ .	
Estimate: _____	I have _____ groups of ten and _____ extra ones, which equals _____ .	_____ is greater than _____ .
Estimate: _____	I have _____ groups of ten and _____ extra ones, which equals _____ .	
Estimate: _____	I have _____ groups of ten and _____ extra ones, which equals _____ .	_____ is greater than _____ .
Estimate: _____	I have _____ groups of ten and _____ extra ones, which equals _____ .	
Estimate: _____	I have _____ groups of ten and _____ extra ones, which equals _____ .	_____ is greater than _____ .
Estimate: _____	I have _____ groups of ten and _____ extra ones, which equals _____ .	

Build-a-Number Cards

A

Build each number using only groups of ten and leftover ones. Draw a picture showing your work. Record the number using expanded notation.
(39 = 3 tens and 9 ones)

B

Build the largest number. Build the smallest number. Compare the numbers using "greater than" and "less than." Write a number sentence to go with your pictures using > and <.

C

Build and record the number that is 10 larger than your number. Build and record a number that is 10 less.

D

Find the difference between the two numbers. You might place the base ten blocks on top of each other and see what is left uncovered. Or use the class counting tape or a hundreds chart to find the difference.

Build-a-Number Recording Sheet

Name _____

Card _____ Card _____

Card _____ Card _____

Comparing Numbers

Names _____

We rolled these three: _____ _____ _____

Here are the numerals we will build: _____ _____ _____

Put your numerals in order here:

	smallest		greatest
numeral			
drawing			

Rounding Bingo Board

Rounding Bingo Recording Sheet

Name _____

My Roll	Rounded to the Nearest Ten

Name _____

My Roll	Rounded to the Nearest Ten

See How We Find the Difference

Names _____ _____

Draw a picture in the box to show your thinking.

Our numbers: _____   _____
Which is greater? _____
How many more? _____
How do you know?

Our numbers: _____   _____
Which is greater? _____
How many more? _____
How do you know?

Our numbers: _____   _____
Which is greater? _____
How many more? _____
How do you know?

Alike and Different

Names	Our Shapes
_____ _____	
How They Are Alike	**How They Are Different**

Guess My Shape Cards

My shape has 3 sides and 3 vertices.

Guess my shape.

My shape has 4 equal sides.

Guess my shape.

My shape has 6 sides.

Guess my shape.

My shape has 4 corners. The sides are not all equal.

Guess my shape.

My shape has no corners.

Guess my shape.

If you put together two of me, you will get a rhombus.

Guess my shape.

Guess My Sort

Name _____

Label your sort.	Draw what you sorted.

Shape Hunt

My shape is a _____

I found it _____

Cards for Building 3-D Shapes

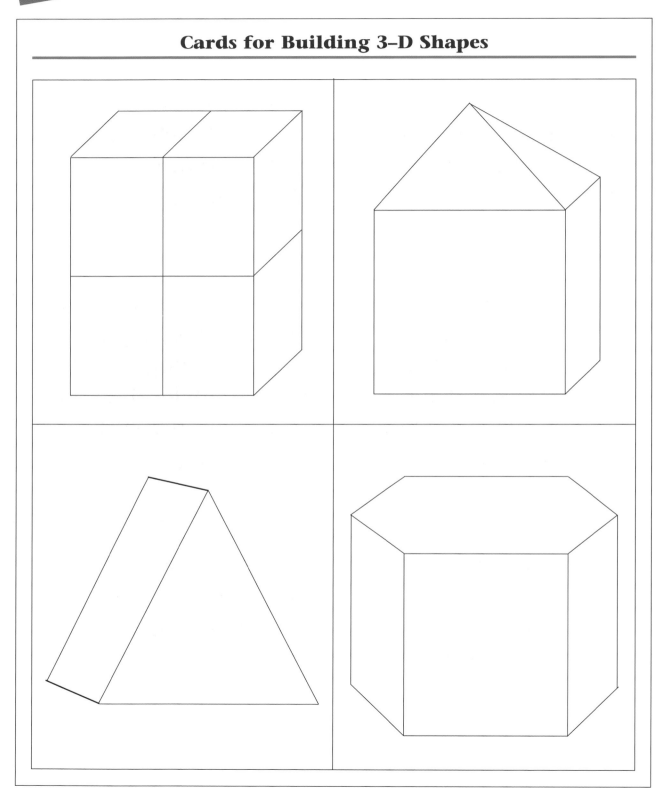

Ed Emberley Drawing Cards

Find and copy a picture that uses rectangles. How many rectangles did you use in your drawing?

Find and copy a picture. Which shape did you draw first? Which shape did you draw last?

Find and copy a picture. Which shape did you use the most? Which shape did you use the least?

Find and copy a picture that uses triangles. How many triangles did you use in your drawing?

Find and copy a picture that uses circles. How many circles did you use in your drawing?

Find and copy a picture. Label some of the shapes you used.

Treasure Chest for Find the Hidden Treasure

Sample Shape-Sorting Cards

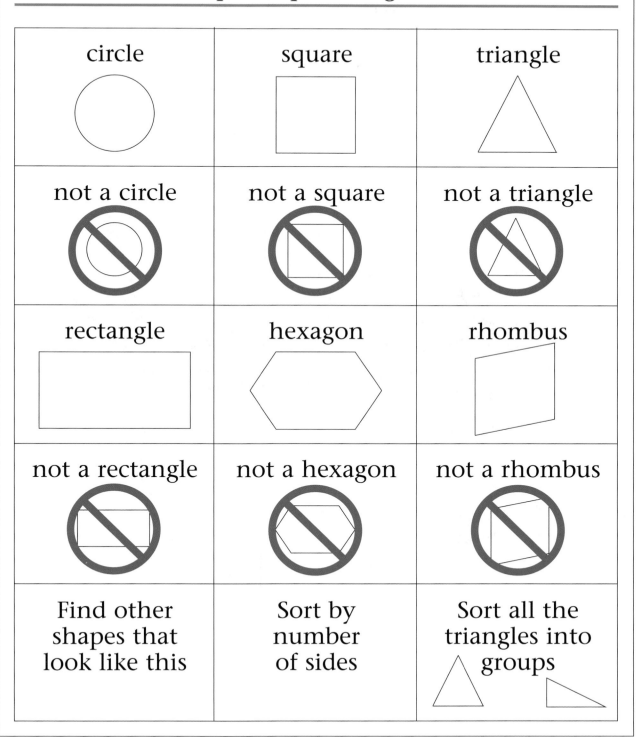

circle	square	triangle
not a circle	not a square	not a triangle
rectangle	hexagon	rhombus
not a rectangle	not a hexagon	not a rhombus
Find other shapes that look like this	Sort by number of sides	Sort all the triangles into groups

Problem-Solving Cards for Geometry

If you trace a face of a cube, what shape would you get? Find other shapes that have the same face.	How many triangles could you build with 12 popsicle sticks?
How many hexagons could you build with 10 popsicle sticks?	How many pieces of yarn would it take to make 2 squares?
I drew 3 different triangles. What might they have looked like?	How many different designs can you make using 5 trapezoid pattern blocks? Try this with a different shape.

Problem-Solving Cards for Geometry *(continued)*

If you trace the face of a rectangular prism, what shape would you get? Find other shapes that have this same face.	If you wanted to build a cube, what pattern blocks would you need? How many?
How many different shapes with 4 sides can you make?	Using the triangle pattern block shape, build other triangles.

Math Work Stations: Independent Learning You Can Count On, K–2 by Debbie Diller. © 2011. Stenhouse Publishers.

Planning Sheet for Math Work Stations

What We're Teaching	Materials We'll Use	Math Work Stations

Longer, Shorter, Same As Recording Sheet

Name _____

I measured with _____

longer	shorter	same as

Guess and Check Weight or Length

Names _____

We measured with _____

Object	Estimate	Actual	How We Measured and What We Found Out

Crooked Paths for Measurement

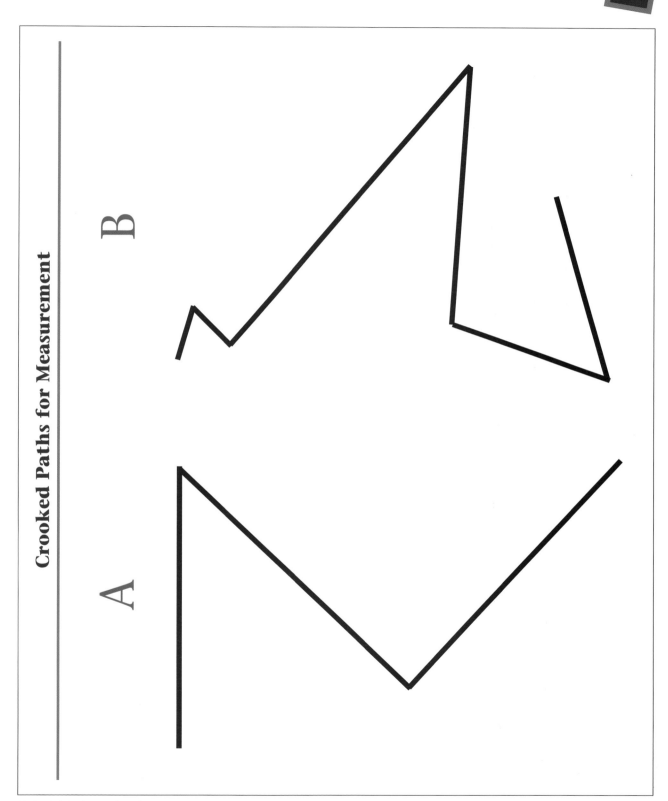

Curved Paths for Measurement

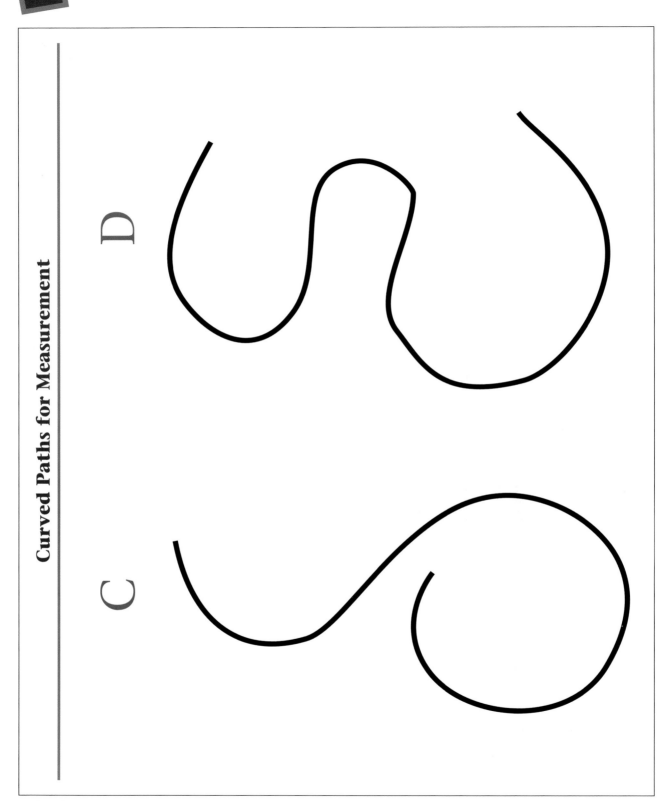

D

C

Which Weighs More?

Name _____

Compare 2 objects. Circle the one you think will be heavier.
Draw a picture of a scale to show what you found. Which weighs more?

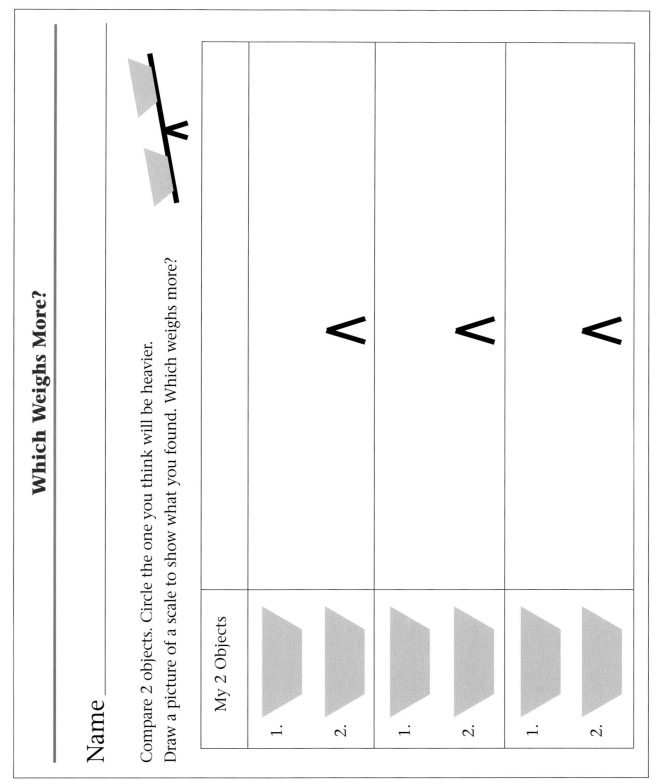

My 2 Objects		
1. 2.	<	
1. 2.	<	
1. 2.	<	

Which Holds More?

Names_____ P = prediction A = actual
_____

We predict it will take more _____ to fill the container.
(Use the SAME container.)

 container P _____

A _____

 container P _____

A _____

It took more _____ to fill the container.

We predict it will take more _____ to fill the container.
(Use the SAME container.)

 container P _____

A _____

 container P _____

A _____

It took more _____ to fill the container.

Guess and Check Capacity

Names_____   _____

Container	Estimate	Actual

Draw and write about how you measured. What did you find out?

What Takes Longer?

Names _____   _____

What we did:	Time
	Our estimates: _____ _____ How long it took: _____
	Our estimates: _____ _____ How long it took: _____

We learned _____

_____

_____

Problem-Solving Cards for Measurement

Get a box. Estimate which ribbon is long enough to go around the box and be tied in a bow. Choose that ribbon and give it a try. What did you find out?

We are getting a new table for our classroom. It must fit through the doorway. Which string shows how long the table could be?

Problem-Solving Cards for Measurement *(continued)*

How many things can you find that are about an inch long? List them.

How many things can you find that are about a foot long? List them.

Problem-Solving Cards for Measurement *(continued)*

How many things can you find that are about a yard long? List them.

During the summer, I am trying to read for one hour each day. What time might I start and when might I finish? List some possible starting and stopping times.

Problem-Solving Cards for Measurement *(continued)*

The teacher must measure the bulletin board to cover it with new paper. Which tool should she use to measure? Tell about your thinking.

Which fruit do you think weighs more? Look at the pictures and put the pictures in order from lightest to heaviest. Then weigh each fruit and put the fruits in order from lightest to heaviest. Check your thinking.

Problem-Solving Cards for Measurement *(continued)*

We have to fill up a fishbowl for a new class pet. Which would be the best tool to use for measuring the capacity of the bowl? A teaspoon, a large cup, a ruler, a piece of string, or a cube? Why do you think that?

We have 1 minute before lunch. What could do we do in 1 minute? We have 1 second before lunch. What could we do? We have 1 hour before lunch. What could we do?

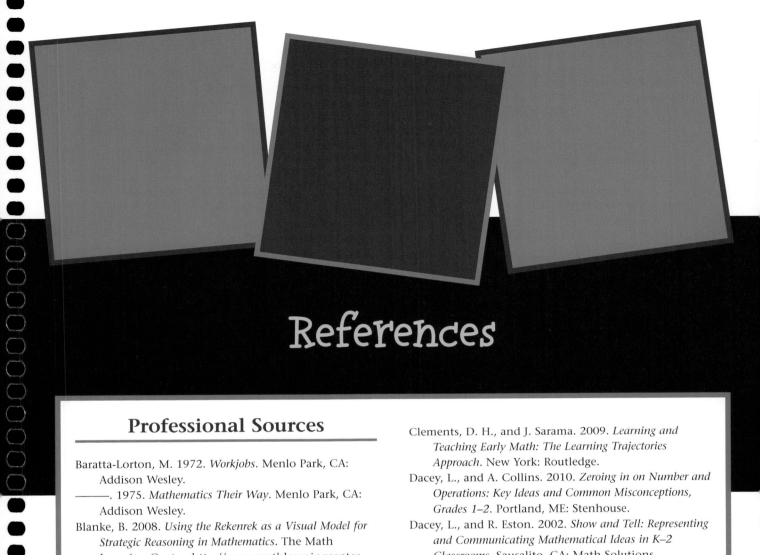

References

Professional Sources

Baratta-Lorton, M. 1972. *Workjobs*. Menlo Park, CA: Addison Wesley.

———. 1975. *Mathematics Their Way*. Menlo Park, CA: Addison Wesley.

Blanke, B. 2008. *Using the Rekenrek as a Visual Model for Strategic Reasoning in Mathematics*. The Math Learning Center. http://www.mathlearningcenter.org/media/Rekenrek_0308.pdf.

Burns, M. 1975. *The I Hate Mathematics! Book*. Boston: Little, Brown.

Burns, M., and S. Sheffield. 2004. *Math and Literature: Grades K–1*. Sausalito, CA: Math Solutions.

Cambourne, B. 1988. *The Whole Story: Natural Learning and the Acquisition of Literacy*. Auckland, NZ: Ashton-Scholastic.

Carpenter, T. P., E. Fennema, M. L. Franke, L. Levi, and S. B. Empson. 1999. *Children's Mathematics: Cognitively Guided Instruction*. Portsmouth, NH: Heinemann.

Chapin, S. H., C. O'Connor, and N. C. Anderson. 2009. *Classroom Discussions: Using Math Talk to Help Students Learn, Grades K–6*. 2nd ed. Sausalito, CA: Math Solutions.

Clements, D. H., and J. Sarama. 2009. *Learning and Teaching Early Math: The Learning Trajectories Approach*. New York: Routledge.

Dacey, L., and A. Collins. 2010. *Zeroing in on Number and Operations: Key Ideas and Common Misconceptions, Grades 1–2*. Portland, ME: Stenhouse.

Dacey, L., and R. Eston. 2002. *Show and Tell: Representing and Communicating Mathematical Ideas in K–2 Classrooms*. Sausalito, CA: Math Solutions.

———. 2007. *Math for All: Differentiating Instruction, Grades K–2*. Sausalito, CA: Math Solutions.

Diller, D. 2003. *Literacy Work Stations: Making Centers Work*. Portland, ME: Stenhouse.

Fosnot, C. T., and M. Dolk. 2001. *Young Mathematicians at Work*. Portsmouth, NH: Heinemann.

Frayer, D., W. C. Frederick, and H. J. Klausmeier. 1969. *A Schema for Testing the Level of Cognitive Mastery*. Madison, WI: Wisconsin Center for Education Research.

Gardner, H. 1993. *Frames of Mind: The Theory of Multiple Intelligences*. New York: Basic Books.

Gillespie, J., and P. Kanter. 1996. *Math Every Day*. Lexington, MA: D. C. Heath.

———. 2005a. *Every Day Counts Partner Games, Grade K*. Wilmington, MA: Great Source.

————. 2005b. *Every Day Counts Partner Games, Grade 1.* Wilmington, MA: Great Source.

————. 2005c. *Every Day Counts Partner Games, Grade 2.* Wilmington, MA: Great Source.

Hechtman, J., D. Ellermeyer, and S. F. Grove. 1998. *Teaching Math with Favorite Picture Books.* New York: Scholastic.

Hyde, A. 2006. *Comprehending Math: Adapting Reading Strategies to Teach Mathematics, K–6.* Portsmouth, NH: Heinemann.

Jensen, E. 1998. *Teaching with the Brain in Mind.* Alexandria, VA: Association for Supervision and Curriculum Development.

Kanter, P., and J. Gillespie. 2005a. *Every Day Counts Calendar Math, Grade K.* Wilmington, MA: Great Source.

————. 2005b. *Every Day Counts Calendar Math, Grade 1.* Wilmington, MA: Great Source.

————. 2005c. *Every Day Counts Calendar Math, Grade 2.* Wilmington, MA: Great Source.

Lake, J. 2009. *Math Memories You Can Count On.* Markam, Ontario, Canada: Pembroke.

Morgenstern, J. 2004. *Organizing from the Inside Out.* New York: Holt.

Patall, E. A., H. Cooper, and J. C. Robinson. 2008. "The Effects of Choice on Intrinsic Motivation and Related Outcomes: A Meta-Analysis of Research Findings." *Psychological Bulletin* 134 (2): 270–300.

Pearson, P. D., and M. C. Gallagher, 1983. "The Instruction of Reading Comprehension." *Contemporary Educational Psychology* 8: 317–344.

Richardson, K. 1984. *Developing Number Concepts Using Unifix Cubes.* Menlo Park, CA: Addison Wesley.

————. 1998a. *Developing Number Concepts, Book 1: Counting, Comparing, and Pattern.* Parsippany, NJ: Dale Seymour.

————. 1998b. *Developing Number Concepts, Book 3: Place Value, Multiplication, and Division.* Parsippany, NJ: Dale Seymour.

Van de Walle, J. A., and L. H. Lovin. 2006. *Teaching Student-Centered Mathematics: Grades K–3.* Boston: Pearson.

Children's Books

Readers should see also the book lists in Chapters 4–8 for books relating to specific concepts.

Carle, E. 1996. *1, 2, 3 to the Zoo.* New York: Philomel.

Beaumont, K. 2006. *Move Over, Rover!* New York: Harcourt Children's Books.

Chrismer, M. 2006. *Odd and Even Socks.* Danbury, CT: Children's Press.

Emberley, E. 1994. *Ed Emberley's Drawing Book of Animals.* New York: LB Kids.

Franco, B. 2004. *Counting Our Way to the 100th Day: 100 Poems.* New York: Margaret K. McElderry Books.

Hoban, T. 1996. *Shapes, Shapes, Shapes.* New York: Greenwillow.

Jonas, Ann. 1984. *The Quilt.* New York: HarperCollins.

Murphy, S. 1997. *Betcha!* New York: HarperCollins.

————. 2000. *Beep Beep, Vroom Vroom!* New York: HarperCollins.

NY Metropolitan Museum of Art. 2005. *Museum Shapes.* New York: Little, Brown Young Readers.

Rauen, A. 2008. *Measuring at the Dog Show.* New York: Gareth Stevens.

Ryan, P. M., and J. Pallotta. 1996. *The Crayon Counting Book.* Watertown, MA: Charlesbridge.

Tompert, A. 1997. *Grandfather Tang's Story.* New York: Dragonfly Books.

Web Sites

Beginning Number Concepts

www.learningplanet.com

http://pbskids.org/curiousgeorge/games/#1

http://nlvm.usu.edu/en/nav/category_g_1_t_3.html

Addition and Subtraction

http://resources.oswego.org/games/Powerlines/powerlines1.html

http://www.hicolor.jp/puzzle/en/trial/index.html

www.aplusmath.com

www.arcademicskillbuilders.com

www.funbrain.com

http://www.abcya.com/math_bingo.htm

http://www.mathplayground.com/PartPartWhole.html

www.illuminations.nctm.org

www.mathstories.com

Place Value

http://nlvm.usu.edu/en/nav/category_g_1_t_3.html
http://www.gamequarium.com/placevalue.html

Geometry

http://nlvm.usu.edu/en/nav/category_g_1_t_3.html

Measurement

www.apples4theteacher.com
http://www.abcya.com/telling_time.htm
http://www.shodor.org/interactivate/activities/
    ClockWise/
http://www.woodlands-junior.kent.sch.uk/maths/
    measures/measure.html
http://www.online-stopwatch.com/online-alarm-clock/

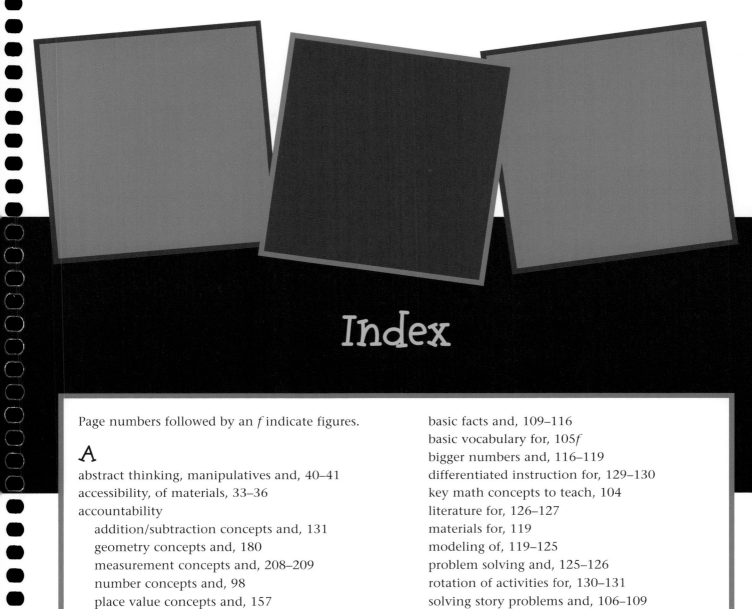

Index

Page numbers followed by an *f* indicate figures.